THE POETRY OF JAMES WRIGHT

THE POETRY OF

ANDREW   ELKINS

JAMES WRIGHT

THE UNIVERSITY OF ALABAMA PRESS   •   TUSCALOOSA AND LONDON

Copyright © 1991 by
The University of Alabama Press
Tuscaloosa, Alabama 35487–0380
All rights reserved
Manufactured in the United States of America

∞

The paper on which this book is printed meets the minimum
requirements of American National Standard for Information Science-
Permanence of Paper for Printed Library Materials, ANSI Z39.48-1984.

Library of Congress Cataloging-in-Publication Data

Elkins, Andrew, 1950–
    The poetry of James Wright / Andrew Elkins.
        p.   cm.
    Includes bibliographical references.
    ISBN 0-8173-0496-7 (alk. paper)
    1. Wright, James Arlington, 1927–
—Criticism and interpretation.   I. Title.
    PS3573.R5358Z67   1991
    811'.54—dc20   90-10879

British Library Cataloguing-in-Publication Data available

*The jacket illustration is based on a photo-portrait of James Wright
by Gerard Malanga.*

Contents

Acknowledgments

My interest in James Wright's poetry began when I was a graduate student at Northwestern University from 1976 to 1980. The professors who served on my dissertation committee deserve acknowledgment for their generous encouragement and criticism: Paul Breslin, Gerald Graff, and Harold Kaplan.

The Research Institute of Chadron State College twice granted me funds to work on this project. I want to acknowledge gratefully that committee's assistance.

I was greatly helped by the anonymous readers at The University of Alabama Press, but, as always, my most perceptive and patient reader was Mary Ellen Elkins.

Finally, I would like to thank the following for permission to reprint copyrighted material:

Dylan Thomas: *Poems of Dylan Thomas.* Copyright © 1952 by Dylan Thomas. Reprinted by permission of New Directions Publishing Corporation.

Denise Levertov: *Poems 1968–1972.* Copyright © 1970 by Denise Levertov Goodman. Reprinted by permission of New Directions Publishing Corporation.

Ezra Pound: *The Cantos of Ezra Pound.* Copyright © 1948 by Ezra Pound. Reprinted by permission of New Directions Publishing Corporation and Faber and Faber, Ltd.

From *This Journey,* by James Wright. Copyright © 1982 by Anne Wright. Used by permission of Random House, Inc.

From "In Memory of W. B. Yeats," from *Collected Poems,* by W. H. Auden, edited by Edward Mendelson. Copyright © 1976 by Edward Mendelson, William Meredith, and Monroe K. Spears, executors of the Estate of W. H. Auden. Used by permission of Random House, Inc.

Reprinted with permission of Macmillan Publishing Company from *The Poems of W. B. Yeats: A New Edition,* edited by Richard J. Finneran. Copyright © 1924 by Macmillan Publishing Company, renewed 1952 by Bertha Georgie Yeats, Michael Butler Yeats, and Anne Yeats.

Reprinted with permission of Atheneum Publishers, an imprint of Macmillan Publishing Company, from *The Carrier of Ladders,* by W. S. Merwin. Copyright © 1969, 1970 by W. S. Merwin. Originally appeared in *The New Yorker.*

"In a Dark Time," copyright © 1960 by Beatrice Roethke, Administratrix of the Estate of Theodore Roethke. From *The Collected Poems of Theodore Roethke.* Used by permission of Doubleday, a division of Bantam, Doubleday, Dell Publishing Group, Inc., and Faber and Faber, Ltd.

"I Cry, Love! Love!" copyright © 1950 by Theodore Roethke. From *The Collected Poems of Theodore Roethke.* Used by permission of Doubleday, a division of Bantam, Doubleday, Dell Publishing Group, Inc., and Faber and Faber, Ltd.

Excerpt from #48 from *77 Dream Songs* by John Berryman. Copyright © 1959, 1962, 1963, 1964 by John Berryman. Reprinted by permission of Farrar, Straus and Giroux, Inc. and Faber and Faber, Ltd.

Excerpt from "At the Fishhouses" from *The Complete Poems* by Elizabeth Bishop. Copyright © 1947 and renewal copyright © 1974 by Elizabeth Bishop. Reprinted by permission of Farrar, Straus and Giroux, Inc.

Excerpt from "Seele in Raum" from *The Complete Poems* by Randall Jarrell. Copyright © 1945, 1951, and 1955 and renewal copyright © 1973 by Mrs. Randall Jarrell. Reprinted by permission of Farrar, Straus and Giroux, Inc. and Faber and Faber, Ltd.

Excerpt from "Skunk Hour" from *Life Studies* by Robert Lowell. Copyright © 1956, 1959 by Robert Lowell. Renewal copyright © 1987 by Harriet Lowell. Reprinted by permission of Farrar, Straus and Giroux, Inc. and Faber and Faber, Ltd.

Excerpt from "The Waste Land" in *Collected Poems 1909–1962* by T. S. Eliot, copyright © 1936 by Harcourt Brace Jovanovich, Inc., copyright © 1964, 1963 by T. S. Eliot, reprinted by permission of Harcourt Brace Jovanovich, Inc. and Faber and Faber, Ltd.

Excerpts from "The Dry Salvages" and "Burnt Norton" in *Four Quartets*, copyright © 1943 by T. S. Eliot and renewed 1971 by Esme Valerie Eliot, reprinted by permission of Harcourt Brace Jovanovich, Inc. and Faber and Faber, Ltd.

The lines from "Diving into the Wreck" are reprinted from *The Fact of a Doorframe, Poems Selected and New, 1950–1984*, by Adrienne Rich, by permission of the author and W. W. Norton & Company, Inc. Copyright © 1984 by Adrienne Rich. Copyright © 1975, 1978 by W. W. Norton & Company, Inc. Copyright © 1981 by Adrienne Rich.

Excerpts from *To a Blossoming Pear Tree* by James Wright. Copyright © 1973, 1974, 1975, 1976, 1977 by James Wright. Reprinted by permission of Farrar, Straus and Giroux, Inc.

Excerpts from the following poems: "A Little Girl on Her Way to School," "A Poem about George Doty in the Death House," "Erinna to Sappho," "The Horse," "On the Skeleton of a Hound," "My Grandmother's Ghost," "Elegy in a Firelit Room," "A Fit against the Country," "The Seasonless," "Eleutheria," "The Fishermen," "Lament for my Brother on a Hayrake," "Three Steps to the Graveyard," "A Presentation of Two Birds to My Son," "She Hid in the Trees from the Nurses," "Morning Hymn to a Dark Girl," "Sappho," "To a Fugitive." Copyright © 1971 by James Wright. Reprinted from *The Green Wall* by permission of Wesleyan University Press.

Excerpts from the following poems: "Complaint," "Paul," "Old Man Drunk," "A Note Left in Jimmy Leonard's Shack," "At the Executed Murderer's Grave," "Sparrows in a Hillside Drift," "In Shame and Humiliation," "All the Beautiful Are Blameless," "The Morality of Poetry," "On Minding One's Own Business," "The Ghost," "The Alarm," "A Girl Walking into a Shadow," "In a Vienesse Cemetery," "A Prayer in My Sickness," "At the Slackening of the Tide," "The Refusal." Copyright © 1951 by

James Wright. Reprinted from *Saint Judas* by permission of Wesleyan University Press.

Excerpts from the following poems: "As I Step over a Puddle at the End of Winter, I Think of an Ancient Chinese Governor," "Three Stanzas from Goethe," "Goodbye to the Poetry of Calcium," "Rain," "Milkweed," "Two Spring Charms," "A Message Written in an Empty Wine Bottle That I Threw into a Gully of Maple Trees One Night at an Indecent Hour," "Having Lost My Sons, I Confront the Wreckage of the Moon: Christmas 1960," "Autumn Begins in Martins Ferry, Ohio," "Fear Is What Quickens Me," "Stages on a Journey Westward," "Two Hangovers," "Beginning," "Depressed by a Book of Bad Poetry, I Walk toward an Unused Pasture and Invite the Insects To Join Me," "From a Bus Window in Central Ohio, Just before a Thunder Shower," "Arriving in the Country Again," "In the Cold House," "Trying to Pray," "March," "Two Poems about President Harding." Copyright © 1959 by James Wright. Reprinted from *The Branch Will Not Break* by permission of Wesleyan University Press.

Excerpts from the following poems: "A Christmas Greeting," "The Minneapolis Poem," "Inscription for the Tank," "I Am a Sioux Brave, He Said in Minneapolis," "Gambling in Stateline, Nevada," "The Poor Washed Up by the Chicago River," "An Elegy for the Poet Morgan Blum," "Old Age Compensation," "Before a Cashier's Window in a Department Store," "Speak," "Outside Fargo, North Dakota," "The Frontier," "Listening to the Mourners," "Youth," "Rip," "The Life," "Three Sentences for a Dead Swan," "Brush Fire," "The Small Blue Heron," "Lifting Illegal Nets by Flashlight," "To the Poets in New York," "Poems to a Brown Cricket," "In Terror of Hospital Bills," "To the Muse." Copyright © 1960 by James Wright. Reprinted from *Shall We Gather at the River* by permission of Wesleyan University Press.

"Saint Judas," copyright © 1951 by James Wright. Reprinted from *Saint Judas* by permission of Wesleyan University Press. "The Jewel," copyright © 1962 by James Wright. Reprinted from *The Branch Will Not Break* by permission of Wesleyan University Press.

"A Blessing," copyright © 1961 by James Wright. Original poem first appeared in *Poetry*. Reprinted from *The Branch Will Not Break* by permission of Wesleyan University Press. "In the Face of Hatred," copyright © 1960 by James Wright. Reprinted from *The Branch Will Not Break* by permission of Wesleyan University Press.

"Spring Images," copyright © 1968 by James Wright. Reprinted from *The Branch Will Not Break* by permission of Wesleyan University Press.

"Lying in a Hammock at William Duffy's Farm in Pine Island, Minnesota," copyright © 1961 by James Wright. Reprinted from *The Branch Will Not Break* by permission of Wesleyan University Press.

"In Fear of Harvests," copyright © 1959 by James Wright. Reprinted from *The Branch Will Not Break* by permission of Wesleyan University Press.

"Living by the Red River," copyright © 1960 by James Wright. Reprinted from *Shall We Gather at the River* by permission of Wesleyan University Press.

Excerpts from *Two Citizens* by James Wright. Copyright © 1970, 1971, 1972 by James Wright and copyright © 1986 by Anne Wright. Reprinted by permission of Anne Wright. Excerpts from "The Quest" by James Wright, copyright © 1971 by James Wright. Reprinted from *Collected Poems* by permission of University Press of New England. This poem first appeared in the *New Yorker* magazine.

Excerpts from "Small Frogs Killed on the Highway" by James Wright, copyright © 1969 by James Wright. Reprinted from *Collected Poems* by permission of University Press of New England.

Excerpts from "Many of our Waters: Variations on a Poem by a Black Child" by James Wright, copyright © 1971 by James Wright. Reprinted from *Collected Poems* by permission of University Press of New England.

Excerpts from "A Secret Gratitude" by James Wright, copyright © 1971 by James Wright. Reprinted from *Collected Poems* by permission of University Press of New England.

Excerpts from "Some Translations" by James Wright, copyright © 1971 by James Wright. Reprinted from *Collected Poems* by permission of University Press of New England.

THE POETRY OF JAMES WRIGHT

Introduction

James Wright (1927–80) wrote his life into his poetry. His entire body of work, consisting of seven major books of poetry, numerous reviews of other poets' works, many published poems that never made it into a book, and several small-press chapbooks of poems, is really one epic poem, a continuing quest, like Wordsworth's *Prelude,* for the poet's self, his identity. In fact, Wright "is perhaps the most 'questing' of all contemporary poets," as Peter Stitt notes,[1] agreeing with other critics. Exactly what to call the stages of the quest, however, is not always agreed upon, but most agree on the general outline—from despair to joy, from alienation to community—and suggest similar analogues. Hank Lazer claims that Wright's career resembles "a mystical journey, one whose stages resemble those delineated by Evelyn Underhill in her classic, *Mysticism:* Awakening or Conversion, Self-knowledge or Purgation, Illumination, Surrender or the Dark Night, and Union."[2] Stitt contends that Wright's quest is "more clearly circular than linear," ending where it began, a quest for recovery of the poet's lost "childhood radiance and joy," similar to Wordsworth's quest in his "Ode: Intimations of Immortality from Recollections of Early Childhood." "The positive 'pole,'" Stitt says, "is located both at the beginning . . . and at the end . . . of man's life."[3] I like to think of Wright's career in terms of the romantic poet's career as outlined by Robert Langbaum in *The Poetry of Experience*. Romanticism, Langbaum says, is not a particular belief or set of beliefs, but a movement from rejection of tradition (what he calls the "Everlasting No," taking that term from Carlyle) to reaffirmation (the "Everlasting Yea"), based on one's subjective and conscious choice to believe: "It makes no difference whether the romanticist arrives in the end at a new formulation or returns to an old one. It is the process of denial and reaffirmation which distinguishes him from both those who have never denied and those who, having denied, have never reaffirmed."[4] I have to agree with Langbaum, as opposed to Stitt, that "although many romantic careers look like a working back to what had been originally rejected, it would be a mistake to suppose that the position returned to could ever again be the same as the original position. For the position returned to has been *chosen*, and that makes it a romantic reconstruction rather than a dogmatic inheritance."[5]

The differences in terminology do not seem all that important to me. One conclusion from the above does seem important, however: Wright's work is a whole and should therefore be read and understood from beginning to end as one continuous statement by a man, a likable guy as we discover, who seeks that pure self somehow beneath or beyond the taint of the culture's guilt. Like all of his formidable ancestors on the same quest, he refuses to trust the socialized self he finds attached to his soul, refuses to be diminished or circumscribed by any society's definition of himself. He works in the great tradition of the adamant individualists in our literary heritage (even though a "tradition" of "individualists" might sound like a contradiction). We hear echoes of someone as far removed as Freneau, who lamented being born "On these bleak climes . . . / Where rigid Reason reigns alone"; Thoreau is present; so is the Emerson who said, "Insist on yourself; never imitate." And the romantics of Britain, those sometimes naive-sounding believers in the individual's centrality and the power of common speech, are also here. Wright's occasional antirationalism, his love of nature and the pastoral, the dominance of lyrical poems in his body of work, his belief in the insights of dreams, his longing for the innocence of children and animals, his exaltation of the exiled individual, and especially the sense in his work of a "something" in reality that is larger than anything science or logic can explain also define him as a twentieth-century romantic. Present also are the ironic moderns trying to make a home for themselves in their imaginations, resisting commitment, reviling the Unreal City and the evils of "usura." Wright has a host of ancestors, then, and his individual struggle, taking place as it does in the last half of the twentieth century in America, dramatizes the central problems of the creative individual in a late industrial society as he tries to turn his life into art.

There are tensions in the poet that vivify the work, as we hear him being poet, being rebel, being proud son of the "dumb honyak" who broke his back in a glass factory all his life, being despiser of bourgeois materialism, being patriot, being iconoclastic denigrator of the violence done in this country in the name of progress, power, and affluence. The body of poetry is like a novel whose protagonist is James A. Wright, the boy from Martins Ferry, Ohio, struggling to deny his heritage, intent on being "European," but finally realizing that, amazingly, one can be an Ohioan *and* an artist. He is, in the end, the man who can curse the stupidity and greed of uprooting elder trees to erect chiropractors' signs and denounce the false dreams that America has sold its young, while also accepting the complex cultural heritage of "America, that brutal and savage place whom I still love." Over the course of his lifetime, he works his way from a single-minded affection for the "beautiful" but outcast, coupled with a single-minded scorn for the "ugly" and conventional, to a larger sympathy that understands the necessity and inevitability (two distinct issues) of both. In the process, he becomes both angry curser and quiet lyricist, neither by itself being a complete art, just as neither rejection nor capitulation, neither denunciation nor apology, can be the sole foundation for a complete life. Wright's understanding of the complexity of his role in the world thus parallels his understanding of his role as artist: he realizes simultaneously that to be complete he must embrace, or "gather" as he says, the "ugly" around him, as well as the "ugly" components of his own soul, and write a poetry open to all prosodic possibilities. His poetry's evolution exemplifies and embodies his life-struggle to reconcile the opposing tensions in his mind.

His work passes through several stages before it reaches this synthesis, and the story of the poet's wrestling with his demons is the story of this book. In the beginning, we hear him as a petulant young lyricist, angry with everyone of the conformist "upper world," while writing merrily along in some of the most formally conventional poetry of the late fifties, dominated by iambs, end rhyme, and regular stanzas, and influenced, as Wright readily admitted, by Frost, Hardy, and Robinson. The solid citizens Wright opposes to his vital innocents and animals only fool themselves if they believe they ever truly waken from their self-imposed "Death in the body, stupor in the brains":

> Now in the upper world, the buses drift
> Over the bridge, the gulls collect and fly,
> Blown by the rush of rose; aseptic girls
> Powder their lank deliberate faces, mount
> The fog under the billboards. Over the lake
> The windows of the rich waken and yawn.

As Wright asks us to "pity" these "rising dead who fear the dark," he sounds assured, but that confidence is a pose; his youthful enthusiasm lets him carry off the act of self-righteous and certain reformer. His diction is formal or even consciously "poetic" (we see "orplidean shoulders," for example, as well as "cobbled hills" and "burgeoning . . . golden skin"), while his tone is superior, at times almost sneering: "Warm your hands at the comfortable fire, / Cough in a dish beside a wrinkled bed." His first two books, *The Green Wall* (1957) and *Saint Judas* (1959), are formally impressive, as has often been noted, and in his early poems, Wright is a proficient practitioner of a formal poetry that he later, in his next two books, rejects as confining and oppressive. But the first two books also begin many themes—affection for the underdog, desire for a truer self, rebelliousness—that are central to Wright's whole career and make them a necessary first stage in his lifelong quest. These initial books, then, are a rejection of tradition contained in a traditional form, a muted call for rebellion spoken in the voices of others.

In *The Branch Will Not Break* (1963) and *Shall We Gather at the River* (1968), Wright exchanges poetic fathers, rejecting Robinson,

Frost, and Hardy in favor of Neruda, Trakl, and Vallejo. We see what seems a radically new form—a more "organic" poetry employing longer lines, few rhymes, unpredictable stanza breaks, more obviously autobiographical content, and the speech of the "common man"—which has been prepared for by Wright's translations (with Robert Bly) of European and South American poets and has been made necessary by his desire to speak in his own voice. Precisely what that voice may be is not entirely clear yet, but Wright is confident it must sound more like Neruda and Trakl than Robinson and Frost. In these books, he also steps down from his perch as enlightened poet to rub shoulders with the "social outsiders" he celebrates from above in his earlier books; as he does so, his confident tone becomes diffident, despairing, disturbed. One lesson of maturity is that freedom can be just loneliness and exclusion. It is not as easy as he had thought to be a romantic outcast:

> Soon I am sure to become so hungry
> I will have to leap barefoot through gas-fire veils of shame,
> I will have to stalk timid strangers,
> On the whorehouse corners.

He must suffer the painful alienation that the logic of his first two books demanded. These are his years of wandering in the desert, the "period of travel and experience" that Langbaum identifies as the middle stage of the romantic poet's career, between the angry "Everlasting No" and the heartfelt "Everlasting Yea."[6] (Stitt agrees that in the middle of his career, the quester "must pass through the vale of tears, the valley of the shadow of death, which he finds such a prominent component of everyday reality."[7]) This middle stage is a period of maturation during which the poet feels more confident of his voice—we hear Wright speaking consistently for the first time in the persona he introduced in *Saint Judas* ("James A. Wright, . . . born / Twenty-five miles from this infected grave, / In Martins Ferry, Ohio")—but during which he also feels the implication of his alienation.

In Wright's case, this is also the period during which he most deeply doubts his own vocation as poet. Everything created, including his poetry, he realizes, adds to the muck, impinges upon the creator's neighbors, occupies space, asks for time—uses up all those precious and limited commodities that we can no longer take for granted. Is Wright simply adding more "dreck" to the world? He fears he may be. He distrusts his writing and its impetus as just so much more muscle-flexing in an era when sometimes only desperate acts of muscle-flexing can convince one that one is alive or different, that one matters. Are all creative acts, including taking words and shaping them into a form designed to win praise, acts of greed and ego, acts of aggression, products of the need to make oneself felt in the world, of the desire to reshape the world in one's image? He wonders if perhaps to create or assign or constitute meaning is not just one more oppressive, egotistical act of the mind. Is any creation unbearable hubris in a world that demands our humility before offering up the truth? Builders of shopping malls ignore the beauty they destroy because they value their concrete blight more highly. Is the poet any better for valuing his or her "this and that," the poet's art, the words, more highly than the silence they displace? Does art simply give the poet a culturally approved way to express his or her own egotistical needs? Are not shopping malls also culturally approved expressions of will?

Wright thus assumes the burden of the creative artist in postmodern America: the acute sense of loss of self in the midst of vast bureaucracies, the need to hear himself to believe he exists, the fear that even poetic speech is simply one more form of pollution in a world already overburdened with garbage. He curses "them" for bulldozing his America but secretly fears he may be a partner in their conspiracy to appropriate the world for selfish needs. He is told, he believes, to be quiet and content yet knows he needs to shout to live. But to shout is, perhaps, to add one's own voice to the drone of steam shovels spewing smoke to satisfy others' (less honorable?) desires to carve their names on the world so that they can be sure of their own identities. The dread of not speaking and being nothing balances the dread of speaking and being one of "them," those he curses throughout his first four books.

In Wright's last three books, *Two Citizens* (1973), *To a Blossoming*

Pear Tree (1977), and *This Journey* (1982, published posthumously),
he achieves the synthesis his poetry has been leading him toward: he
is the confident poet of the first two books, but without needing to
feel superior; he uses any form—sonnet, prose poem, rhymed cou-
plets, free verse—appropriate to his rhetorical and aesthetic goals;
his work is autobiographical, not distanced, as at first, or self-con-
scious, as in the second two books. He settles into a poetry of more
restrained imagery, explicit statement, and simple diction. He be-
comes, in short, the mature poet who has come to realize that truth
is not only beauty but ugliness as well, them as well as us, formality
as well as informality, hate as well as love, and that all truth is cause for
celebration. The world stands forth as fresh again to the dying poet:

> The moon and the stars
> Suddenly flicker out, and the whole mountain
> Appears, pale as a shell.

He works his way forward from a midcareer flirtation with anarchy,
characterized by a willful and often angry rejection of the forms he
mimicked so well in his initial books, to a consciousness of "wise
innocence" that accepts all it sees. He learns to live and write being
grateful for what he has, "my Ohioan," as he says, realizing that to
sever all cultural, social, historical ties would be to destroy the very
taproot of his life and creativity. The honest affirmation of his life
and culture makes his poetry not only central to its developing tradi-
tion but bracing to readers of any time. Wright's final two books are
the best examples, I believe, of an earned, open-eyed affirmation of
self, history, and culture that one can find in recent American poetry.
 Eliot tells us that "the important difference [between major and
minor poets] is whether a knowledge of the whole, or at least a very
large part, of a poet's work, makes one enjoy more, because it makes
one understand better, any one of the poems. That implies a signifi-
cant unity in his whole work."[8] The desire to write down the
"knowledge of the whole" motivated this study. What follows will, I
hope, reveal a "significant unity" in Wright's work and strengthen
his claim for recognition as a major American poet.

1

"Had you
been strong
enough to dare"

James Wright's first book, *The Green Wall* (1957),[1] a Yale Series of Younger Poets selection, chosen and introduced by W. H. Auden, is caught between earth and air, between the poet's desire to be one of the brave souls who live fully in this world and his longing for escape from this "rifted paradise" into a realm "beyond the names / Of sludge and filth of which this world is made." This desire to be both of the earth and off the earth, to live gracefully and fully in this land of beauty or to escape this land of death, is at the heart of all of the poet's later work. We hear in these poems the contrasting attitudes implicit in what Northrop Frye calls the "language of immanence" and the "language of transcendence."[2] At times, Wright speaks as if a meaningful life is to be lived with one's feet planted firmly on earth, and we hear the "language of immanence": values are to be found in the things of this world and our life among them. In these poems, as we shall see, Wright advocates an active ethics: to live well is to run and jump and do. In other poems, those in which we hear the "language of transcendence," Wright implies that all meaning is elsewhere, off this earth, above it or below it, and we find passive heroes and heroines, listening to the music of the spheres rather than the rhythm of the seasons. The root of this ambivalence is the conflict between the poet's desire, on the one hand, to live fully among the concrete details he affectionately describes—hawks, horses, and hounds—and his fear, on the other, that to do so is to be implicated in mankind's profound guilt, a guilt born of his need to alter, tamper with, and destroy those very things he loves as he expresses his exuberance and will. There is, then, a political, as well as religious and philosophical, component to this ambivalence. Wright will move, in seven volumes, toward a synthesis of these attitudes, call it an active passivity. The activity will be the writing of poetry itself; the passivity, the careful, slow, and nonaggressive observation of the life before his eyes, what Hank Lazer calls "the ideal of receptivity" in his essay on Wright's last book.[3] The ethics will finally be one of active observation: one looks closely, reverently, apparently passively, to see and then to release in words the value immanent in all life's phenomena. He finally accepts "immanence" because he no longer feels bound to dissociate himself from those he deems guilty.

That wise reconciliation, however, takes time, and his opening poems are a complex fallacy of bifurcation: either I live here on my own terms and without compromise, or I will be damned to mediocrity, conformity, commonness, and bad faith; either I flee this rotting globe (to where?) or be doomed. Even the fullest life is a doomed life; anything less than the fullest life is a damned lie. The "world of *The Green Wall* is without redemption," as Jerome Mazzaro notes, but where else can Wright go to be redeemed?[4] The inability to align himself squarely with either "immanence" or "transcendence" shows up in the poems in the suspension of characters in midair. Sometimes the speaker himself is "hung in poise / Between the air and the damp earth" ("A Little Girl on Her Way to School"). Sometimes a character is "hung":

> Caught between sky and earth,
> Poor stupid animal,
> Stripped naked to the wall,
> He saw the blundered birth
> Of daemons beyond sound.
>   ("A Poem about George Doty in the Death House")

When Sappho, in "Erinna to Sappho," is lured from her lover's side by a "hollow spirit," Erinna literally drags the poet back where she belongs, cleverly using Sapphic stanzas to describe the feat:

> I leaped, above the ditch of earth,
> Bodily, clung my arms around
> Your poising knees, and brought us both
>   Back to the ground,
>
> Where we belong, if anywhere,
> To hide in our own hollowed dust.
> Whatever I gave, I gave no bare
>   Pain of a ghost.

Whether or not "we belong" here is the problem. If we do, how can we live well *here*?

The tension or "hanging" is also clear in those poems in which Wright celebrates animals in both worldly and otherworldly terms, apparently uncertain where his heroic horses and hounds should reside. The horse in "The Horse," for example, is introduced as a sort of Platonic ideal of the beast, hot out of the ovens of creation, "dripping with the dew of lawns" and soaring in a realm far above the "Death in the body, stupor in the brains" that characterizes earthly life. The horse is almost pure disembodied action, romping above this earth, and in the first two stanzas, Wright frequently disrupts the poem's basic iambic beat by starting a line with a strongly accented verb that stresses the animal's vitality: "Rose," "Leaped," "Jerked," "Spun naked." Yet later in the poem, the horse descends to this world and is palpable enough to throw off his rider, the speaker's wife. In "On the Skeleton of a Hound," Wright inspects a hound's remains and imaginatively supplies the animal with a hare-chasing past firmly rooted in this world ("I saw the two leaping alive on ice, / On earth, on leaf, humus and withered vine"), but

> Then, suddenly, the hare leaped beyond pain
> Out of the open meadow, and the hound
> Followed the voiceless dancer to the moon,

To dark, to death, to other meadows where
Singing young women dance around a fire,
Where love reveres the living.

One could call this a simple apotheosis, common enough in poetry, or could object that we expect poetry to leave the hard ground of mayapple and crowfoot to "race between the stars." Yet so many of Wright's subjects in *The Green Wall* get suspended between here and there, between this world and some other that is always pictured as a better place, purer, cleaner, more alive, that the suspension or movement becomes conspicuous, part of the book's central theme. In the sonnet "My Grandmother's Ghost," for example, the octave has the spectral relative sampling the pleasures of berries, a "shallow stream," and damp leaves. In the sestet, however, the ghost makes her way back underneath the ground once she is satiated with the momentary joys of sunshine and sight-seeing:

And then, forgetting what she wanted there,
Too full of blossom and green light to care,
She hurried to the ground, and slipped below.

In some cases, this transportation between realms is facilitated by images that sound realistic but are impossible to visualize. The reader is coaxed from a realistic setting to a fantasized world:

Instead of paying winter any mind,
I ran my fingerprints across the glass,
To feel the crystal forest sown by wind,
And one small face:

A child among the frozen bushes lost,
Breaking the white and rigid twigs between
Fingers more heavenly than hands of dust,
And fingernails more clean.
　　("Elegy in a Firelit Room")

As we read the first two lines of the second stanza quoted (the third stanza of the poem), we may believe the child outside the window is real, though experience makes us suspect that the child is not. By the third line, we are sure that the child is imagined, and by the fourth, we are in a pure world where the words make sense but are impossible to visualize. What, after all, do fingernails more clean than "hands of dust" look like?

All the examples cited can be explained as appropriate to the subjects of the poems, but that is not the point. The point is that Wright chooses, in this first volume, subjects that lend themselves to this treatment that floats the reader from the palpable to the impalpable, the real to the imagined, earth to air, time to eternity, limited life to unlimited imagination, or, sometimes, life to death. Realistic-looking characters are not painted for their own sake, but for the sake of Wright's intention. As Mazzaro has noted, "Will prevails in *The Green Wall,* and landscape seem[s] mainly 'setting' or 'idea.' Nature [is] the projection of various subjective states. . . ."[5] Despite the fact, then, that *The Green Wall* is loaded with concrete nouns and distinct, realistic settings, our feet always seem to be drifting off the earth and toward a realm of ideas, either heavenward or downward, in any direction as long as it is away from this tainted land where repression and convention are the rules of order. If one could simply live, be like the hound who "lived the body out, and broke its laws, / Knocked down a fence, tore up a field of clover," then one could remain firmly planted here. But one cannot, or rather—and this distinction will be important for the direction of Wright's poetry—"they" will not let one simply and purely live. So one must escape. The forces of society, and often they are as vague as that phrase implies, prevent one from living one's life truly. In this volume, Wright celebrates those who manage to live innocently (primarily animals and children) or who avoid society's rules (the "social outsiders," as Auden calls them in his "Introduction"[6]), and who are thus not only true to themselves but also untainted by the culture's dark guilt, as it selects for and rewards those who are conformist, complacent, and content with their assigned roles. However, the poet also implies, by his many images of physical or imaginative flight, that such a life "beyond" convention and constraint is impossible if one is human, wants to live very long, or wants to live within the bounds of—and share the fruits of—a culture that is inherently repressive. The poems in *The Green Wall* remind one at times of Yeats's early visions of a fairyland that is seductive but inhuman, an Arcady "Where the wave of moonlight glosses / The dim grey sands with light," but where "the calves on the warm hillside" and "the kettle on the hob" ("The Stolen Child") are both absent. How can one enjoy both the free, intoxicating life of "there" and the human life of "here"? Can one? Or does the fairyland of freedom and fulfillment exist only between realms, only in poetry? The questions will trail the poet throughout his career.

His poems are the young poet's attempts to set the world straight, to lead it to a clean place only dimly apprehended by the writer himself but believed in passionately. He fears growing old and becoming self-satisfied and complacent, of course, but just as importantly, he fears being defined, while he is alive, by a culture in which he feels an alien. These poems, although their metrical regularity and conventionality do not hint at Wright's later experiments in prosody, begin the poet on the quest that will be the focus of his entire poetic oeuvre, the quest for a way to live as a creative being. What comes through consistently in Wright's first book is the poet's longing for relief from human pain and confusion, a desire for love, peace, and an undistorted view of "the way." He sets down the terms of his struggle in "The Quest," first published in 1954, although not part of the original version of *The Green Wall:*

> So, as you see, I seek your bed
> And lay my careful, quiet ear
> Among the nestings of your hair,
> Against your tenuous, fragile head,
> And hear the birds beneath your eyes
> Stirring for birth, and know the world
> Immeasurably alive and good,
> Though bare as rifted paradise.

The effortless and unannounced movement from the realistic details that begin this poem's final stanza, and which are characteristic of its first three stanzas, to the fantastic image of "birds beneath your eyes" is typical, as I indicated above, of these poems' suspension between a loving concern for the facts of this world and a desire, usually calm in this volume but to become more desperate later, to get "behind" those facts' surfaces to some land where decay and disintegration do not threaten the speaker's existence. The longing for a meaning for a world that is neither divinely ordered (we find no affirmation of a traditional deity in Wright) nor a fiction created in response to the poet's consciousness of the loss of such a divinely inspired significance is a typical longing among postmodern American poets.[7] Like many of his contemporaries, Wright wants to believe in his life and find a stable ground for it. Existential "nausea" and an existence that is mere existence will not do.

However, while he gives with one hand ("the world / Immeasurably alive and good"), he immediately takes away with the other ("Though bare as rifted paradise"), as though distrusting his own affirmations. The early poems are informed by the realization, or perhaps only the hope, that something "Immeasurably alive and good" does reside here and may guide or inspire the poet, but with the equally held conviction that such goodness is doomed, which only increases the poet's despair and urgency. As Wright said in an interview with Dave Smith, he learned from E. A. Robinson that this world demands hope but simultaneously shatters it.[8] Quietly, these poems hold before our eyes the beauty that can be nature, but they also remind us that death and decay are the inevitable fate of all things living. All manner of things rot and "fall" here—apples, pears, sparrows, chickens, tanagers, hay, fish, hounds, and, occasionally, human beings disintegrate before the reader's eyes. The odor of organic death permeates the poems, beginning with "A Fit against the Country":

> Odor of fallen apple
> Met you across the air,
> The yellow globe lay purple
> With bruises underfoot;
> And, ravished out of thought,
> Both of you had your share,
> Sharp nose and watered mouth,
> Of the dark tang of earth.

The landscape does occasionally blossom, of course, but summer
is usually only a memory to keep one warm while snow covers the
ground:

> When snows begin to fill the park,
> It is not hard to keep the eyes
> Secure against the flickering dark,
> Aware of summer ghosts that rise.
> The blistered trellis seems to move
> The memory toward root and rose,
> The empty fountain fills the air
> With spray that spangled women's hair;
> And men who walk this park in love
> May bide the time of falling snows.
>   ("The Seasonless")

Spring is mentioned in the past tense, here in lines that echo "Fern
Hill":

> When I went there first,
> In the spring, it was evening,
> It was long hollow thorn
> Laid under the locust,
> And near to my feet
> The crowfoot, the mayapple
> Trod the limbs down
> Till the stalk blew over.
>   ("Three Steps to the Graveyard")

But rarely do we find spring in the present tense. We are occasionally
given glimpses of spring, but the picture of winter or autumn. Life is
a continuing process of loss, redeemed only, if at all, by the soft, dark
beauty of decay:

> The moments ride away, the locust flute
> Is silvered thin and lost, over and over.
> She will return some evening to discover
> The tree uplifted to the very root,

> The leaves shouldered away, with lichen grown
> Among the interlacings of the stone,
> October blowing dust, and summer gone
> Into a dark barn, like a hiding lover.
>   ("Eleutheria")

We are all pursued, as is Eleutheria, by time: "the pale year follows her." Furthermore, to live improperly, that is, not to live completely, is to die metaphorically. The shadow of death—as a figurative or literal presence—forces the question of how to live. Wright's subjects, then, ultimately are mortality (to be doomed), spiritual enervation (to be damned), and the relationship between them: can this doomed life be led fully and morally here, thus avoiding damnation (which is not a religious term but specifically the "stupor in the brains" he so fears)?

These are the poems of a young man, as I said, not of an old one looking back and brooding on mortality. That much is clear, first, because the poet takes too much sensual delight in his images of death ("Bewildered apples blown to mounds of shade"); second, because the poet tells the world how to live, or "be," as young poets are wont to do ("Be leaf, by hardwood knots, by tendrils crossed / On tendrils, stripped, uncaring; give no shade"); and third, because the poems are not particularly sympathetic to old people gone hollow inside:

> You showed me how their faces withered
> Even as we looked down
> To find where they left off and sea began.
> And though the sun swayed in the sea,
> They were not moved:
> Saurian faces still as layered lime,
> The nostrils ferned in smoke behind their pipes,
> The eyes resting in whorls like shells on driftwood,
> The hands relaxing, letting out the ropes;
> And they, whispering together,
> The beaten age, the dead, the blood gone dumb.
>   ("The Fishermen")

This is one of several poems in *The Green Wall* in which Wright shows off his image-making power, here at the expense of the old fishermen. The fact that the poet can use the old men's infirmities as material for his verbal pictures, with no sympathy for or identification with the image he draws of his subject, says to the reader that the writer is young, flexing his poetic muscle, writing more about himself than about the "dried fishermen" he has come to frame.

And what does this poem, and the others in the volume, say about the writer, other than that he is young? Primarily that he believes himself, and those he associates and identifies with, to be superior: he has not allowed, and will refuse to allow, his "twine" to "go slack," as these fishermen and others of the conventional world have. The fishermen "were not moved" by the "sun" that "swayed in the sea," being too busy at their work to notice the beauty about them. The implication of the line is that the speaker and his companion were moved, and not, as we might suspect, because they were at leisure to observe idly the working fishermen, but because theirs is a superior, a more moral vision than the fishermen's. This may seem to be drawing too much out of a single poem, but the tone here is clearly that of the condescending young artist sneering at the old wage-slave's predicament, and it returns in other poems, slightly modified and with less obvious targets. Even the speaker's wife in "The Horse" is mocked for her timidity after being thrown from the exemplary horse mentioned earlier:

> Run to the rocks where horses cannot climb,
> Stable the daemon back to shaken earth,
> Warm your hands at the comfortable fire,
> Cough in a dish beside a wrinkled bed.

Earlier in the poem, Wright had included himself among the timid ("Now we have coddled the gods away," "wild / Arenas we avoid") but now points his finger directly at "you."

The speaker's brother, too, is shown throwing away his life, this time as he is hunched over a hayrake:

Cool with the touch of autumn, waters break
Out of the pump at dawn to clear my eyes;
I leave the house, to face the sacrifice
Of hay, the drag and death. By day, by moon,
I have seen my younger brother wipe his face
And heave his arm on steel. He need not pass
Under the blade to waste his life and break.
("Lament for My Brother on a Hayrake")

The poet has his eyes "clear" and can see the "sacrifice," both of the hay and of the lives spent harvesting the hay. The younger brother, however, is not only "broken" but is blind to the fact as well. The tone is not mocking, as is the tone of "The Horse," but it is too dispassionate to be termed sympathetic, either. If you are afraid of the horse's vitality or are content to waste your life in common labor (common because conventional, not merely because physical), if fear, lack of imagination, or simple conventionality breaks your spirit, the poet will shed no tears for you. Turn yourself into a sickly caricature of what you have the potential to be if you please, he says, but do not look to me for sympathy.

Who, then, does get the poet's nod? As James Seay has noted, Wright's hopeful experiences in *The Green Wall* "usually involve a surrender of the Self to another living thing [the horse and hound, for example] which the poet senses is in closer touch with the mystical forces of nature, a surrender that is motivated by the hope of sharing that state of being."[9] In *The Green Wall*, those characters who truly live, those whose "state of being" Wright would like to share, live beyond the bounds of society and may not be the best models, or even possible models, for the rest of us. They are inhuman, insane, or on the fringes of culture. Hence, horses, murderers, hounds, lesbians, children, prostitutes, and lunatics are rather violently yoked together to form one group, that of the living innocents whose sheer naive vitality (in the case of the animals and the children) or courageous defiance of conventionality (in the case of the various "outsiders," mostly women) makes them heroic. Wright's symbolic animals run, jump, and fly, trusting their muscles:

THE GREEN WALL 🦌 19

Look up and see the swift above the trees.
How shall I tell you why he always veers
And banks around the shaken sleeve of air,
Away from ground? He hardly flies on brains;
Pockets of air impale his hollow bones.
He leans against the rainfall or the sun.
    ("A Presentation of Two Birds to My Son")

By contrast, the "chicken" (not a very subtle pun) is afraid to leave
the secure ground:

Chicken. How shall I tell you what it is,
And why it does not float with tanagers?
Its ecstasy is dead, it does not care.
Its children huddle underneath its wings,
And altogether lounge against the shack,
Warm in the slick tarpaulin, smug and soft.

Wright gives us "smug" in the last line when we expect "snug" and
makes the chicken not only timid but morally repugnant. That the
chicken grasps earth rather than soars overhead is not only a biolog-
ical fact but a moral one, and the swift (also appropriately named) is
credited with "genuine ecstasy," a code phrase for the result of a
properly lived life. Both chicken and swift are "clods," but the latter
at least has known the "agony" of flight that is also "ecstasy, a kind
of fire / That beats the bones apart / And lets the fragile feathers
close with air." Like the hound's life, the swift's is doomed and
"meaningless," but at least it is not "plain," as the chicken's is. Sheer
action becomes one form of morality, one definition of a "full life."

One can only talk for so long, however, about the morality of ani-
mals before realizing that the term is misplaced. People are moral or
immoral, not animals, and in *The Green Wall*, Wright also gives us
human models, people who are approved of for defying convention
in whatever form. The mental patient who refuses to respond to the
curfew whistle in "She Hid in the Trees from the Nurses" is a case in
point. "She," the mad patient, is called from the woods by the atten-
dants' "whistles":

> She too must answer summons now,
> And play the chimes inside her brain
> When whistles of attendants blow;
> Yet, for a while, she would remain,
>
> And dabble her feet in the damp grass,
> And lean against a yielding stalk,
> And spread her name in dew across
> The pebbles where the droplets walk.

Here it is not action that is moral, but a passive resistance to authority. Who is truly maladjusted, Wright wants us to ask, the patient or the keepers? Who truly lives: the raw, unsocialized self of the madwoman or the agents of society and denial who "summon" the female patient from her reverie back to official reality? Is it true that, as Roethke says in "In a Dark Time," "madness" is "but nobility of soul / At odds with circumstance"? Is it better to be insane by official definition when one lives in an insane land? Does not that make one all the saner? Or, as R. D. Laing says in *The Politics of Experience*, "Our society may itself have become biologically dysfunctional, and some forms of schizophrenic alienation from the alienation of society may have a sociobiological function that we have not recognized."[10] The assumption is that there are portions of the self, largely untapped and buried deep in our unconscious, that we could ride to full awareness if we would only surrender to them. The problem for modern humankind is that we have "coddled the gods away" and drawn "grass over our childhood's lake of slime" ("The Horse"). The "slime" that we hide from ourselves is not disgusting at all, however, but is the source of new life if we would rediscover it. As Jung says when discussing the role of progression and regression in the libido theory,

> What the regression brings to the surface certainly seems at first
> sight to be slime; but if one does not stop short at a superficial
> evaluation and refrains from passing judgment on the basis of a
> preconceived dogma, it will be found that this "slime" contains not
> merely incompatible and rejected remnants of everyday life, or
> inconvenient and objectionable animal tendencies, but also germs
> of new life and vital possibilities for the future.[11]

"Surrendering" to one's "slime" rather than to society's demands returns us to the right path, in much the same way as does the surrender of Emerson's "traveller" in "The Poet": "As the traveller who has lost his way throws his reins on his horse's neck and trusts to the instinct of the animal to find his road, so must we do with the divine animal who carries us through the world."[12] Trust that the "horse," the unconscious, prerational portion of the psyche so at odds with the time clock, knows the way. Listen to the rhythms deep within yourself, as "she," the mental patient, does. Recover the eland, the vital link between the inner and outer worlds, that the wife in Jarrell's "Seele im Raum" conjures up from her psyche and then seats at the supper table as a member of the family: "To own an eland! That's what I call life!"

The problem with this advice, however, is that elands and horses are usually unwelcome guests at dinner. Jarrell's speaker had her imaginary eland taken from her—"it was ill, they told me." Is it possible to let loose the reins on one's "horse," to recover one's "slime," and still live in an organized society with established and sometimes rigid rules of decorum and order? If it is impossible, do we give up the "horse" and "slime" or society? What do we lose, and gain, in either case? The implication of "She Hid" is that we would lose much less by giving up society than by failing to listen to our inner voices. The fairly regular iambic tetrameter mimics the keepers' world, where there is no room for the aberrant patient or the extra syllable. The "summons" and the poet's meter are both external forms of order imposed upon the woman. The "chimes" in her brain are associated with the "whistles of attendants" and further emphasize the externality and unnaturalness of summoning her away from her quiet pleasure. There is a clear opposition made between the woman's reality and the hospital's, which, by extension, is the reality of the society at large, which establishes and supports such places. Wright makes us wonder why the woman must be denied her harmless pleasures:

> But why must she desert the shade
> And sleep between the walls all night?

Why must a lonely girl run mad
To gain the simple, pure delight

Of staying, when the others leave,
To write a name or hold a stone?
Of hearing bobwhites flute their love
Though buildings loudly tumble down?

Having the "buildings" of officialdom "loudly tumble down" stacks the deck in the woman's favor. The "simple, pure delight" of the bobwhites' love that she listens to is meant to be not only pure and innocent but part of something eternal as well, while the culture's monuments to itself make their only coarse music as they fall apart. It is becoming clear that one of the virtues of alienation is not only inculpability for a society's crimes, but also escape from the fear of mortality. The woman is listening to something—a Jungian collective unconscious, perhaps, or some great undefined ground of being that underlies all forms of life, human and inhuman—that is outside of clock time, measuring whistles, plodding meter, and societal fashions. Her peace is the peace that passeth not only understanding but also individual mortality, for it is the peace of listening to the music of the spheres or the single heartbeat beating through all nature.

One need not be mad, of course, to feel this life-force. Several sane, "dark" females in the volume also seem to be in touch with a vitality that denies convention and forestalls or neutralizes the fear of death. Betty, the black prostitute in "Morning Hymn to a Dark Girl," is one such character. She lives next to a river, beneath a bridge, and beneath the streets of the city's daily commerce. She is literally and figuratively on the edge of society and explicitly contrasted to the "upper world" of light, where men become "stone" as they go about their stultifying daily rounds:

Summoned to desolation by the dawn,
I climb the bridge over the water, see
The Negro mount the driver's cabin and wave
Goodbye to the glum cop across the canal,

> Goodbye to the flat face and empty eyes
> Made human one more time. That uniform
> Shivers and dulls against the pier, is stone.

One can almost hear the speaker thinking, like Eliot's speaker in *The Waste Land* as he walks with the morning crowds across London Bridge, "I had not thought death had undone so many."

Wright repeatedly uses the word "dark," even to the point of making the light around Betty "dark light," which she graces "darkly." The light and the coming of dawn, when the speaker must leave Betty, signify the state of man "made human one more time." Light and human are used here in ways contrary to their normal poetic usage and contrary to the way Wright will use them so effectively in his last book, *This Journey*, where, in a more affirmative mood earned by years of struggle, he employs light more conventionally: as a symbol of knowledge, illumination, deliverance, celebration.[13] He longs there to be part of the light, to bathe in its blessing:

> I am going home with the lizard,
> Wherever home is,
> And lie beside him unguarded
> In the clear sunlight.
>   ("Wherever Home Is")

To be part of the "light" world here, however, is to be one of the "rising dead who fear the dark," one of those who rise in the morning to greet the solid assurance of another day, but who fear the dark of their own souls, open to them at night in dreams or in the love Betty offers. The "rising" is opposite to the "rising" others do in this volume as they rise to love. These risers of the town's populace are those who deny and avoid love, the body's secrets, and themselves. They prefer to live in "the pale town" where their "flat face[s] and empty eyes" can be safe among other empty eyes, and where they can take their appointed places, "dull against the pier."

The words associated with the upper world are revealing: glum, empty, dull, aseptic, dank, fog, dune, stone, pale. Wright depicts a wasteland, "dune on dune" of infertility. Betty, by contrast, resides beneath these streets of daily activity, in the "fearless" portion of our psyche that we normally allow ourselves to see only in dreams. "Dream on," the poet tells the dark girl, "scatter the yellow corn / Into the wilderness, and sleep all day." Betty is the fecund, grain-scattering woman of the "wilderness," of the unconscious, untamed, primeval forest of the psyche. She is at home in the animal and vegetable world:

> Your shivering ankles skate the scented air;
> Betty, burgeoning your golden skin, you poise
> Tracing gazelles and tigers on your breasts,
> Deep in the jungle of your bed you drowse;
> Fine muscles of the rippling panthers move
> And snuggle at your calves; under your arms
> Mangoes and melons yearn; and glittering slowly,
> Quick parakeets trill in your heavy trees,
> O everywhere, Betty, between your boughs.

The sensuous lyricism of the alliteration seems perfectly suited to the wild creature who will later "slide / Silkily to the water" and greet orangutans and crocodiles, animals chosen, like mangoes and melons, for their exotic sound. When Wright gets to Betty, and away from the conventional phrasing that begins the poem ("Summoned to desolation by the dawn"), his paean to the "dark girl" is a joy to read, as one imagines the "rippling panthers" snuggling Betty's calves. The reader's natural curiosity about this "dark girl" and Wright's clever use of verbs at the ends of lines to create momentary suspense pull the reader through the verses and bind the lines one to the next.

Another "living thing which the poet senses is in closer touch with the mystical forces of nature" is the speaker in "Sappho," who is left alone when her lover is "pluck[ed]" away "like an apple" by her jealous husband. The abandoned speaker, however, cannot have her memories tarnished, not even by the "sly voices" that condemn her:

> But I have turned away, and drawn myself
> Upright to walk along the room alone.

Across the dark the spines of cactus plants
Remind me how I go—aloof, obscure,
Indifferent to the words the children chalk
Against my house and down the garden walls.
They cannot tear the garden out of me,
Nor smear my love with names.

The speaker is "beyond the names" and need not defend herself: "I keep the house and say no words," Wright has her think twice. Like religious truth, her knowledge is intuited directly rather than understood verbally. Yet "they," those of conventional wisdom and morality, *must* "smear" her to make themselves feel clean, for hers is a deviant and infertile desire (like the mad patient's, and one with a long history, as the title suggests) that threatens "their" unexamined complacency:

For I know that I am asked to hate myself
For their sweet sake
Who sow the world with child.
I am given to burn on the dark fire they make
With their sly voices.

The irony of "sweet sake" and of a "dark fire" supposedly fueled by "their" pure motivations is in keeping with the poem's underlying moral paradox. The woman reverses the Edenic myth and declares herself made innocent by her knowledge and by her experience of passion:

There is a fire that burns beyond the names
Of sludge and filth of which this world is made.
Agony sears the dark flesh of the body,
And lifts me higher than the smoke, to rise
Above the earth, above the sacrifice;
Until my soul flares outward like a blue
Blossom of gas fire dancing in mid-air:
Free of the body's work of twisted iron.

In Wright's Heraclitean world, the way up is the way down, and the flame of physical passion causes one to burn and "rise" above the smoke and earth. The speaker's calm voice contrasts with her detractors' harsh words and makes her refusal to sacrifice herself on their altar of repression seem not only convincing but also morally correct. Her restrained defiance elicits the reader's sympathy and approval as "their" excoriations cannot.

Wright gives us another innocent in this volume, this time a young girl in "A Little Girl on Her Way to School." It seems that all of nature talks to the girl (stones cry out under her feet, while a catbird, a pigeon, and a swan all give her directions as she walks), but she does not talk back, at least not in a language most humans would understand. For, like the speaker in "Sappho," this little girl has no need for words: "She listened, but she would not speak, / Following the white swan through the hedge." Presumably she can speak but chooses not to. It is not ignorance Wright shows us, but, on the contrary, a higher knowledge, a superior vision. The little girl is guided so well by her mystical communications with nature that she can move effortlessly "through the hedge," "following the white swan" on her way to school. She is like Cook Ting of the Chinese parable, who used the same knife for nineteen years without sharpening it because he was able to "go along with the natural makeup" and let the "spirit move where it wants."[14] Barriers offer no more resistance to her movement than oxen joints did to Cook Ting's knife, because she follows the spirit where "perception and understanding have come to a stop."[15] She is "beyond" understanding as those of the adult, light world know it—beyond rational, logical, discursive knowledge, which is always associated here with the cultural repression that constructs walls (or builds hospitals) on which others bruise themselves.

These early muses of Wright, by their very unreality, pure sensuality, or idealistic innocence, betray the poet's youth, his own innocence. There is a continuity of muses in Wright's poetry. Betty and the young girl belong to the poet's early work and are almost fairy-tale muses. Later women will initiate Wright into, and eventually lead him through, more difficult times. Jenny, who appears in what I call the middle stage of the poet's career, his third and fourth books, is, like Betty, "dark," but dark in a much more complex way. She is dead, lost to the poet, and sits at his shoulder as he works his way through his most difficult poetic and personal crises. She leads him through hell, and he almost stays there, fearing himself too beaten to return to the living and, it must be added, enjoying his self-pity. The final muse, Annie, Wright's actual second wife, is the muse of the light, as light is used in the poet's final stage, hopefully and joyously. She leads him through Europe, where he comes to terms with his past and his country's past, discovering how to live on the far side of despair, learning what will suffice, or, as Wright says it, recovering "the river gold" that is always present but often inaccessible. Betty and the schoolgirl seem pure constructs of the poet's imagination, controlled by Wright, rather than leading him where they will, as Jenny and Annie do to a more vulnerable or open poet.

Wright's muses in *The Green Wall*, then, are innocent and acceptable enough, for the most part. It is one thing to praise horses and little girls, though, and quite another to idolize a murderer, as Wright does in "A Poem about George Doty in the Death House":

> Close to the wall inside,
> Immured, empty of love,
> A man I have wondered of
> Lies patient, vacant-eyed.
> A month and a day ago
> He stopped his car and found
> A girl on the darkening ground,
> And killed her in the snow.
> . . . .
> But I will mourn no soul but his,
> Not even the bums who die,
> Nor the homely girl whose cry
> Crumbled his pleading kiss.

Why is Doty mourned? What do we know of him to justify, or make us sympathetic with, Wright's judgment? Not a great deal: Doty is "alone" and "clean shaven." Other than those facts, we only know what the poet imagines Doty to be: one who has seen "the blundered

birth / Of daemons beyond sound," one who "rose / For love" be-
cause he was "Sick of the dark," one who has "to bear / What no
man ever bore." The poeticizing ("blundered birth / Of daemons"),
romanticizing ("For love"), and exaggerating ("What *no man* ever
bore"?) of Doty's condition tells us more about Wright, and the lim-
itations of his radical rejection of moral convention, than about
Doty. Loneliness and darkness have acquired a life of their own and
carry the poem on by their own insistent echoes of other poems in
this volume, in which they are associated with creatures of superior
vision and instinctive morality. Doty, by this account, "sees" some-
thing that the "bums" in his cellblock do not. These complaining
bums, we begin to suspect, are meant to represent those of the
"light" world, those cultural criminals who imprison helpless vi-
sionaries. But there just is not enough justification given in the
poem for valuing Doty or for believing that he—a real murderer, by
the way—was motivated by anything noble, even by anything
"darkly" noble.[16] In the opening lines Wright tells the reader that he
has been "Lured by the wall, and drawn / To stare below the roof."
He has been "lured" and "drawn" rather by his own poetic diction to
accord Doty the status of one of his noble outsiders. And his facility
with the form—iambic trimeter, a stanza of two envelope-rhymed
quatrains—encourages him to keep going smoothly on to a planned
conclusion, apparently while giving little thought to the implica-
tions of his sympathy. The lines roll one into the next, as we have to
imagine the poet's mind did as he smoothly flowed along on the pull
of the meter and rhyme, until he filled up the last stanza with a
predictable—for the poet, we must imagine, as well as for the
reader—conclusion. Wright should have remembered one of Frost's
rules: "No surprise for the writer, no surprise for the reader."[17]

Wright makes a simple dichotomy, in "A Poem about George Doty
in the Death House" and throughout *The Green Wall*, between "us,"
including the poet and all his enlightened readers, and "them." Just
as "they" define the various "social outsiders" as evil, Wright defines
"them" as oppressive by making them crude, boorish, narrow-
minded straw men—evil cops, heartless businessmen, sadistic jail-
ers—whom the poet sets up to knock down with the innocent good-

ness and vitality of his protagonists. But the poet's own piety and smugness, evident, I think, in the passages quoted here, damage his credibility as the messenger of humility and egolessness. Even a more subdued, or humane, tone, however, would not make the moral universe Wright constructs here any less simplistic. All issues are phrased in either/or terms in *The Green Wall*. We are of the world or off it; we are in society or out of it; we are moral or immoral. In the poet's first two books, his "Everlasting No," the world is typically composed of good guys (in the black hats this time) and bad guys, leaving the reader few areas of moral grayness. But if moral problems were so clear-cut, they would not be problems at all, as Wright surely knew when he wrote *The Green Wall*. The reader gets the impression that the words begin to move forward under their own power, thanks to their own momentum, after Wright provides the impetus. "Darkness" overwhelms all questions of moral ambiguity as Wright plays with the paradox of a dark (but pure) and silent (yet communicable) knowledge that promises a childlike happiness beyond the culture's bounds, which seduces the poet and the reader with the hope that such a happiness is not only possible but also desirable for an adult in this world. What Wright's romantic forebears knew—that one cannot be morally pristine without being a Keatsian "sod," that the very act of framing the terms of purity distances one from that prelapsarian world—seems to have been forgotten. And what anyone in twentieth-century America should know—that to be outside the culture of power is to be the victim of it, that to refuse to participate in a guilty society only ensures that society's continued culpability—seems to have been ignored.

Children, horses, hounds, swifts, lunatics, murderers, prostitutes, lesbians—all are conferred with automatic innocence because they are outside the dominant culture that Wright implicitly condemns. The silent women and the mute animals, by their "higher" knowledge, carefree egolessness, and instinctive behavior, become for Wright symbols of the unconscious life-force that we have buried, again at the culture's insistence, beneath layers of rationality, lies, and coercive socialization. In "The Politics of Anti-Realism," Gerald Graff calls this "assumption . . . that a parallelism exists between psychological, epistemological, esthetic, and political categories of experience" "cultural radicalism."[18] Graff goes on to define the term more fully:

> The central assumption here is that objective thought is the psychological and epistemological counterpart of political tyranny. There are several senses in which this is held: objective thought requires us to repress our emotions, to take a "valueless" stance in the interests of operational efficiency. This "reification" destroys the unity between ourselves and what we perceive and turns the "other" into an alien thing, ripe for domination and manipulations. In a parallel fashion, Western civilization turns both nature and human beings into manipulable things through technological mastery on the one hand and colonialism and exploitation on the other. . . . It follows that the cultural revolution must be conceived as a revolt against the reality principle in the name of the pleasure principle, as the overcoming of repressive reason by imagination— or by a new "reason" based on Eros, fantasy, non-aggressive desire.[19]

The individual who denies his dark heart is, on his own small scale, the model for the father who tyrannizes his child, the scientist who creates Frankensteinian mutants in his lab, the general who "saves" a village by obliterating it, the president who administers a colonial empire. Wright wants to make very sure that his poetry does not belong on the list of parallelisms, a list that, ironically enough, appeals only to our rationality, that human faculty that delights in seeing connections. He wants his words to express his emotions, voice his values, and maintain and strengthen the bond between himself as poet and perceiver and his subjects. He will work, then, toward a poetry that resists the urge to dominate or manipulate purely for the gratification of the writer's ego.

Wright, however, like many contemporary poets, by rejecting the intellect as oppressive, falls victim to "a new dissociation of sensibility," a term employed by Stephen Stepanchev in *American Poetry since 1945*.[20] Stepanchev questions the logic of this conscious narrowing of the range of poetry and we should, too. As Stepanchev states, "Bodily and emotional processes . . . represent only a part of the life of man."[21] Are the pleasure principle, as exemplified by the madwoman's desire to sit and listen to the bobwhites' song and Betty's dark eroticism, and the imagination sufficient by themselves to cleanse either the speaker or the culture? Can the characters in the poems, attractive as some of them are at times, serve as models? Do we want to live like Doty or Betty? Could we, even if we wanted to, live like the horse, the hound, or the little girl on her way to school? I can hear some readers about now shouting that I am asking the wrong questions: poetry does not give us role models; Wright is not writing hagiography for us to model our lives after. To think so is to butcher poetry unmercifully, in the way newspaper editors do when they extract "words to live by" to fill a blank space at the bottom of page thirty-five. But those objections will not do because, first, Wright clearly wants these poems to be guiding lights, to tell the reader about his own life. In a 1972 interview, Wright said this of *The Green Wall*: "I tried to begin with the fall of man, and acknowledge that the fall of man was a good thing, the *felix culpa*, the happy guilt. And then I tried to weave my way in and out through nature poems and people suffering in nature because they were conscious. That was the idea."[22] "The idea," then, according to the author, is to show us how wrong we are to interpret our "fall" as our curse. The speaker's wife who falls from the horse in "The Horse" is wrong to let her fall keep her down. She suffers unnecessarily: "I think that most of the people who are alive in the world right now are very unhappy. I don't want people to be unhappy, and I'm sorry they are. I wish there were something I could do to help. I'm coming to face the fact that there isn't much I can do to help. And I think I've been trying to say that ever since I've started to write books. That's what my books are about."[23] He tries to help his readers be happier, even though he realizes his efforts are probably futile. The poems do, then, imply authorially approved ways to live.

Even if we subscribe to the gospel of the intentional fallacy and deny the validity of Wright's opinions of his poems' effects, we can surely not deny our own ears:

Hurry, Maguire, hammer the body down,
Crouch to the wall again, shackle the cold
Machine guns and the sheriff and the cars:
Divide the bright bars of the cornered bone,
Strip, run for it, break the last law, unfold,
Dart down the alley, race between the stars.
("To a Fugitive")

The preacher's voice is unmistakable: Wright is not talking to Maguire, but to us. Run for it, he says, escape the guilt that shackles your life to others' notions of good and bad: "Race between the stars." The poems beg to be read, and evaluated, as moral indictments and instructions. We have a duty, I think, not only to question the internal consistency of a poet's ideas, but also to discuss and evaluate those ideas. I agree with Charles Molesworth on this point:

> . . . I am suggesting something further, namely, that criticism must be willing to engage in Discourse as well as to elucidate Form. Too often poetry is greeted with benign neglect, or facile enthusiasm, or polemical maneuverings. For contemporary poetry some of this is profitable and even necessary, if only as precritical activity, a way of preparing what are often the stringencies of truly innovative poetry for a larger audience. But criticism of a more considered kind, operating with the advantage of at least limited hindsight, must be willing to discuss the content, the argument, the philosophical assumptions and implications of contemporary poetry.[24]

To his credit, Wright values his art highly enough to ask it to do noble work. To his discredit, however, at least in this early book, he asks his readers to accept a simplistic linking of all rationality and compromise—including necessary compromise to external demands of daily living—with tyranny, repression, and oppression.

Of course, if we believe that Wright was conscious of the assumptions that underlie *The Green Wall*, we would expect him to have eschewed the traditional verse structures that dominate the volume. That is, we would expect him to have abandoned the poetic form that "dominates" its subject in favor of a form that gives the subject free rein. But, as Wright says in a later interview, he was tyrannized by his iambic heritage. He also learned early—first from John Crowe Ransom while an undergraduate at Kenyon College from 1948 to 1952, and later from Theodore Roethke while a graduate student at the University of Washington taking Roethke's creative writing class in the spring of 1954—a great respect for craftsmanship, which he apparently took to mean traditional, tight forms at this early stage in his career. Like many other American poets writing since the 1940s (I am thinking especially of Lowell, Berryman, Dickey, Merwin, Roethke, Levertov, Simpson, and Kinnell), he soon threw off or began to distrust and use more sparingly the regular stanzas, meters, and rhymes that are every English-speaking poet's heritage and every young, English-speaking poet's bonds. The Lowell of *Lord Weary's Castle* (1946) is not the Lowell of *Life Studies* (1959), any more than the Wright of *The Green Wall* is the Wright of *The Branch Will Not Break* (1963), his third book. Both poets, like many of their contemporaries, had to find new forms and new voices to convince themselves they were writing their verse, not an updated version of their forebears'.[25]

The change in style is a subject for a later chapter, but one question is relevant here: why did so many poets of Wright's era begin their careers as they did? In his book *From Modern to Contemporary: American Poetry, 1945–1965*, James E. B. Breslin examines ten "first books" written in America during the forties and fifties. Wright's first book supports Breslin's contention that "in the postwar period, poetry characteristically began as a not-too-disorderly retreat to preexisting positions," in large part because of "the poet's persistent presentation of the self as powerless, passively suffering the burdens of a splintered, chaotic world."[26] Often enough in this volume we have seen just such "passively suffering" victims—the outsiders, those only peripherally part of a world they have no control over. The victimized self retreats to a comfortable spot from which to make silent protest, and the poet speaks from within the comfortable framework of a poetic tradition he has mastered. We notice the absence of any real protest, any revolutionary dialogue or calls to political action. Very few characters protest here, and if they do, their dissatisfactions are private: the silent housecleaning of the woman in "Sappho" is perhaps the most vociferous protest we hear. Like that woman, Wright in these poems often shakes his fist at the "splintered, chaotic world," but from inside a clean home or while retreating. The speaker carves out a comfortable world within the poem, a spot that, as I have said, is believed to be innocent of the outside world's violence, somehow "above" or "beyond" the "sludge and filth of which this world is made." Despite the fact that he instructs his readers on how to live, the poet seems to have little faith in his power to effect change. These doubts are not expressed directly but are evinced by the firm conventionality of the verses—a radical change in style, even the possibility of one, seems now beyond the poet's imagining. The poems, then, even as they celebrate daring, are timid; as they preach hope, they are defeated. Their form, while in conflict with the poet's celebration of anarchic energy and a boundless life-force, gives Wright an ordered, calm spot, an eye in the storm whose course he records but feels powerless to alter. The technique ensures the poet's purity but does little to dispel the evil that he wants to remain free of. To keep the "sludge and filth" at bay, Wright must remain "aloof" from the very demonic forces and darkness that he wants to appropriate as the source of the imagination's vitality.

The tension between poetic method and poetic goal is revealed to the reader in the conflict between the writer's desire for freedom and his attachment to a secure past, between his desire to be both of this world (secure and grounded) and off it (free and soaring), which I mentioned at the beginning of this chapter. Even his announced affection for Frost and Robinson might be seen as a halfhearted attempt to be free of a stifling, modernist inheritance while still keeping within a tradition. He chooses to be mildly rebellious—by naming as his mentors modernist figures less celebrated and therefore less intimidating than Yeats, Eliot, or Stevens, and by flirting with outcasts in his frustratingly confining verses—because the tension between content and form, between that which he believes in and that which he still needs to rely upon, is as yet unresolved in his mind. He is an "angry young man" trying to break free, but afraid of complete independence.

It would be wrong, however, to think that Wright is merely a poet for late twentieth-century America, shortsighted to believe that his concern with the problem of living a moral, clean life in a corrupt culture is strictly a contemporary identity crisis in verse. His rejection of contemporary American culture as oppressive and corrupt and his consequent hope for a home elsewhere place him squarely in the mainstream of American literature, whose most persistent theme from its Puritan beginnings, according to A. N. Kaul in *The American Vision*, "may be described as the theme of separation from an established society in search of a more satisfying community life."[27] Wright, although he has reversed the moral values of light and darkness, joins this continuing war between the forces of light and the forces of darkness that was begun by the Puritans; was carried on by Thoreau as he temporarily abandoned Concord in favor of Walden Pond; was continued by Melville as he sent Ishmael to sea; was furthered by Eliot, Hemingway, Fitzgerald, and others as they sought proper soil for their art in Europe; and was perpetuated by countless more writers who either lamented living in such an unromantic, pragmatic, and materialistic culture hostile to art, the artist, and the artist's personal integrity, or who literally abandoned the culture altogether. This "antinomian, Adamic impulse," as Roy Harvey Pearce demonstrates in *The Continuity of American Poetry*, is central to the American poetic tradition.[28] The problem Wright faces, "the problem of reconciling individual freedom with a mode of social life to which the individual can give his allegiance without danger of impairing his moral, spiritual, or psychological integrity,"[29] is the same problem faced by all major figures in the history of American imaginative literature. How can the individual remain true to the deepest impulses of his or her soul while pledging allegiance to a society that demands, for its stability and productivity, that we all subjugate part of ourselves for the common good? Must the individual's insistence on personal freedom and integrity lead to isolation, selfishness, irresponsibility, and a loss of cultural heritage? Or is there some way to reconcile the individual's needs to the group's and thereby retain both the benefits of the group's support and its history as well as the strength derived from remaining true to one's personal morality? Wright, by his continuous and ultimately successful attempt to come to terms with his native land and his poetic heritage, assumes his role as one of a long series of disenfranchised, alienated American writers.

2

"My name is James A. Wright"

*S*aint *Judas* (1959),[1] Wright's second book, looks, on the surface, like a continuation of *The Green Wall.* We encounter the same formal patterns, the same dominance of iambs, the same insistent end rhyme, or so it seems. If we look closely, however, we can see a difference as the poet begins to doubt the efficacy of those inherited conventions and of language itself. Wright turns in *Saint Judas* to what may be the most important themes of poetry in the twentieth century—the flirtation with silence, the distrust of language's power to communicate or heal, and a profound sense of the responsibility and guilt attendant upon creation. His words bring only bad news of the world. He feels criminal for having spoken. Whether these terms are explicit or subtly underlie the poems' thematic structure, they are ominously present in almost all of the verses in this volume. Can the language Wright has at his command help him live? Is that poetry's function? If not, what is the use of speaking? Can words make honest statements about the world they seem to describe and give meaning to, or does the very act of uttering a phrase do violence to the phrase's subject? As bearer of bad news, is not the poet somehow responsible for creating what might have gone unnoticed? In his need for love and communion, does he do more harm than good to the people he touches? How is he—or is he—different from the murderer George Doty, who, "for love," raped and killed a girl? (We, of course, can see that he is, can realize, as Robert Bly says, that "a convicted rapist-murderer is a different piece of goods from James Wright."[2] Wright, however, does not always see this.) Does language simply domesticate the world, make it easier to bear? Or can it reveal its subject? How can it be made to bear witness, to communicate the deepest truths to others? Or, as William Meredith worded the problem when discussing the "mock-aphorisms" in Roethke's *Praise to the End!*, "can knowledge be *worded*, once it has been felt?"[3] And a more technical problem: are the forms that have been useful throughout the history of English poetry still valid? These are the questions that Wright, directly or indirectly, wrestles with in *Saint Judas.*

The book's first two poems, "Complaint" and "Paul," are helpful here. The subject in both is the death of a woman, probably a wife in both cases. In "Complaint," the speaker, after identifying the woman as "my love, my moon or more" in line 1, refuses to mourn her passing for the next fifteen lines, thinking of her only as a "hag," as little more than a domestic servant who kept the civil peace in his house:

> She chased the chickens out and swept the floor,
> Emptied the bones and nut-shells after feasts,
> And smacked the kids for leaping up like beasts.

She is defined as women so often are in American literature: as those who give order to the chaotic adolescence of the children and sweep up as needed:

> And who will dump the garbage, feed the hogs,
> And pitch the chickens' heads to hungry dogs?

The lines conceal a grief that the speaker wants to control by his pose of indifference, which finally breaks down in the final couplet:

> New snow against her face and hands she bore,
> And now lies dead, who was my moon and more.

"More," placed as it is as the poem's last word and echoing with "my moon," rings in our ears with the recognition that the poet has been faking it, denying his loss, being "cool." The woman, who "dumbly bore such pain," was not only the speaker's lover, she was also his mentor, for he, too, tries to bear his pain "dumbly," tries to hold it at bay by not expressing it. The tension between the speaker's words and the pain they suppress provides the poem's energy. It is the sort of effective understatement we find in Pound's "The River-Merchant's Wife: A Letter," but it also raises a question: why did the speaker try not to reveal his loss to us or to himself? In Pound's poem, the understatement intensifies the reader's sense of the lovers' affection, which their culturally conditioned sense of decorum does not allow them to express openly. In Wright's poem, with a different speaker in a different culture, the refusal to mourn not only intensifies the reader's sense of the speaker's loss but also implies the speaker's skepticism about speech's cathartic power, its usefulness as a means of understanding or relieving pain. If language cannot help us understand loss but only hide or heighten grief, what good are words? Speaking of the loss only reminds us of it: may it not be better to bear pain "dumbly"? If language only points to the wound—and we have to remember the wound the poet feels, his scar of separation from his culture—and cannot pretend to hide or salve it, why speak? Why make poems?

Paul's wife is dead, too, in "Paul." The speaker remembers her for Paul:

> I used to see her in the door,
> Simple and quiet woman, slim;
> And so, I think, Paul cared the more
> The night they carried her from him,
> The night they carried her away.

For the doctor who pronounces her dead, "There was not anything to say" (which would have been more naturally stated as, "There was nothing to say," but Wright needed the extra syllables for his tetrameter line), just as the speaker in "Complaint" tried not to say what he felt about his wife, knowing that no expression could change the fact. The world is clearly more powerful than the word in these poems. Paul himself dumbly bears the loss:

And did Paul shriek and curse the air,
And did he pummel with his fist
Against the wall, or tear his hair
And rush outside to bite the mist
That did not have a thing to say?

He sat upon the ruffled bed
And did not even look at me.

Of course Paul is too shocked to speak, but as we see more instances of characters unable to speak, we realize that language can possibly (and only possibly) sugarcoat grief but cannot solace the aggrieved. The death in "Paul," for example, is related in nursery rhyme cadence that makes the loss sound like the end of a parlor game ("she was resting now, / And would not wake, and that was all") or in flat, clipped phrases from which all emotion has been surgically removed ("She was lovely, she was dead"). Words are the speaker's enemies, the treacherous utterances from his own pain that force their way out, almost against his will. Language seems to have no real role in relieving the burdens that touch us most deeply, such as grief. When a loved one dies and the world seems to have lost its sense, language is tested. These poems are brief case studies, then, of language's efficacy, its human worth. If words can make pain comprehensible, they are valuable—they thus help us establish our relationship to the shaky world outside us. If they only point to pain as a fact, what have they done for us? And what has the poet or speaker done except inflict pain? Here, in these opening poems, language's only function is description, and the world language describes is better left undisturbed by words that only sharpen its pain. It is true, as Bly says, that the "most pronounced emotion in *Saint Judas* is guilt."[4]

It would be helpful if we could at least lie well, but that, too, seems out of the question. Not only can the speakers of "Paul" and "Complaint" not fool themselves, others seem incapable of any therapeutic deception. The old man of "Old Man Drunk" cannot use words as "treachery" and thereby avoid offending and hurting his daughter with the news of her lover's death:

He would have lied to her, were he not old:
An old man's fumbling lips are not defiled
By the sweet lies of love.

The messenger is held accountable for his bad news:

. . . His daughter struck him in her grief
Across the face, hearing her lover dead.

We sympathize with the helpless old man (and Wright obviously does, too, perhaps seeing his own predicament in the character's), but also with the many speechless who do not know how to make language into a shape that will not offend, will not hurt, but will appease and aid. The speaker, whom I think we have to identify as Wright, also "can say nothing," can only sit and watch the old man drink through the night, "lost in the blind bewilderment of love" and unable to make sense of his daughter's "meaningless despair." All the poet can offer is a "vague alas," parodying the poetic grief meant to soothe but which is now trite, worn-out, ineffective, a condolence offered from a lost age.

The speaker cannot lie and cannot make life or its pain meaningful. Suffering can be, has been, the path to redemption; we expect tears to be meaningful. But what if the speaker cannot utter or believe the terms necessary to suffering's transformation? Those phrases of condolence and promise are not available to Wright, so why speak at all? All he can cause is grief to others and guilt to himself; all he can bear is bad news. In "A Note Left in Jimmy Leonard's Shack," Beany ("the kid whose yellow hair turns green") tells the poet to find Jimmy and report that his brother, Minnegan, is drowned. The speaker fears Jimmy's reaction:

You might have thrown a rock at me and cried
I was to blame, I let him fall in the road
And pitch down on his side.

As we may expect by now, the speaker first tries to be brutally honest and dispassionate about the death he is reporting ("Your brother

Minnegan, / Flopped like a fish against the muddy ground"). Without some balm for the wounds of the life he records, he first feigns indifference, pretending not to be injured, but his attempts to be callous fail him. By the end of the poem, although Minnegan is still "Rolled in the roots and garbage like a fish," he is also "The poor old man." The poet tries to dissociate himself from the death, but as the end of the poem nears, he realizes he must make an accurate statement, knows he no longer can dance around the corpse and pretend not to care about the dead man. He cannot distance himself from others' grief, nor can he fail to report the loss. He is, after all, the poet. He is trapped with his words, must speak, and, in speaking, must finally tell the truth as he sees it. The impulses to honesty and verbalization (impulses, one suspects, common to most poets), coupled with the desire to help those he is compelled to hold before our eyes (an impulse especially identified with this poet) doom Wright to fill the world with messages of unremediable anguish.

But is the poet just a messenger of doom? A messenger who has lost the technique of making the bad news bearable? Who has not the courage to deliver the news without making it bearable? Who is not interested in sanitizing the bad news? We hear Wright speaking of his own dilemma when he has his persona say,

> Well, I'll get hell enough when I get home
>   For coming up this far,
> Leaving the note, and running as I came.

Saint Judas is the "note" that Wright is reluctant to drop, and the note says not only that Minnegan or Paul's wife is dead but also that something much larger is amiss—the culture is in decline, is in fact a culture of death, one in which dying is all that can be done well: "Dying's the best / Of all the arts men learn in a dead place" ("At the Executed Murderer's Grave"). His reluctance to feel the deaths he reports is, in larger terms, his reluctance to face the culture's death, which he rather blithely, and we now suspect inauthentically, announced in *The Green Wall*; his reluctance in *Saint Judas* ironically masquerades as a hard-nosed stoicism at the beginning of a poem, yet it is really the result of his fear that language and its forms, as he now employs and understands those forms, have failed him, as he in turn fails those he addresses. Language points to dark truths, but words do not explain those phenomena to him or help him to make sense of his data for his audience. Perhaps there *is* no sense to the world—why should he implicate himself in that meaninglessness by reporting what he cannot cure? Or perhaps words, because they function as interpretations, because we have to order them into sentences that look like explanations, falsify inexplicable experience. Speech of any kind is suspect because it is not raw perception (and is therefore not naked truth) and because its mock explanations do not substitute a quantity of understanding equal to the immediacy they displace and the pain they make us face. Language alienates the speaker from his own perceptions by codifying that data, making new experiences fit old words, promising a precision it cannot deliver, promising that things can be understood when they strike the speaker as unintelligible.

Metered verse is especially suspect, for it is one more step removed from experience. As Karl Malkoff, in *Escape from the Self*, has noted, "The important characteristic of meter . . . is that it exists as a rationally apprehensible construct in the poet's mind before the poem is written, in fact, before the experience that is the occasion of the poem exists."[5] Consequently, the poet may feel, as Wright now begins to feel, that he has "been imposing a logical system on reality, distorting it rather than objectively describing it."[6] Precise, decorous forms imply an order that Wright suspects violates the reality of the subjects trapped inside. He is like the sparrows of "Sparrows in a Hillside Drift," those "pitiful dupes of old illusion, lost / And fallen in the white," who perch on the boughs of an oak as if they still lived in summer. Wright is at the beginning of his poetic winter. Something has died or is at least very ill—his faith in his words, his belief in his role, the assurance of the young poet, his faith in the forms and voice he has inherited and assumed as his own—and nothing has yet sprouted to replace that loss or to convince him that the illness is not terminal. "Somewhere the race of wittier birds survive[s]," he says in the same poem, but "somewhere" is a very vague place. Those "wittier birds," the poets who have found "an alternative method of organizing experience,"[7] as Malkoff puts it, are "alive / Like some secure felicity of phrase." This "bird," however, Wright himself, is still in search of a method and felicitous phrases that he can believe in.

He employs an oxymoron that describes the frozen sparrows and also captures his predicament: ". . . these few blunderers below my hands / Assault the ear with silence on the wind." The profound silence of the frozen birds assaults Wright's ears with its conviction of the impossibility of singing in this frozen season. "Man is the listener gone deaf and blind," Wright says, not qualifications for the ideal listener, we think to ourselves. He cannot discern the sparrows' words, only the winter winds and the chimney whispering to "a cloud of snow." He has only dead words, frozen sounds, to help him understand this "gathering of the cheated and the weak." The struggle is important for the poet because he does not, we can infer, intend his words to be independent of the world they describe, to be neutral signifiers in a sign-system that chases its own tail. He writes to draw the lines of his own face and so cannot really be indifferent to his words' effect, even though he occasionally tries to trick himself into believing that he can remain aloof from his own words or that those words can be fooled into expressing emotions and ideas not his own. In fact, we may infer that he agrees with Arnold's dictum that "we have to turn to poetry to interpret life for us, to console us, to sustain us,"[8] the most important life for him right now being his own. As we have seen, however, the language we use to compose the poetry that may "sustain us" is also the language that, thus far in *Saint Judas*, often betrays us.

Wright's ambivalence about language is one of the most striking features of these early volumes. He is unable to decide whether he should ignore language as unnecessary for true knowledge (as he often did in *The Green Wall*), distrust language as a hindrance to real communication, or praise language as the only means by which we can be fully human. This last attitude is most clearly articulated in "In Shame and Humiliation," a poem from the second section of this volume:

What can a man do that a beast cannot,
A bird, a reptile, any fiercer thing?
  He can amaze the ground
With anger never hissed in a snake's throat,
  Or past a bitch's fang,
Though, suffocate, he cannot make a sound.

This ambivalence derives, I think, from several sources. First is Wright's awareness that language, as a manifestation of the rational mind, distances nature as it codifies and packages it; but that language, as the manifestation of humans' unique self-consciousness, enables people to speak their own names and identify themselves and their relationship to the world outside:

That fire, that searing cold is what I claim:
What makes me man, that dogs can never share,
  Woman or brilliant bird,
The beaks that mock but cannot speak the names
  Of the blind rocks, of the stars.

In his poetry, Wright wants to speak his own identity ("He will not deny, he will not deny his own"), which obviously requires language. Yet, unlike the "starved, touristic crowd" of "All the Beautiful Are Blameless," he also wants to root his identity in the prelinguistic and animalistic portions of the self. How can he use language to reveal those sublinguistic parts of his psyche that may be the storehouse of meaning and hence redemption? How can he not? This distrust of language is both romantic (in that it results from the poet's desire to be more like the silent world of nature) and contemporary (in that it incorporates the post-Freudian notion that language is one of society's methods of socializing the speaker).

Another source of Wright's ambivalence toward his words is his desire to discover "exactly what *is* a good and humane action" and "why an individual should perform such an act," as his statement on the cover of *Saint Judas* tells us. For the poet, words are acts, and Wright's words are not now, he believes, "good and humane" acts.

They have not "helped anyone else to solitude, and [have] not helped him toward solitude," as Bly says.[9] The guilt of *Saint Judas*, indicated as early as the title,[10] derives in part from the poet's suspicion that the anger and malice of "In Shame and Humiliation" cannot become the compassion he seeks. "Working through malice to compassion becomes one way of determining the need for 'good and humane action,'"[11] Jerome Mazzaro reminds us, but how can Wright's words help effect that "working through"? If malice is one result of being expelled from Eden, as Mazzaro suggests,[12] how can Wright in poetry convert that malice to compassion and, if not reenter the Garden, at least discover some community, some end to the isolation from others that his very role as bearer of bad news—as poet, in other words—seems to entail? Perhaps simply being quiet is as close as one can get to a "good and humane action." (The title character, as one may have guessed, must provide the clue and will be discussed later.)

I would suggest that the poet's distrust of language is also a political statement. As Charles Molesworth says, in *The Fierce Embrace: A Study of Contemporary American Poetry,* "public language in America is intended to deceive, to foster a false consensus, or to lubricate the gears that mesh induced appetites and shabby products."[13] For a poet, like Wright, who wants to speak honestly, disrupt the consensus, and strip the gears of conformity, the public language is naturally suspect. To call attention to the lies that "the language of the tribe" enforces—for example, that life's tears will be wiped away in a blissful, heavenly beyond—is to call attention to the culture's lies. We do not see much in *Saint Judas* that identifies itself as "political poetry," but the very act of questioning the language that we use daily to bear up is political in the broadest sense, for it makes us wonder if our terms of conciliation are not just drugs fortifying us against the reality of our pain. We tell ourselves "it will be all right" so we can get up, go to work, and keep the machine rolling. Wright says it is not all right, he cannot make it all right, and we lie to ourselves if we declare differently or go about our business as if that business were a meaningful compensation for all we have lost— honesty, humility, each other. For a poet with Wright's beliefs, then, distrust of language is more than just a poetic problem he wishes he could solve—it is a movement toward silence, a sort of work slow-down, a strike against business as usual, a defiant act rooted in his conviction that something is very wrong and that we need to stop and find ways to talk honestly and unflinchingly about it. Speech always carries "guilty social overtones," as Roland Barthes tells us,[14] and to flirt with silence is to say, in effect, "By God, I didn't start this mess," as Wright says in "Two Poems about President Harding" (*The Branch Will Not Break*).

The poet is in a real bind, however, because of course he cannot really be silent—by definition he has to speak, if only to say he would rather not; even the speaker of "Sappho" has to *say*, "I keep the house, and say no words"—and because any kind of writing is eventually taken over and neutralized by the culture, no matter how revolutionary the author's intentions were when choosing his words. The sixties and their aftermath taught us that much. The hip, often obscene, phrases and gestures of the counterculture, de-signed to shock "uptight" members of the middle-class establish-ment, have since become the diction and imagery of advertising, movies, television, and journalism. A consumer culture consumes practically everything with no signs of indigestion. As Barthes says, ". . . there is no writing which can be lastingly revolutionary, and . . . any silence of form can escape imposture only by complete abandonment of communication."[15] Total silence, then, seems the only really revolutionary "statement," and total silence obviously will not do for a poet who wants to remain a poet. Wright certainly wants neither "imposture" (speaking about not speaking, for exam-ple) nor "complete abandonment of communication." What he wants is a way to speak that will allow him sincere, honest com-munication that denies the cultural assumptions (the dominance of the ego, the willful manipulation of the world for selfish ends, the anthropomorphic appropriation of all the contingent world to man's realm) of the language he uses to communicate. This is a painful struggle for the very life of the poet, and we should expect am-bivalence about the medium that both facilitates and hinders the poet's quest.

Nowhere is this ambivalence more evident than in "The Morality of Poetry," in which Wright meditates upon the poetic process while contemplating the wild sea below him:

> I stood above the sown and generous sea
> Late in the day, to muse about your words:
> Your human images come to pray for hands
> To wipe their vision clear, your human voice
> Flinging the poem forward into sound.
> Below me, roaring elegies to birds,
> Intricate, cold, the waters crawled the sands,
> Heaving and groaning, casting up a tree,
> A shell, a can to clamber over the ground:
> Slow celebration, cluttering ripple on wave.

The poet is "late": he follows the modernist masters who have given him a style he finds confining. The words of the poet Gerald Enscoe, to whom this poem is dedicated, are juxtaposed with the noise of the "roaring" sea: words and world, in the same stanza, are separate but distinct, one an ordered human sound, one a "cluttering." The sea's noise is rough and anarchic, a "slow celebration." The poet stands "above" this chaos, separated from it physically and by his rational musings, and wonders how it can survive:

> I wondered when the complicated sea
> Would tear and tangle in itself and die,
> Sheer outrage hammering itself to death.

He imagines his words, his *mot juste,* harmonizing these discordant noises:

> And, for the ear, under the wail and snarl
> Of groping foghorns and the winds grown old,
> A single human word for love of air
> Gathers the tangled discords up to song.

He proposes to tame the sea and order it with his voice, making pattern out of puzzle.

In so doing, however, he loses the sea's variety and fertility, its "sown and generous" nature, preferring to strip it to its bare bones, to keep it spare and lean, a skeleton that can be understood:

> It thrives on hunger, and it rises strong
> To live above the blindness and the noise
> Only as long as bones are clean and spare,
> The spine exactly set, the muscles lean.
> Before you let a single word escape,
> Starve it in darkness; lash it to the shape
> Of tense wing skimming on the sea alone. . . .

He prescribes a poetics of minimalism, order, and control, a poetics of restraint of nature's vigor, fullness, noise, and spontaneity. The tone is the same tone the poet uses to describe the tough person, the one who can live courageously despite the fears that such living brings, the person who is hard, cold, lean, tautly drawn. His prescription is for a poetics of man and mind, a modernist avowal of craft and impersonality that aims to tame the sea's exuberance, its "sheer outrage," and its "heaving and groaning." It is a poetics appropriately captured in a skeleton image.

The white space between the first and last section is the poet's uncertainty and indecision about his prescription. As the second section begins, he quickly recants and vows to let the sea go its anarchic way:

> So through my cold lucidity of heart
> I thought to send you careful rules of song.
> But gulls ensnare me here; the sun fades; thought
> By thought the tide heaves, bobbing my words' damp wings;
> Mind is the moon-wave roiling on ripples now.

"Now" mind and nature are reconciled rather than juxtaposed, or so we are told. But is that reconciliation possible? The poem concludes:

> In a mindless dance, beneath the darkening air,
> I send you shoreward echoes of my voice:

The dithyrambic gestures of the moon,
Sun-lost, the mind plumed, Dionysian,
A blue sea-poem, joy, moon-ripple on wave.

As we can see, Wright does not "let all measures die," as he urges us to do, and the celebration of a Dionysian "moon-ripple" is phrased in nearly flawless iambic pentameter. Metrically, the "dithyrambic" gestures of the second section are indentical to the "spare" lines of the first. The mind has changed—one of the "Lunar Changes" that are announced in the title of this first part of *Saint Judas*—but the meter has not. The claims to synthesis were premature. What Wright gives us is, first, the thesis in the poem's opening section and, second, the antithesis in the closing section. But there is no synthesis of mind and moon: despite the clever phrase "sea-poem," we are given only a picture of opposing forces and the dominance of the shaping poet's "cold lucidity." How can a poem celebrate the life-affirming "dithyrambic" gestures of section two rather than the life-denying "clean and spare" bones of section one?

This is the same as asking what "the morality of poetry" is. In what ways is a poem "moral"? Is it moral by being dithyrambic, by being a "sea-poem" rather than a poem about the sea? By being true to its subject's identity, by admitting the priority of the world and of the subject, rather than simply using the subject to evoke the mood the poet wants evoked, thus assuming the priority of the poet's intention rather than of the world's existence? By reverencing the world and its inviolability? By respecting the things one uses and incorporates but necessarily distorts by writing about them? By immersing oneself in the flux, chaos, and clutter of life rather than standing above it pure and pristine, removed from commitment and personality, dedicated instead to cold, unnatural forms that imprison rather than reveal the objects they mold? Yes, to all of the above, I think the poet would answer. He wants, or again we can infer from his poems that he wants, a form and diction that will "receive" rather than shape and subdue those things that can still make this winter world bearable.

But how does one achieve such a moral poetry? That, of course, is the problem, and we see it wrestled with again in "On Minding

One's Own Business." The subject is love, something that may balance pain in this world. Can love be approached through the poet's words, which seem to destroy rather than liberate? In the poem, Wright and another paddler in a boat, gliding near the shore, spot a shack, "Above us, up the bank, / Obscure on lonely ground." They silently "wander out of sight" and, because "Somebody may be there," they vow not to "land to bear"

> Our will upon that house,
> Nor force on any place
> Our dull offensive weight.

We recognize the "somebody" from *The Green Wall*:

> All hunted criminals,
> Hoboes, and whip-poor-wills,
> And girls with rumpled hair,
> All, all of whom might hide
> Within that darkening shack.

So Wright and his companion, stealthily, carefully, without saying a word, glide back across the water, leaving the imagined group of lovers and outcasts alone. To make a sound would be to impose his will, to interfere with the silent workings of love, to violate one place that may harbor that "race of wittier birds" capable of surviving life's chill. There must be a way, then, to receive rather than to force, to accept rather than to oppose, a way to gather rather than to impose. But can that receiving be done through language, or does language necessarily impose the speaker's will? Is silence perhaps the only answer—an untenable one, obviously, for a poet—to the question of how to live in the world? Or can the poet figuratively enter the shack of love and report on its workings as he has reported on death's? Would entering that inviolate place destroy its sacredness and thereby taint with his willful aggressiveness any message he managed to return with?

The answer is not yet given explicitly, but we can see again that, in his own practice at least, the poet's fears are well founded. He seems unable to avoid imposing himself. "On Minding One's Own Business" is like an argument, a series of statements arranged to lead the inquisitive reader to a predetermined conclusion. There is no sense of a meditation unfolding along its own lines, but of an argument being carefully plotted to lead a questioning reader to precisely the spot where the poet wants to leave him. Even the diction of the final stanza sounds like that of some bizarre combination of a lawyer's closing argument and a poet's statement:

> Lovers may live, and abide.
> Wherefore, I turn my back,
> And trawl our boat away,
> Lest someone fear to call
> A girl's name till we go
> Over the lake so slow
> We hear darkness fall.

And if we look at the individual lines of the poem, we notice how often Wright (and this is characteristic of many of his poems, as I noted in chapter one) ends a line with a verb, an accented syllable, or some suspended action that carries the reader over to the next line where the action is completed:

> Ignorant two, we glide
> On ripples near the shore.
> . . . .
> And men in boats alight
> To see the day subside.
> . . . .
> All evening fins have drowned
> Back in the summer dark.

The technique works—it draws us along as surely as the paddle propels the boat in which the speaker rides. But as we see, it is perfectly suited for writing couplets that stack into quatrains that become stanzas that combine into poems that round out neatly in the last couplet's action or thought. It works, but it is as far as one can get poetically from a form that, like the darkening shack of the poem, "receives the night." The poet clearly bears his will on his materials as he is telling us of his reluctance to bear his will on this refuge of lovers. The poet might now agree in theory with Roethke when the latter calls reason "That dreary shed, that hutch for grubby school-boys!" ("I Cry, Love! Love!"), but in practice, Wright's own willful rationality—in the form of intelligent manipulations of the reader's interest and pace—too often intrudes between himself and the shack or birdsong he is trying to pass on to the reader. Wright agrees with Roethke: "The hedgewren's song says something else." But what "else"? And how can one hear it without distorting it? And how then can one convey it without disfiguring the notes? He is competent to describe suffering, but the more delicate act of living happily, an almost impossibly subtle art in this winter world, re-quires a skill he fears he, armed only with his coarse words, does not possess.

The conflict of freedom and restraint is not just a poetic problem; it is a cultural one, too, and when one asks how to capture the moon-ripple in a poem without distorting that silver image or how to describe love without molesting it, one could just as easily ask how to reconcile society and culture as arbiters of values and goals with the individual's needs, which often exist in direct conflict with the group's. How can the poet get what he wants without violating his subject's integrity? Can society get what it needs without violat-ing the citizen's individuality? The poet, faced with his own ano-nymity and unimportance in a world that has no time for his slow meditations or observations, is as endangered as the moon-ripple. After all, who needs another poet when there are almost as many self-described poets today as there are readers of poetry? Who can bother to attend to a moon-ripple when one just like it will float by tomorrow night and we have so much to do now? Wright fears for his own "sown and generous nature" as well as for the sea's, and well he might.

It is not, I think, mere fashionable cultural criticism to contend that most public language is designed to deceive (and that the contemporary American poet who wants to speak the truth, as he or she sees it, has few readers except other contemporary American poets and professors of English) or to note that most of the attention contemporary poetry gets is focused on only one aspect of poetry, its linguistic structures. Wright wants to bring us truth, but who looks for that in a poem now? As Christopher Clausen claims in *The Place of Poetry*,

> Since the rise of science to intellectual preeminence, poets have been less able either to show equal claim with scientists to clarify the problems western civilization has (perhaps wrongly) seen as most important, or to incorporate and epitomize the conclusions of their rivals. . . . The claims of poetry to be the best source of knowledge about human nature and experience came to seem unconvincing to most readers in the age of the social sciences, whose collective name at least carried the promise of greater system and rigor.[16]

Where does the poet in the boat, the bearer of bad news, the thrasher about the waters of language, belong in late twentieth-century America? His work is hermetically sealed away in aggressively small magazines that no one reads; serves as filler for more widely circulated and respected journals such as *The Atlantic Monthly*, *Harper's*, or *The New Republic*, which, to preserve their image as purveyors of culture, must publish at least *some* poetry; or is fodder for the latest linguistic or semantic theory. His work is merely a "text" to be deconstructed, reconstructed, or ignored. Wright believes that poetry can be moral, that it can teach one how to live, or at least help one to discover how to live, and, furthermore, that the writing of poetry is itself a moral act. He believes in the first of Clausen's "two opposed assertions" about poetry: "the poetic imagination provides a kind or kinds of truth at least as valuable as anything science can give us."[17] Autonomy is not his goal; truth is. We have seen that he mistrusts his own language and the traditional poetic forms used to make that language meaningful. He also has to realize, in some part of his brain, that his readers, or potential readers, have even less confidence in the value of poetry, seeing it more

and more as " 'just personal,' inherently an esoteric entertainment
. . . of no real or public importance."[18] He is compelled to keep try-
ing but cannot be sanguine about the results of his efforts.

To add to the poet's troubles is the fact that he has not yet mas-
tered the "morality of poetry": as we have seen, his poems are not
yet the sort of moral acts he wants them to be. Recognizing what
Wright wants us to understand about poetry and morality, it is odd
to reflect that so many of the poems in this book are not very con-
crete or convincing. Many of the poems are like corpses (and corpses
are frequent visitors in *Saint Judas*) into which the poet wants to
breathe new life. Yet they refuse; they exhale air but make no real
sound, just the sickly wheeze of a dying style that can no longer do
what the poet wants it to do. In some of these enervated poems, the
poet claims to be in limbo again, trapped somewhere between the
living and the dead. He is right:

> I cannot live nor die.
> Now shadows rise nor fall,
> Whisper aloud nor weep.
> Struck beyond time and change
> To a claw, a withering thing,
> A breath, a slackening call
> To cold throats out of range,
> I fade to a broken hope.
>   ("The Ghost")

> Neither the living nor the dead I stood,
> Longing to leave my poor flesh huddled there
> Heaped up for burning under the last laments.
> I moved, to leap on spider webs and climb.
> But where do spiders fling those filaments,
> Those pure formalities of blood and air,
> Both perfect and alive? I did no good.
> The hands of daylight hammered down my ghost,
> And I was home now, bowing into my dust,
> To quicken into stupor one more time,
> One of the living buried like the dead.
>   ("The Alarm")

This is the last stanza of "A Girl Walking into a Shadow":

> Something of light falls, pitiful and kind.
> Something of love forgot the dark embrace
> Of evening, where the lover's eyes go blind
> With dreaming on the hollows of your face.

We find two "somethings" in the first two lines of the last stanza of a poem about a girl and her shadow, spoken by an unidentified, older admirer. The poem is rather "shadowy" itself, struggling with its vagueness and portentousness. "With darkness deepening everywhere," the phrase that immediately precedes the quoted stanza, exists only for its alliteration and assonance. Wright should have listened more carefully to his own advice in "In a Viennese Cemetery": "Bodiless yearnings make no music fall." Too often he is "buried" in his iambs and rhyme, filling in the meter as one fills in the blank spaces of a coloring book. Everything looks completed and sounds intelligent, but the poet himself can hear that the words neither command the reader's attention nor compel his sympathy: "Only the living bodies call up love" ("In a Viennese Cemetery"). Does anyone care if the speaker of "The Alarm" is alive or dead? Wright seems afraid to leave the familiar past but eager to plunge into the uncharted future. The flesh may be willing, but the spirit is not, or not yet. He is still an "alien in my self" ("A Prayer in My Sickness"). Just as "The Morality of Poetry" wavers between two opposed notions of poetry, so do many of these poems waver between life and death. That chasm between the two realms is again underneath the poem's surface, as it is in *The Green Wall*. Added to it now is the equally threatening doubt about the ability of the poet to use his language to help him jump the gap, make his poetic leap of faith from the deadly and ghostlike (for him, at least) ground of secure tradition to the new life (he hopes) of the other side, wherever and whatever that may be.

Of course, it is easy to find fault, and certainly I do not want to imply that Wright's voice fails him completely. If we listen to and compare, for example, "All the Beautiful Are Blameless" and "At the

Slackening of the Tide," we will see how Wright can predictably, and then successfully, handle the same subject in different poems. "All the Beautiful Are Blameless" wants to be a concrete poem about a girl who drowned, but it cannot resist mythologizing her death to the point that what we hear is the poet talking about her and lose sight of the girl completely. We can see the tension in the second stanza:

> Two stupid harly-charlies got her drunk
> And took her swimming naked on the lake.
> The waters rippled lute-like round the boat,
> And far beyond them, dipping up and down,
> Unmythological sylphs, their names unknown,
> Beckoned to sandbars where the evenings fall.

It does no good to call these sylphs "unmythological," for we hear the poet drifting into mythological realms when he drowns his subject in "lute-like" waters. The poet muses on the girl as he walks along shore:

> Slight but orplidean shoulders weave in dusk
> Before my eyes when I walk lonely forward
> To kick beer-cans from tracked declivities.

Wright is getting "poetic," and we wonder where the girl has disappeared to. She is no longer the subject of the poem: "orplidean" and "declivities" are. Wright tells us that "the ugly curse the world" and offer "the dead / Hell for the living body's evil." He wants to dissociate himself as much as possible from "the ugly," and one tool he has is his poetic diction. But that diction also distances him from the girl whom he ostensibly celebrates as one of the "beautiful," one of those who will be "blameless now" that she has escaped this "starved, touristic crowd." The voices he curses are not only those of the ugly crowd but also those in his own brain, the echoes of his mentors that terrorize him.

"At the Slackening of the Tide," by contrast, while it, too, tells of a drowning victim, comes alive:

Today I saw a woman wrapped in rags
Leaping along the beach to curse the sea.
Her child lay floating in the oil, away
From oarlock, gunwale, and the blades of oars.
The skinny lifeguard, raging at the sky,
Vomited sea, and fainted on the sand.

The subject is really the drowned child and his mother's anguish, not the poet's desire to write a poem or his quarrel with "them." The language discovers the subject rather than distances it. The diction sounds as if it were inspired by the subject rather than by the poet's thesaurus. True, Wright cannot resist including "naiads," but the "mollusks," "seagulls," and "human howls" dominate. We feel the woman's grief and hear the sea's indifference, "far off / Washing its hands." When the poet considers dying in "The Alarm," he simply talks about it as if wishing to die were something to do to kill time on a dull Sunday afternoon. Here, when he flirts with self-pity, actually wondering "What did I do to kill my time today" while the child was drowning and the mother was cursing the sea, we believe he means it, we do not dismiss the question as mere self-indulgent whining.

All these poems seem prelude to the revealing of the liberated Wright—liberated from consciously poetic diction, from other poets' voices, from simplistic moralizing, and from the fear of hearing himself speak—the Wright we hear in "At the Executed Murderer's Grave," the most satisfying poem in *Saint Judas*. It is, as Wright recognized, a "watershed poem."[19] The poem is divided into seven sections, but the first four sections are really one long, cathartic *mea culpa* and extended self-flagellation as the poet abuses himself for his former "lies." The ostensible object of this abuse is George Doty, the murderer we met in *The Green Wall*, but Doty is here Wright's dark double, "Dirt of my flesh, defeated, underground." Both Wright and Doty are lovers—Wright of his poems and their subjects, Doty of "A girl on the darkening ground" whom he "killed . . . in the snow," as we were told in the earlier Doty poem. Both lovers' touches are murderous—Doty raped and killed the young girl he stopped for; Wright has been metaphorically raping and killing, or so he implies, the subjects of his poems by speaking of them falsely in a false voice. As Wright denies Doty in sections 1 through 4, he simultaneously denounces himself, or the "lies" of his earlier poetry. Both men's loves are destructive, foolish, misguided. He both pities and hates Doty and himself for their frantic, blinding need to express their love. That expression crushes the beloved in its arms.

Wright, of course, is too hard on himself and on his earlier poetry, as we would expect of one feeling the first flush of guilt long buried. He has been going around talking and talking, making a fool of himself in other people's voices, he feels, and is now disgusted with himself. He wants to shed his old skin completely, lose his old voice (which was not really his in the first place), confess his sins without blinking, be forgiven, and start a new life. After confession comes self-pity (earned this time) and a resolution to do right, to live right, to be himself. Ohio killed Doty for murdering his beloved; it will not get Wright, if he can help it. However, he must be wise enough to stop his destructive and self-destructive course before he is silenced forever, as Doty has been. The first four sections, the poem's first forty-nine lines, begin with Wright naming himself for the first time in his poetry ("My name is James A. Wright") and end with his determination to continue to be himself ("I kick the clods away, and speak my name"). In between is the battle with himself. He calls Doty an "idiot," but we hear that he is really angry with himself. He has "made [his] loud display, / Leaning for language on a dead man's voice" and is now "sick of lies." He chastises himself for his "easy grievance"; he "burn[s] for [his] own lies"; he "run[s] like the bewildered mad / At St. Clair Sanitarium"; he "croon[s his] tears at fifty cents per line"; and his "sincerity" and "widely printed sighing" are "paid." The self-disgust that permeates the first four sections leaves little doubt about whom Wright is really disappointed with, even if he had not later in the poem explicitly identified himself with Doty and all sinners ("We are nothing but a man").

He must atone for his earlier false voice. It is as if he suddenly looks at himself in a mirror (Doty plays mirror as well as double), recognizes who he is ("My name is James A. Wright"), is nauseated to recall the false picture he has been presenting to the world ("Now sick of lies, I turn to face the past"), and resolves to set the record straight. His task is the "labor of disclosure."[20] He has come back to Ohio, if only in his mind, "to testify, to bear direct witness to the personally apprehended life" his poetry "rises from," as Warner Berthoff claims is characteristic of "the most accomplished writing since the 1940s."[21] The poem is not only his confession, it is his declaration of poetic independence and his revisionist history of his own past, now spoken honestly, with the implicit promise that he will always speak truly in the future. I will be my own man and my own poet from now on, he declares: "I kick the clods away, and speak my name." We realize now that he has mistrusted speaking not only because he doubts his (or anyone's) words' efficacy, but also because he has not been speaking for or through his own mouth but the mouths of others. The "anxiety of influence" has tempted him to silence. He needs to tell the truth, which means telling his tale in his own words. He is not "James A. Wright" unless and until he can utter that identity in his words, not in the words of others. His identification of himself in line 1 is a challenge to himself as much as it is his declaration of his identity: I *am* James A. Wright, and I had better begin to sound like him, he says in effect. He tries to sound tough ("I waste no pity on the dead that stink"; "I do not pity the dead, I pity the dying"; "Nature-lovers are gone. To hell with them"), but he is not tough at all: he is barely able to speak his name, barely able to talk, almost overwhelmed by fear that he cannot speak, that he has lied too long to recognize the sound of his own voice: "The hackles on my neck are fear, not grief."

Yet he cannot deny Doty or himself any more than the speaker of "Complaint" could disguise his affection for his lost love, "my moon or more." He risks annihilation if he dares speak in his own terms, for he has relied on others'. So it is appropriate that his two faces—the Wright one and the Doty one—meet over this murderer's grave whose "gash festers." It may be the grave of the poet James Wright, if he leaves behind what he knows well for the risky job of being himself. Risks propel our lives into the world, promise the greatest rewards as well as the greatest dangers. Death may be the price of not risking; it may be the price of accepting the challenge. He cannot tell. He may die (metaphorically, as a poet) if he stays (that is, continues to tell "lies"), or he may die if he leaves (speaks for and by himself). He is intensely ambivalent, like the child deciding whether or not to leave the cozy home of his parents. This is his own possible death (even if it is *only* his death as a poet) he is contemplating, not just death as a handy topic for a poem. As Richard Howard noted, "It is not until [Wright] is able to see the entire earth and all its processes of fruition and decay *inside* himself, contained by the arena of his own body . . . that he can stop separating, can stop alienating himself from . . . the ghosts and criminals and lunatics and perverts, the dispossessed who haunt him from the start."[22] He now steps down with the rest of us ("We are nothing but a man"), ready to risk making his way with the feeble language he has at his command. Now that he has exposed himself—as lovers and poets do—he does not have much choice. He can no longer pretend to be someone else, can no longer lean "for language on a dead man's voice." He reveals his secret sins—his inauthentic voice—to his most intimate friends (his readers, his audience, those who respect him the most but also expect the most from him), knowing that when he does so it will be impossible for him to be inauthentic again. It is like confessing your most troubling secret to your spouse, knowing that those words can never be recalled.

He feels cleaner, more honest after his confession, and the splenetic tone of sections 1 through 4 changes in sections 5 through 7 to a pleading, apologetic, humble, almost prayerful tone. He has ventilated what needed to be let out; he has spit and sputtered. The supplicant is an unfamiliar role for Wright—an unimaginable role for the Wright of *The Green Wall*—and his knees audibly creak a bit as he bows down:

> . . . and we dead stand undefended everywhere,
> And my bodies—father and child and unskilled criminal—
> Ridiculously kneel to bare my scars,
> My sneaking crimes, to God's unpitying stars.

He has said something like this in his earlier poems. He has always embraced the "outsider." We even hear the same iambic pull in the lines. But, as I said to begin the chapter, something is subtly different in this book, and we see it most clearly, or finally, here. He *has* embraced the outcast before, and even this specific outcast, but not in his own words—in the inherited words of Hardy, Frost, Robinson, and other poets he admires. The idea may be the same, but the poem is different because the poet is different. He is now speaking for himself and as himself. He is true to himself as James A. Wright of Martins Ferry, Ohio, the man, and to himself as James A. Wright of Martins Ferry, Ohio, the poet. He has no great hope here that such an embracing will be fruitful, but he recognizes it as the only possible solution left him. Like Judas in the book's title poem, Wright has discovered a man, himself, beaten, "Stripped, kneed, and left to cry." Like Judas, he pulls that stranger to him without any guarantee that the embrace will help either one: "Flayed without hope, / I held the man for nothing in my arms." It is a charitable act of loving oneself and of loving all others who are part of the same human community. For Wright, there is only a negligible difference, if that, between the poetic self and the personal self, so to gather oneself and all other sinners, come as they are, is to gather one's own voice, come as it may, and to take the leap of faith into the unknown world of speaking "the names / Of the blind rocks, of the stars" in one's own tones.

Saint Judas is a record of the poet's struggle against his own inherited limitations. The book is, in one sense, a paradoxical celebration of the poet's defeat, a defeat that makes him whole, that empowers him to speak, a defeat that is necessary before he can make "At the Executed Murderer's Grave." The poet says he will "Devour the locusts of my bitterness." Like Baudelaire, Rimbaud, Rilke, Dostoyevsky, and any number of other artists, Wright claims he is not fully human until he has recovered his own degradation, not to redeem or purify it by speaking it, but to shout it in defiance of the "Serpent or bird or pure untroubled mind." Perhaps that meal of "bitterness" is precisely what nourished him enough to spit out "At the Executed Murderer's Grave." His urge to confess in "In Shame and Humiliation," an earlier poem in *Saint Judas* and in many ways a necessary precursor of "Grave," manifests itself not as a confession—as it does in "Grave"—but as a defiant shout, a curse that only thinly disguises the profound guilt that underlies the poet's motivating anger. His curse of the "pure" is a cathartic curse of his own felt cowardice, his own lack of nerve in the face of the demands of free poetic creation. The book is the necessary curse of himself—as man and as poet—which he has to utter if he is to continue speaking at all. He clears the land and shouts that to speak we must suffer defeat, must be forced down from the throne of impersonality. He has pulled down his vanity, flopped himself "like a fish against the muddy ground," and finally learned to love himself, "the poor old man" who ultimately won the sympathy of the speakers of other poems in *Saint Judas*. As we read through the poems of *Saint Judas* successively, we discover the new poet emerging, feel his emerging strength, and, perhaps, if this is not attributing too much to poetry, we, too, feel that the strength to make our own lives is available, even here and even in (or through) language.

So, then, does Wright achieve redemption or recover Eden? Certainly not. Redemption is impossible in Wright's world, "a world where God has ceased to exist," as Mazzaro characterizes it.[23] However, "consolation," again using Mazzaro's term,[24] is possible, and that in the figure of Judas. "Saint Judas," the final poem in the book, while formally more traditional than "At the Executed Murderer's Grave," is Wright's ultimate statement of independence from all fathers and precursors and his definition of "exactly what . . . a good and humane action" is. Judas denied Christ and, by extension, God, the Father of all. This is the final, most blasphemous, and most daring denial we know of. Judas is the guiltiest man in the universe, guiltier even than Doty, guiltier even than Wright can imagine himself:

> When I went out to kill myself, I caught
> A pack of hoodlums beating up a man.
> Running to spare his suffering, I forgot
> My name, my number, how my day began,
> How soldiers milled around the garden stone
> And sang amusing songs; how all that day

Their javelins measured crowds; how I alone
Bargained the proper coins, and slipped away.

Banished from heaven, I found this victim beaten,
Stripped, kneed, and left to cry. Dropping my rope
Aside, I ran, ignored the uniforms:
Then I remembered bread my flesh had eaten,
The kiss that ate my flesh. Flayed without hope,
I held the man for nothing in my arms.

Once again this day, Judas must decide between giving and withholding his love. Now the man who needs his help is a simple man like himself, a victim whose only power over Judas, unlike Christ's or the Roman soldiers', is his humanity, his human "suffering." Under these altered circumstances, when the one needing Judas is neither God nor soldier, a man Judas neither loves, respects, nor fears because of his power, he emerges from himself. Judas, "for nothing," for no promise of silver, security, or heaven, holds, loves, and comforts a fellow man for the sheer sake of that person's suffering humanity. It is an act of true selfless compassion, a model for us all, "a good and humane action."

Judas emerges as the archetypal symbol of the isolated individual—the "I alone"—romantically defiant to the end, and, in Wright's inverted theology, replaces Christ as our spiritual exemplar. Wright canonizes Judas, as Peter Stitt notes, "not because he has lived a pure life away from the harsh demands and temptations of reality, but because, a man like all men, he has redeemed his unspeakable act of betrayal through an act of love. . . . Judas . . . is thus a kind of hero for Wright, representing the most that man can achieve (endurance and love) within the fallen world."[25] He also provides the example of how malice (Judas's sin and denial) can become compassion by stripping away all one's claims to compensation and forcing one's actions to be selfless. From sin and suffering, then, and the attendant guilt of the criminal that Wright clearly feels, can come love, charity, and some community. This is the meaning of the poem, I think, but to understand that is not necessarily to be convinced of it. Bly, for one, was not persuaded:

The transformation of Judas from a criminal who did something despicable into a saint is too quickly done—it is as if a man were to claim he dug a hole for one day and immediately comes out of the other side of the earth. Kierkegaard and others have defended awareness of guilt as one of the most valuable sensitivities. To say, however, that taking acts which increase guilt is a way toward sainthood is to give impossible directions. The poem is really an attempt to bend together, with his imagination, two ends of an iron bar—Wright's conviction that he is in some sense a criminal, and his conviction that he is somehow a man of goodwill.[26]

I am less bothered by the speed of the conversion, however, than by another point. The son, Judas here, having paid the price for us all, that is, having once and for all defied the father so that he and we, his descendants, could be free, goes on to his own death. It is precisely that death, the sacrificial act that perversely echoes Christ's crucifixion, that bothers me. The price for this total freedom is so high that we are left with less than the sense of final fulfillment that this poem, I think, is meant to convey. If self-defeat is the only victory, it is a dismal victory, indeed. If denial is the catalyst that finally enables Judas to act "for nothing," then we are left with a victory that is fatal. Must we bring this intolerable burden of guilt and loneliness to bear in order to achieve the free identity that Wright tells us is our only true identity? Perhaps the death of Judas is meant to be a death-into-life and my too cynical ears fail to respond; what I do hear is an almost masochistic reverence for a course of action destined to end in failure. The final, brief act of compassion or ascendance is valued absolutely over a lifetime of less dramatic action. "Small Frogs Killed on the Highway," a later poem from the "New Poems" section of Wright's *Collected Poems*, echoes this idea, showing how tenacious a hold it has over the poet:

> Still,
> I would leap too
> Into the light,
> If I had the chance.

The quest for the light, for illumination, knowledge, or what Hank Lazer identifies as "self-transformation and self-transcendence," that is, the heroic act of self-identification and self-discovery, still "involves a self-annihilating, violent end. . . . The price paid for the leap into the light becomes part of its attraction."[27] It is not until the very end of Wright's career that he passes "gently . . . beyond the former violence that sought purgation."[28] So, while "Saint Judas" is Wright's final word in this volume, it is by no means his final word. His course is simultaneously self-creative and self-destructive, as we will see most clearly in discussing the next two books. But, as I noted in my introduction, Langbaum assures us that between the romantic poet's "Everlasting No" and his "Everlasting Yea," his final reaffirmation, must intervene a "period of travel and experience,"[29] a period of maturation during which the poet understands the implications of both casting "them" out and being in turn cast out by "them." That is the period we turn to now.

3

"Look: I am nothing"

The first title we come across in *The Branch Will Not Break* (1963)[1] is eighteen words long ("As I Step over a Puddle at the End of Winter, I Think of an Ancient Chinese Governor") and describes an event, not a subject. What has happened to "The Ghost," "The Refusal," "The Alarm," or "The Accusation"? Confused but undaunted, we press on, determined to survey the territory. Readers who turn directly from *Saint Judas* to *Branch* can be excused for feeling for a moment like readers who come upon the opening sentence of Kafka's "The Metamorphosis": "As Gregor Samsa awoke one morning from uneasy dreams he found himself transformed in his bed into a gigantic insect." We see we have entered an alien land and instinctively stop, look around, and ask ourselves what the characteristics and rules of this new world are. We search for laws to explain what, in our familiar world, is unexpected, to say the least, and perhaps inexplicable. Nothing looks the same; the landscape is so disorganized. The old signposts of rhyme, meter, predictable line length, and consistent stanza length are gone. We find ourselves "lost in the thicket," as many of Wright's characters are, with the smoothed paths of orderly verse nowhere to be seen. The final few poems of *Saint Judas* prepared us for a change, a new voice, but not for the change in style that some critics have hailed as almost a religious conversion from the heretical practice of closed form to the popular open form of free verse, juxtaposed images, and psychic "leaps." Many critics agree with Robert Bly that the new poems also deal with "deeper and more painful" subject matter.[2] Wright himself, however, preferred to speak of his form's evolution as "a continuous exploration,"[3] and I have been contending, and will continue to contend in this chapter, that Wright's themes remain remarkably consistent throughout his career, that his subject matter has always been as "painful" as possible, and that there is much less of a radical break between Wright's second and third books than was once believed or as there first seems to the reader who simply turns the page from the last poem of *Saint Judas* to the first poem of *Branch*.

Branch created a shock when it was first published, in part because it came four years after *Saint Judas*. It seemed as if Wright had gone into poetic hibernation and then produced this brand new work. As Nicholas Gattuccio has convincingly shown, however, "twenty-eight poems, roughly two-thirds of *The Branch*, were written between 1959 and early 1961 . . . literally on the heels of *Saint Judas*."[4] So there really was no temporal gap between the poems of *Saint Judas* and those of *Branch*. The book also seemed revolutionary rather than evolutionary, in part because readers underestimated the importance to Wright, and the duration of that importance, of the foreign poets he and Robert Bly had translated. Trakl, Vallejo, and Neruda, in particular, were very influential on the direction of Wright's style, and it was not as if he just happened on them after completing *Saint Judas* and while looking around for new ways to write. He describes first hearing Trakl's work read in a University of Vienna classroom, into which he accidentally wandered, in 1952, five years before publishing *The Green Wall* and nine years before he and Bly published *Twenty Poems of George Trakl*: "It was as though the sea had entered the class at the last moment. For this poem was not like any poem I had ever recognized. . . ."[5] Clearly, then, this "new poetry" had been simmering in Wright's brain long before it boiled over in *Branch*; to speak of a sudden change is to misrepresent Wright's career. Yet *Branch* is a definite and noticeable stylistic change, as I admit, from *Saint Judas*, and that stylistic change has to be understood as the result of the strong influence of poets outside of the Anglo-American tradition. Lest we get the cart before the horse, though, let us first listen to and look at the opening poems of *Branch*, gather some evidence so that we can make an inductive conclusion about the shape of this verse, note its thematic similarities to Wright's earlier verse, and then return to the question of the influence of foreign poets on Wright's style.

"As I Step" begins with Wright addressing an ancient Chinese governor:

> Po Chu-i, balding old politician,
> What's the use?
> I think of you,
> Uneasily entering the gorges of the Yang-Tze,
> When you were being towed up the rapids
> Toward some political job or other
> In the city of Chungshou.
> You made it, I guess,
> By dark.

The second line is not only a statement but also an attitude throughout the poem. The speaker sounds apathetic, afraid, or afraid to be anything but apathetic. He is sometimes precise (lines 4 and 5), but sometimes carefully imprecise (lines 6 and 8), as if he could not be bothered to find out what job Po Chu-i was being towed to or whether he got it. "What's the use?" One's fate is an indifferent matter, for success seems out of the question.

We think of Pound's use of historical figures to create a community of heroes and villains from all ages, to draw from a usable past for his present needs. Po Chu-i may be just such a character from the past, a Jefferson or Madison or Confucius for Wright to use, but the tone of the second stanza makes that doubtful:

> But it is 1960, it is almost spring again,
> And the tall rocks of Minneapolis
> Build me my own black twilight

> Of bamboo ropes and waters.
> Where is Yuan Chen, the friend you loved?
> Where is the sea, that once solved the whole loneliness
> Of the Midwest? Where is Minneapolis? I can see nothing
> But the great terrible oak tree darkening with winter.
> Did you find the city of isolated men beyond mountains?
> Or have you been holding the end of a frayed rope
> For a thousand years?

There is no real hope that Po Chu-i will find "the city of isolated men" or that such a mythical community exists. Wright looks to the past for succor but not with Pound's confidence, perhaps Pound's intimidating confidence, that any fruitful connection can be made to that history. He can imaginatively identify himself somewhat with the Chinese governor—he imagines his own Minneapolis "black twilight / Of bamboo ropes and water"—but the link is tenuous and questionable, as the interrogative nature of stanza 2 indicates.

"Three Stanzas from Goethe," a translation of part of Goethe's "Harzreise im Winter," is similar in intention to "As I Step." Wright plunders the past to "quicken" the present, this cold and dark Minneapolis (which occasionally replaces Ohio as the symbol for all of America). Wright (or Wright's version of Goethe) begins with a question:

> That man standing there, who is he?
> His path lost in the thicket,
> Behind him the bushes
> Lash back together
> The grass rises again,
> The waste devours him.

The lines of stanza 1 increase in terror, from simple loss of direction, to suffocating enclosure, to disappearance amidst the "waste" that is a dominant image of this book. Everywhere we, or Wright's characters, turn, we find waste—weeds, thickets, slag heaps, black water, splintered trees. The apparently neutral presentation of a fact—

grass does, after all, "lash back together" once we walk through it—
is transformed into a horror tale. Grass, bushes, even thickets, are
not in themselves "waste," unless viewed from the proper perspec-
tive, that of the self-defined victim masochistically or purgatively—
or both—lashing himself with his own despair. The poet sees not
merely adjacent objects but rows of threats to his physical, psycho-
logical, and moral integrity. The "man" of Goethe's poem is the
poet's double, so Wright has again managed to find an analogue in
the past for his predicament, but the retrieval from history does
nothing except affirm the speaker's own desolation:

> Once despised, now a despiser,
> He kills his own life,
> The precious secret.
> The self-seeker finds nothing.

"Finds nothing" because there is, he fears, nothing to find except the
horrible truth of his own hollowness. The "secret" is that there is
nothing to guard, nothing to find, nothing the poet can drag from
inside himself to bring to life. The land is dry: the rejuvenating
water has receded from the Midwest, to be replaced by weeds. But
this wasteland is the man's "own desert"—he has created the ste-
rility himself, just as Wright felt he had squeezed the life from his
poems by his own mastering of technique. The flowers he wants to
celebrate die on the vine because he does not have the water of po-
etic imagination to make them bloom. This book is the story of the
poet's efforts to find precisely the right method to release, as Wright
said, "whatever poetry may be in me." And, as I noted at the end of
chapter two, releasing that poetry is a moral as well as an aesthetic
act. He will release himself as well as his verses, or, by releasing his
verses he will release himself.

We notice in the first four poems the introduction of two almost
mythical figures, in addition to Po Chu-i and the "man" from
Goethe, whom Wright hopes may bring him back to life:

> Mother of roots, you have not seeded
> The tall ashes of loneliness

For me. Therefore,
Now I go.
      ("Goodbye to the Poetry of Calcium")

Oh Father of Love,
If your psaltery holds one tone
That his ear still might echo,
Then quicken his heart!
      ("Three Stanzas from Goethe")

Wright is invoking two minor muses that are part of a series of muses, already referred to in chapter one, that range from Betty of *The Green Wall* to Jenny of *Shall We Gather at the River* and Annie of *Two Citizens*, his next two books. He asks that his poetry be looked over, guided to the life he hopes is in it. He needs some outside source to seed or quicken his lines, for his own efforts, he fears, have been futile. Failing himself, he turns to the hope of a life-source immanent in a spiritualized universe. We get the impression that we are eavesdropping on prayers and feel a bit uneasy. The supplicant's voice dominates these first four poems; we read them in hushed voices as if we can thus hear them better, understand their gnostic mysteries more fully. There is an irony, however, in Wright's prayers. I am reminded, perhaps idiosyncratically, of the irony in Elizabeth Bishop's precise descriptions, which show us what we know but also remind us of what we cannot know, and which draw dark black lines around the limits of our knowledge. Wright's poems occasionally sound prayerful but remind us more of the absence of hope than of the presence of a guiding force. These poems, and others with the same tone that the reader has probably noticed, do *sound* like prayers, but they implicitly remind us, by the absence of any real hope for an answer, that they are unheard, except by the reader. Instead of faith in a deity and hope of deliverance, the voice of prayer in Wright usually indicates despair and desperation. Occasionally at this stage in his career but more often in later poems, Wright will sound *religious* in the sense that he will try to speak quietly, carefully, and slowly, sensing that he, though not deserving, is in the presence of mysteries, beautiful secrets that he has been allowed momentarily to marvel over. That is a different tone, for those poems do indicate a meeting with something valuable and heartening, as in "A Blessing" in this volume. But when he sounds actually *prayerful*, as in "Goodbye to the Poetry of Calcium" and "Three Stanzas from Goethe," we rarely find hope or beauty. In fact, frustration at not being heard may even prevail, as in "Speak" (from *River*), where the poet becomes increasingly angry as it becomes increasingly clear to him that the Lord he is addressing is not listening, that he is speaking only to himself.

I think, however, that while we may get the tone of these opening poems, we often are frustrated when we try to describe them more specifically. For example, in the lines last quoted from "Goodbye to the Poetry of Calcium," we hear the sincere anguish, but who is the "Mother of roots," and what is the logic of "Therefore"? The poem continues:

> If I knew the name,
> Your name, all trellises of vineyards and old fire
> Would quicken to shake terribly my
> Earth, mother of spiraling searches, terrible
> Fable of calcium, girl.

To utter the terrible name of the god will restore the speaker's power, deliver him from the "weeds" in which, he says, "I crept this afternoon." The images do not want to be deciphered, but they do deliver the tone of fear and spiritual poverty. You have to hear the desperation. The poet strives to deny you the pleasure, or reassurance, of rationally interpreting his pleas for help. He wants the reader to be in the weeds, too; as he has stepped down from his privileged perch above the chaotic sea, so he demands that you imaginatively, as well as rationally, enter the poetic and spiritual labyrinth he has created, if you are to understand the poems at all. Of course this is a rather heavy demand on the reader, who will only respond if he is rewarded for his efforts.

One technique that frustrates even the best intentioned reader's efforts is the poet's reliance on ambiguous pronouns throughout *The Branch Will Not Break*. Examine these examples from later poems in this volume:

It is the sinking of things.

Flashlights drift over the dark trees,
Girls kneel,
An owl's eyelids fall.

The sad bones of my hands descend into a valley
Of strange rocks.
    ("Rain")

I look down now. It is all changed.
    ("Milkweed")

This is a vague, cosmic "it" referring to large terms—life, the human condition, a sensed desperation that is alienation but also a notice of one's status as a member of a group of the alienated and isolated. Wright is using such ambiguous, nonreferential terms to capture the engulfing feeling of life's futility and meaninglessness. He is sending out calling cards to see who responds, who claims membership in the club whose motto might be "It is the sinking of things." This club may be the "city of isolated men beyond mountains" but cannot be a community, for all that its members have to share with each other is their isolation. He is asking for the reader's identification with the poet, quite a different purpose from the modernist masters whose vaunted impersonality keeps the reader's attention on the poem's hard surface. Wright asks us to look at the surface but then hear the individual behind that series of apparently unconnected images. The poet's consciousness is the poem's coherence, it binds the images one to the other, and ultimately we are asked to hear and judge the poet himself. In "Tradition and the Individual Talent," Eliot tells us "that the poet has not a 'personality' to express, but a particular medium, which is only a medium and not a personality, in which impressions and experiences combine in peculiar and un-expected ways. Impressions and experiences which are important for the man may take no place in the poetry, and those which be-come important in the poetry may play quite a negligible part in the man, the personality."[6] Wright obviously is making a different kind of poetry, one in which the "personality" is the subject matter and one in which we make personal and poetic evaluations simultaneously, almost inevitably. It is hard for me to imagine someone reading Wright's poetry without thinking about Wright the man and basing at least part of his response to the poetry on his response to the man as revealed in the poetry.

This sometimes means that we are asked to treat sincerity as a criterion of literary judgment, usually to the detriment of the poem. As Charles Altieri points out in *Self and Sensibility in Contemporary American Poetry,* Wright and many of his peers, like Eliot and other moderns, identify "cultural barbarism in middle-class life" as an "antagonist of the arts," but, unlike their modernist predecessors, many contemporary poets also interpret "high culture . . . as part of the problem rather than a basis for resistance," reject "complicated forms of reasoning and intricate self-reflection," and consequently have "little but the intensity of extreme emotional states, the sharpness of perception, and the sublimity of momentary religious visions as their means for giving authority to their new perspectives."[7] In other words, postmodern American poets such as Wright "impose on themselves the . . . criterion of 'the relative believability of the poem's voice,'"[8] that is, sincerity. One of Altieri's points is that by withdrawing from "demonic lucidity in order to make essentially lyric emotions serve cognitive needs,"[9] Wright "creates something close to what Hegel called the 'bad infinite,' a form of mystery depending more on vagueness and surprise than on any sense that the mind has located structures that genuinely exceed its own powers of comprehension."[10] I think Wright is guilty of the "bad infinite" less often than Altieri seems to believe he is, but there is no denying that some of the poems in this volume and *Branch* lapse into vagueness because the poet expects his sincerity and intense perception to do the poem's work single-handedly, without the "striking imaginative constructs of sufficient emotional and intellectual weight" that Altieri declares are necessary "to make moments of vision do the work of the intellect."[11] Wright is certainly sincere in "The Jewel," for example, but is the poem any good?

> There is this cave
> In the air behind my body

> That nobody is going to touch:
> A cloister, a silence
> Closing around a blossom of fire.
> When I stand upright in the wind,
> My bones turn to dark emeralds.

Bones as dark emeralds by itself strikes me as an impressive image, but perhaps too "hard" to be the product of the silence in line 4. The "this" of line 1 is consciously unpoetic and sounds contrived. How often do we want to read a poet trying not to sound like a poet? "Cloister" and "silence" have religious connotations; we almost imagine the body as the sacred temple of Jesus, a staple idea of most Sunday school teachers, but here without Jesus. The speaker asks us to regard him as a precious object, an emerald, and his secrets as themselves precious, untouchable. We are asked to revere the poet and his interior "blossom of fire" rather than some external object, deity, or the poem as an artifice in itself. Those internal gems are pure, hard, and untainted by the outside world and ratiocination. As in some of Wright's earlier poems, the poet wants to be impenetrable, protected, safe from the corrosive world out there, and he defines this turn inward not as an escape but as a more authentic confrontation with what really matters, the self (with ego absent), or the soul, as more conventionally religious poets might have described it. One problem with the poem, and others like it produced at this time, is that it succeeds too well at being impenetrable because it demands too much acceptance from the reader, demanding that the reader take it as it is, validated by being conceived by the poet and by being a sincere utterance of the poet's predicament. This is a cry for personal acceptance, I think, and not fully formed into a verbal construct that can *compel* the reader's sympathy or understanding.

Even without looking at many more examples from later parts of the book, the reader now has enough data to make some tentative conclusions about the form of the poems of *Branch*. First, the poems sound alike because most are written in the first person. The "I" dominates, replacing, for the most part, the personae of earlier poems. Despite the initial impression we received from "As I Step," the poems's titles are normally short: half have four or fewer words (six have only one word and seven have two); the rest have from five to twenty-three words, but six have ten or more, and the long titles naturally attract more attention, giving the impression that they are more frequent than they really are. Jerome Mazzaro explains that the "deliberate exclusion of discursive reasoning . . . accounts for the necessity of a long, explanatory title."[12] Alan Williamson suggests that the long titles are "a gauntlet flung down to the reader's notions of poetic decorum."[13]

The poems also look alike. Just as a collection of sonnets leaves the reader with an orderly visual impression, these poems, spread out over many pages, leave an image of their own, call it an orderly disorderliness: "orderly" because consistent visually; "disorderliness" because refusing to conform to our memory of what poetry traditionally looks like on a page. They are usually short and, if no longer than fifteen lines, are also written in one, unbroken strophe. If they are longer, however, they are broken into equal stanzas, making the viewer wonder what rhetorical function the stanza breaks perform. Each stanza is simply a conveniently sized package. A row of similar-sized boxes or cans on a supermarket shelf looks more orderly than a haphazard collection of pint and quart jars in a sale bin. So, too, these stanzas look neat and regular, though their rhymes (when they exist) and meter (when it follows a pattern we can define) are not. Again, the impression is of an orderly disorderliness: Wright breaks his old rules but takes care to line everything up neatly. The "conservative"[14] Wright holds onto a semblance of order in one hand as he lets go with the other. The result could be a chaotic indecisiveness but is instead, I think, a bold tension between order and chaos, consistent, in the better poems, with the tension between the promise to be open to rational interpretation and the insistence that we only get to know their whole story by feeling their experiences as well.

The tone is by turns despairing, as if the apocalypse were imminent, and defiant, as if one's internal "cloister" made one the equal of any catastrophe. The poems are consciously ambiguous, relying on pronouns without antecedents as we have seen, but also filled

with abstract terms that defy the reader's attempts to find their defi-
nitions within the poems. The writer insists instead that the reader
make a pact to respond to such phrases as "Mother of roots" with the
religious dread that the poem's very ambiguity and mysteriousness
suggest. The lines are of various lengths, not even a minor distrac-
tion in most cases but surely a change from the tetrameter and pen-
tameter lines Wright had relied on in the past. The syntax is usually
regular, but the elements are occasionally unexpected, as in the
third poem, "In Fear of Harvests." It is short:

> It has happened
> Before: nearby,
> The nostrils of slow horses
> Breathe evenly,
> And the brown bees drag their high garlands,
> Heavily,
> Toward hives of snow.

Again, we begin in the middle of a thought or action, *in medias res,*
our human condition, and are forced to make do with only a fraction
of the data we need to answer our questions. What is "it"? The first
line of the poem makes us expect somewhat of a narrative ("What
has happened?" we respond. "Show us.") but all we really get are two
images connected by a coordinating conjunction in line 5 offering no
sense of temporal or causal relationship between the horses and the
bees. We are stopped short by "snow," for we do not expect the
phrase "hives of" to end with "snow." The bees' "garlands" is a con-
ventional enough comparison of the bees' stripes to a wreath, but
"hives of snow" refuses to be converted to something comfortable
and familiar. Even if we imagine beehives covered with snow, we do
not have the image Wright intends, which makes the hives con-
structed of snow, not merely covered with a white blanket. But we
finally do understand that "snow" is another image of sterility and
cold emptiness, the reason that harvests are feared: no matter how
great the harvest this time, we know that snow will follow, a cliché
Wright makes much more interesting than I can. This is Wright's
reversal of Shelley's rather more optimistic "If Winter comes, can
Spring be far behind?" ("Ode to the West Wind").

We can draw a few more tentative conclusions. Wright's style in *Branch* implies a universal confusion, denies the ability of ratiocination (whose efforts are continually and consciously thwarted) by itself to provide our necessary answers, and offers the poet as witness and arbiter of life's values and experiences. The poems present moments rather than tell stories, they testify to the difficulty of living and making sense of the data that overwhelm us, and they show spots of time rather than debate values. Those spots, however, as we have seen already, imply attitudes toward the world that are themselves values, for they imply a way to live. At work is what Altieri, in *Enlarging the Temple*, which he wrote before *Self and Sensibility* and in which he is more supportive of Wright's technique, calls a "poetic of immanence," in which "aesthetic elements have primarily epistemological rather than interpretive functions. The reader sees style and structure not as imposing order but as articulating modes of thinking and projecting relationships through which latent values and orders can be perceived."[15] This is not a modernist poetic dedicated to the impersonal author's ability to force an order onto the world, whose chaos he greets with anguish and despair. Wright's poetic is more closely related to Wordsworth's: ". . . the Romantic poet must see his poem as embodying experience, as directly presenting the act of prehension, instead of commenting after the fact on the nature of his thoughts or of objects confronting them."[16] But why does Altieri say the romantic poet "must" see his poem in this way? Because "simply to discuss values in a poem was to find oneself trapped in the opposition between thoughts and the world, so the poet needed to imagine his work as directly embodying the experience of value."[17] Like Wordsworth, Wright does not simply want to *structure* the world by using elaborate linguistic and formal patterns. Rather, he wants to *present* his experience—in some order, of course, but validated by the fact that it is his true experience—to the reader, almost as a gift. He wants to step back into the world of objects and reveal, not impose, the value that is immanent in experience itself. He wants to eradicate not only the subject/object dichotomy, but also the fact/value split. His goal is to show, not to tell, and he clearly believes that there is something to show—some goodness inherent in the world's facts that modern man's alienating reason and egotistical categorizing and organizing have hidden from his eyes. His is "a morality of attention," to quote Altieri again,[18] and, as I hope the reader has noticed, this attitude is precisely the one needed to produce the type of "moral poetry" I have already discussed and contended that Wright is trying to write. He wants to draw our attention to the world of the poem, not to the traces of the artist's mind that are left in clever forms and patterns and esoteric diction. Thus Alan Williamson observes that for "the middle generation of American poets," a generation that includes Wright, "the 'I' becomes numb, neutral, universal: a transparency through which we look directly to the state of being or feeling."[19] So, although the first-person pronoun does dominate the verses, it refers not so much to Wright the personal ego as to Wright the "transparent eyeball" who sees for us.

We should now return to the problem I left hanging earlier: to what extent is *Branch* a revolutionary break with Wright's earlier work? We see that if one simply moves from *Saint Judas* to *Branch*, the landscape changes. When *Branch* was first published, critics understandably were puzzled and, judging from the evidence available, concluded that the work was a major change for the poet.[20] However, the poems of *Branch* are the result of many years of searching for a style more suited to the poet's goals. They are the result of a long germination process and not a radical, sudden break with the poet's old habits or a signal of new poetic intentions on the poet's part. Even before Wright published *Saint Judas* in 1959, he was becoming dissatisfied with his work. He had struggled to master the forms of *The Green Wall* and now felt those old iambs were strangling him. In a letter to Theodore Roethke, dated 5 August 1958, Wright says,

> I have been depressed as hell. My stuff stinks, and you know it. . . .
> What makes this so ironically depressing, as I say, is that I am
> trapped by the very thing—the traditional technique—which I
> labored so hard to attain. . . . I work like hell, chipping away
> perhaps one tiny pebble per day from the ten-mile-thick granite
> wall of formal and facile "technique" which I myself erected, and

which now stands ominously between me and whatever poetry may be in me.[21]

We see him formulating a personal poetics, as he reads, translates, and introduces foreign poets to the American audience. In "A Note on Trakl," the introduction to a 1963 translation entitled *Twenty Poems of George Trakl*, on which Bly and Wright collaborated, Wright praises the Austrian poet for not writing "according to any 'rules of construction,' traditional or other," but rather for waiting "patiently and silently for the worlds of the poems to reveal their own natures."[22] Trakl, according to Wright, learned "to open his eyes, to listen, to be silent, and to wait patiently for the inward bodies of things to emerge, for the inward voices to whisper."[23] This patient listening to the subjects of the poems and letting those subjects' qualities, rather than tradition, determine the poems' forms is a characteristic in Gary Snyder's work, which Wright praises in two reviews published in 1961 and 1962, just before *Branch* was published. Snyder, Wright says, wants a line capable of "recording the actual physical details of living things, and allowing those things to speak—or simply exist—in and for themselves."[24] Poems written in such a manner "emerge from within the living growth of each particular poem and most definitely *not* in a set of conventions (such as the classical English iambic, with all its masterpieces of the past and its suffocating influence in the present)."[25] Wright wanted to let the inner demands of the subject shape the poem, rather than rely on metrical patterns that existed prior to the moment the poet and his subject confronted each other, the moment of the poem. Finally, after Wright published his *Collected Poems* in 1971 and drew critical attention to his translations of foreign poets by inserting a selection of them between *Saint Judas* and *Branch*, the continuity between his early work and *Branch* became clearer, and readers could see that *Branch* was the result, in part, of Wright's reading and translating, especially of his and Bly's work with the poems of Vallejo, Trakl, and Neruda. Specifically, as James Seay has noted, "Following the various examples of these foreign poets, [Wright] had in his own work begun concentrating on simplifying the individual line, sharpening the imagery within a given line, making it more obviously receptive to the irrational, and reducing exposition to a minimum."[26] This is not to say that we can, or would want to, attribute all of Wright's poetic evolution to the influence of these poets, nor is it to say that had Wright not read them his work would have remained the same as in *The Green Wall* and *Saint Judas*. Wright clearly was dissatisfied with the form of his first two books and was going to strike out in a new direction. What that direction would have been had he not read Trakl, Vallejo, Neruda, and others, however, is impossible to say. Nor do we want to say, as Dave Smith wisely reminds us, that Wright "abandoned" either "his native traditions in poetry" or "his Ohio Valley," for he did neither.[27] What we can say with some confidence is that there is an unmistakable link between Wright's work after *Saint Judas*, especially his work in his third and fourth volumes, *Branch* and *Shall We Gather at the River*, and his translations of poetry outside of the Anglo-American tradition.

A look at some of the poems from Trakl, Vallejo, and Neruda included in *Collected Poems* will make the transition from *Saint Judas* to *Branch* via South America and Europe clearer.[28] Listen to the first stanza of Trakl's "De Profundis":

> It is a stubble field, where a black rain is falling.
> It is a brown tree, that stands alone.
> It is a hissing wind, that encircles empty houses.
> How melancholy the evening is.

We hear the same ambiguous and portentous "it" and feel the same "melancholy" emerging from the dark images the poet chooses to focus on. The poem begins *in medias res*, and the diction is limited, never consciously poetic. The stanza moves to a conclusion through an accumulation of increasingly heavy images, from a rain that might be beneficial to a bare tree to an unmistakably serpentine wind that makes the speaker's every breath an inhalation of evil, much as we will later see "Lying in a Hammock at William Duffy's Farm in Pine Island, Minnesota" move to its more shocking, but logically and poetically similar, conclusion. In later stanzas we see pastures, villages, fields, and thickets, the same landscape, the same wasteland we have already seen in *Branch:* "At night, I found myself in a pasture, / Covered with rubbish and the dust of stars." The emotion is direct and personal: "I am a shadow far from darkening villages." The tone is apocalyptic and the phrasing cryptic: "I drank the silence of God / Out of the stream in the trees." In other words, if we have read *Branch* first, we say to ourselves, "Trakl sounds just like Wright," before realizing of course that the opposite is the truth.

We see the same directness, the same direct confrontation of the reader with the writer's naked personality, in the selections from Vallejo: "I am freed from the burdens of the sea / when the waters come toward me" ("I Am Freed"); "I feel all right. Now / a stoical frost shines / in me" (White Rose). As in Wright, however, the "I" is meant to be not simply the writer but the writer as spokesman for all the outcast. The "I" in Vallejo is "the symbol of all men," and for Vallejo, as for Wright, "to speak of all men means becoming the lowest common denominator, the most wretched of men, in order to force the reader to contemplate his mirror-image, to inculcate a Christian humility without Christianity."[29] In "Saint Judas," Wright clearly identifies with Judas, but not until *Branch* do we see the poet himself personally debased. Judas was seen from the outside; in *Branch,* we see through the eyes of the outcast, out to the world, just as in these selections from Vallejo:

> This afternoon it rains as never before; and I
> don't feel like staying alive, heart.
>> ("Down to the Dregs")

> My God, I am weeping for the life that I live.
>> ("The Eternal Dice")

> I am calling, I am feeling around for you in the darkness.
> Don't leave me behind by myself,
> to be locked in all alone.
>> ("The Big People")

The longing for deliverance we hear in the above lines is an explicit theme in later Wright, a trait he may have picked up from Vallejo, who, like Wright, frequently imagines himself sailing out over the sea, sometimes toward a promised land, sometimes simply away from a nightmare. A sense of one's limitations, however, is the much stronger emotion in these works, and Vallejo's children in "The Big People" are more typical of the human condition as it is portrayed in these translations and in Wright's third and fourth books. The children wait for the big people to return, inventing fictions of return, rescue, and homecoming, as Beckett's characters invent fictions of Godot's return. The children have played the game according to the rules; they have been good, they have minded, yet they are still abandoned, just as Wright's speaker in "Speak" finds himself alone, despite having "loved Thy cursed, / The beauty of Thy house," and listening for a sign, any sign, of something outside his locked cage. The children then become a single child, further isolated, who begs not "to be locked in all alone." Again, as in Beckett, the characters are progressively immobilized until they cannot move, like the Wright of "Before a Cashier's Window in a Department Store": "In my frayed coat, I am pinned down / By debt."

Trakl's speaker, too, often dreams of escape, but the escape usually means the speaker's or persona's dissolution, just as Wright will flirt with self-destructive desires: "Oh the stony hill. The cool body, forgotten and silent, is melting away in the silver snow" ("A Winter Night," Trakl). Yet, despite the desire for rest and the fear of death we hear in Trakl's speaker, he feels compelled to continue his quest: "With a stiff walk, you tramp along the railroad embankment with huge eyes, like a soldier charging a dark machinegun nest. Onward!" We remember Wright, in "Having Lost My Sons, I Confront the Wreckage of the Moon: Christmas, 1960," also compelled to push on, even in isolation and despair:

> I am sick
> Of it, and I go on,
> Living, alone, alone,
> Past the charred silos, past the hidden graves
> Of Chippewas and Norwegians.

The quest for deliverance, a qualified hope of escape or transcendence coupled with dreams of stasis and petrification, becomes almost an obsession in *Branch*.

Both Vallejo and Trakl take us out into the snow, away from the warmth of human community. For Vallejo, this is the "frigid hour" in the "City of winter." For Trakl, it seems always to be late at night in the dead of winter:

> It has been snowing. Past midnight, drunk on purple wine,
> you leave the gloomy shelters of men, and the red fire of
> their fireplaces. Oh the darkness of night.
> ("A Winter Night")

The winter scene implies the speaker's desperation and hopelessness. Nature participates in man's moods, just as it does in *Branch*: "Black frost. The ground is hard, the air has a bitter taste" ("A Winter Night," Trakl); "This afternoon its rains, rains endlessly. And I / don't feel like staying alive, heart" ("Down to the Dregs," Vallejo).

The stark coloration of Trakl's imagery further reminds us of Wright's black-and-white world in *Branch*. "White sleep" and "white birds," for example, share time with the "deepening twilight" and the "dark pirate ship" of "Sleep"; white snow and black frost divide the world of "A Winter Night"; and a "white moon" and "fantastic shadows" combine to create the "gray malodorous mist" of "The Rats." Like many of Wright's poems in his third and fourth books, Trakl's verses are stark paintings of a pained, solitary figure wandering lonely in a black landscape, searching for an angel that comes out at night only in sleep. His poems are like woodcuts, black and white and in sharp relief. They are like Munch's paintings, and also like Wright's pictures of himself wandering through Minneapolis and across the frozen Great Plains.

Vallejo's influence on Wright's imagery can be seen in two stanzas, the first from "A Divine Falling of Leaves":

> Moon: royal crown of an enormous head,
> dropping leaves into yellow shadows as you go.

> Red crown of a Jesus who broods
> tragically, softly over emeralds!

The moon, shadows, the color of decay, gems—all occur frequently in Wright's next two books and convey the brooding, hopeless, mysterious sense of something valuable lost or let slip through our fingers.

Another stanza, from "Down to the Dregs," prepares us for the leaping imagery of Wright's later work, that imagery often called surrealistic:

> This afternoon in Lima it is raining. And I remember
> the cruel caverns of my ingratitude;
> my block of ice laid on her poppy,
> stronger than her crying "Don't be this way!"

There is nothing incomprehensible about ingratitude as a cavern or block of ice, but there is something unexpected about the connections, especially between the ice and the poppy. The narrative and discursive connectors are omitted, leaving the reader to create a scene and populate it with characters or simply to feel the coldness of the emotion.

Even certain of Vallejo's specific phrases of escape sound uncannily like later phrases in Wright. For example, in "I Am Freed," Vallejo says:

> We shall cover ourselves with the gold of owning nothing,
> and hatch the still unborn wing
> of the night. . . .

Later Wright says, at the end of "The Minneapolis Poem":

> I want to be lifted up
> By some great white bird unknown to the police,
> And soar for a thousand miles and be carefully hidden
> Modest and golden as one last corn grain. . . .

We have to hear not only the same longing, the same identification with the poor, but almost the same phrasing.

There is another, more intangible quality in these poems that is echoed in Wright, call it the presence of emotion, evinced in many ways, including the continued use of "heart" by Vallejo. It is important for these poets and for Wright that not too much ratiocination intervene between the heart that feels and the word that conveys that feeling. The heart is the source of the word, and the absence of rhetoric, explanation, the drawing of conclusions from experiences all point toward the new emphasis on undiluted emotion. The goal is to capture the emotion of the moment rather than convey its significance after one has understood it. As James Seay says,

> . . . after *Saint Judas* Wright became more concerned with the
> question of how the poetic revelation in its unfolding could more
> closely approximate the actual sequentiality of images and ideas
> that led the poet to a given conclusion. That is, assuming some of
> the truths we arrive at are not the results of logical reasoning, how
> the unfolding of a poetic revelation could approximate the fluid
> process of its own realization more closely than a strictly "logical"
> ordering of images and ideas after the fact of discovery.[30]

Reading these selections from Trakl and Vallejo, one gets the sense of an emotion seeking its proper imagery, almost in the way that, often, the emotion we go to sleep with seeks its form in our dreams. We do not as often hear reactions to events or narrations of experiences, true or fictional, as we were likely to in *The Green Wall* and *Saint Judas*, but emotions poured into the shapes of dreams and emerging as poems, as liquid takes the shape of its container. The "I" is always there, even if it is not mentioned. The poems are clearly personal, even when no first person is mentioned. The "I" is the background wash on the canvas, coloring all the images with its presence even if it never announces itself directly.

We see clearly, then, that the images, the tone, the emotion, and the themes of Trakl and Vallejo all remind us of Wright's poetry that we have seen in *Branch* and that we will see in *River*, and that these help explain the apparent disjunction between Wright's second and third books. It is as if the themes latent in *The Green Wall* and *Saint Judas*, those themes present but covered with a lush growth of modernist influence, are freed and brought to the light (or darkness), as Wright hacks away the vines of Robinson, Frost, and Hardy to get to his new voice, the one legitimated by this new family of poetic fathers.

Another important influence is Pablo Neruda. Reading the translations of Neruda has some of the same effects as reading the translations of the other poets: we remember Wright's earlier work (especially note how the lush sensuousness of Neruda's "Some Beasts" sounds just like that of Wright's "Morning Hymn to a Dark Girl"), and the fluidity, images, and line structure point us forward to later poems. But I believe there is a greater affinity between Wright and Neruda, one we hear in the translations from "The Heights of Macchu Picchu," found in Wright's *Collected Poems*. Neruda studies the decline of a once great culture, its early decline almost predicted by its great promise. Alan Williamson contends that Wright, too, is concerned with "the beauty and evil of America, the tragic logic connecting excessive promise to premature old age."[31] For Macchu Picchu, I can read America or Ohio or Minneapolis, which takes Ohio's place from time to time after *Saint Judas*. When we read Wright's translations of "The Heights of Macchu Picchu, III," we hear the daily deaths of the disenfranchised chronicled in *Branch* and *River*:

> each day a tiny death, dust, worm, a light
> flicked off in the mud at the city's edge, a tiny death with coarse
>   wings
> pierced into each man like a short lance
> and the man was besieged by the bread or by the knife. . . .

This "endless / granary of defeated actions," those actions defeated almost before they are taken, is precisely the image of America Wright gives us most explicitly in his third and fourth books. When Wright read Neruda, it must have been like reading himself, or like reading what he wanted his poems to be. If we listen to Wright discuss "Macchu Picchu," we hear not only the despair of his third and fourth books, but also, strangely, the more affirmative tone of his fifth and later books as well, those documents to the living rather than the dead of *Branch* and especially *River*. In a 1968 review of Nathaniel Tarn's translation of "Macchu Picchu," Wright paraphrases Neruda's "argument." The first-person pronoun is simply a technique of the review and is Wright's impression of how Neruda would describe his problem, but when we read it, we realize how prophetic it is of Wright's own "argument":

> ... everywhere I go among the living I find them dying each by each a small petty death in the midst of their precious brief lives. So I ascended to the ancient ruins of the city of Macchu Picchu in the Andes. . . . Look at the gorgeous things they have made. But wait a moment. Weren't their lives just as petty and grotesquely fragmented as the very people who die early and pointlessly in the modern cities . . . ? Yes, they were. And therefore I love the poor broken dead. . . . The silent and the nameless persons who built Macchu Picchu are alive in Santiago de Chile.[32]

The living are dead, as we have seen Wright contend. But the dead living are not therefore to be contemned, as we have heard Wright do; they are to be loved as brothers, fellow broken humanity. The climb up to the heights of Macchu Picchu, away from the "petty and grotesquely fragmented" lives around him, is the movement of Wright's first two books. Discovering that he has so hated those living dead because he is one of them is the movement of Wright's next two books; the discovery that the "gorgeous things" of the past are gorgeous things that cannot compare to the living beings around him, struggling to stay alive as "things" cannot, is the movement of his final books. In these final volumes of affirmation, he says, in effect, "The living are the living, and dead the dead must stay,"[33] making his commitment to the value of ordinary lives, to life as lived without any proof, without any "gorgeous things" to attest to its worth. The movement away in disgust, the realization that what one has left is also valuable, then the return—Neruda's "argument," at least as understood by Wright—is really the "argument" of Wright's entire career of poetry.

If we return now to Wright's poetry, I hope that readers who found themselves somewhat lost after reading the first four poems of this volume will be able to confront the volume's two "anthology pieces" more confidently. "Autumn Begins in Martins Ferry, Ohio" starts by taking us back to the poet's adolescence and memories of high school football[34] but continues to become a picture of an American ritual—fathers sending sons to play football—designed to return power and dignity to the land:

> In the Shreve High football stadium,
> I think of Polacks nursing long beers in Tiltonsville,
> And gray faces of Negroes in the blast furnace at Benwood,
> And the ruptured night watchman of Wheeling Steel,
> Dreaming of heroes.
> All the proud fathers are ashamed to go home.
> Their women cluck like starved pullets,
> Dying for love.
>
> Therefore,
> Their sons grow suicidally beautiful
> At the beginning of October,
> And gallop terribly against each other's bodies.

Each man gets a line all to himself in the first stanza. The images are cameos of disappointment, each patiently drawn. There is no forcing of personae into pentameters here. The Polacks, Negroes, and night watchman are shown as they impressed themselves on the poet's memory at the moment of the poem, not forced to fit patterns established by literary history. There is no vague "Mother of roots" here, but only solid, concrete, middle America facts: specific places, actions, people. We are solidly grounded in time and place, among a cross section of American fathers. James E. B. Breslin contends that "the figure of the father, alternately 'dreaming of heroes' and wishing for his own death, is resented for his impotence, which leaves the son exposed to a variety of dangerous forces."[35] This is true, and the resentment is given an extra edge by the apparent respect, perhaps only sympathy, on the poet's part, since he gives each man as much line as he needs to be expressed in lines 1 through 4 before viciously undercutting them all with "dreaming" and "proud." Lines 5 and 6 are like blind-side blocks on the unsuspecting fathers, who are drawn with almost loving detail in the opening four lines, only to be put into their true places as impotent dreamers incapable of achievement or love.

The teenage boy plays football because the failed fathers dream of heroes, and because he, too, will one day need younger, unbroken boys to run into each other to furnish him with new vicarious dreams of possibility, achievement, heroism. He plays now to ensure that others will continue the ritual of furnishing the blast furnace workers and night watchmen of the world with hope for a future. He pays his dues so that he may have the right later, in a bar in Tiltonsville or Paris, it makes no difference really, to appropriate the boys' fearless rushes at each other for his own dreams. The boys internalize the fathers' ambitions and dreams, thereby dooming themselves to broken dreams and, unless the cycle is broken or transcended, dooming their children, too. "Suicidally," although oxymoronic when modifying "beautiful," is the proper adverb because, as Robert Hass says, "it tries to describe what happens when the inner life can't find its way out of the dark . . .":[36] what is potentially "beautiful" becomes "suicidal." The causal connection, "Therefore," is not as enigmatic as the "Therefore" of "Goodbye to the Poetry of Calcium." Here we can understand how egotistical, false pride paradoxically grounded in failure—or in a futile attempt to deny the failure that faces each father when he awakes—makes love impossible, which causes sons to seek loving approval in ways "proud fathers" can understand and feel free to praise. We understand that rituals perpetuate themselves unless we challenge them and risk expulsion from the doomed, but safe, circle of fathers, sons, and mothers. "Therefore" makes the cycle seem fated to continue forever. (But, as Hass notes, the voice of the poem is that of a man who is no "longer a part of the community he is seeing," even though "it is unlikely that he could see so clearly if he had not been a part of it" once.[37]) A barely controlled violence (football) is the direct result of the frustrated need for love, power, and dignity. The ritual is "an efficient transmutation of lovelessness into stylized violence," as Hass says.[38] The women are pathetic in their dehumanization, and the sons are saved for the last stanza because they are the sacrificial victims. They are like autumn leaves splashing across streets or onto windshields, beautiful in their brief fall. Theirs is a less violent version of Yeats's "terrible beauty," except that in these boys' case, the "beauty" is what is lost, not what is gained, through the "suicidally beautiful" act.

By continuing past stanza 1, Wright enlarges his vision to include not only himself but all American sons, mothers, and fathers. Football is the phenomenon that ties the general loss of love to our specific American culture. He presents his experience to us as a meaningful sequence of events with an internal validation. "This is the way things happen," he says, not just, "This is the way things happened to me." The individual "I" is thrust, by the pivotal "Therefore," into the large category of "sons," and the experience of the "I" is more meaningful because of that association with all sons. The "I" is still the focus of the poem—Wright begins with the individual and then enlarges his circle of reference—but the "I" has cultural significance, too. The individual experience, in other words, exists for itself but also does service to a larger cause. The values "latent" in the experience are drawn out by the poet's vision, and the poem becomes a testament not only to the experience it embodies but also to the poet's imagination, which reveals, rather than imposes, a meaning.

"Lying in a Hammock at William Duffy's Farm in Pine Island, Minnesota," probably Wright's most famous poem, gives us the best example of how images and experiences are allowed to exist fully for themselves but simultaneously reveal meaning and makes clear what Seay meant when he referred to Wright's "sharp" imagery in each line. Wright's debt to another poet, William Carlos Williams, is also clear here: each image describes a numinous moment, fully concrete yet fully abstract. The "ideas" are in the "things." We also hear Hemingway's minimalism and other echoes that perhaps carry us as far back as "the formalized plain speaking of rigorous antinomian purifiers like the early Quakers and Baptists."[39] The moments are meaningful, but their significance can never be apprehended unless they, the specific data, are accurately, honestly, and individually perceived. Here is the poem in full:

Over my head, I see the bronze butterfly,
Asleep on the black trunk,
Blowing like a leaf in green shadow.
Down the ravine behind the empty house,
The cowbells follow one another
Into the distances of the afternoon.
To my right,
In a field of sunlight between two pines,
The droppings of last year's horses
Blaze up into golden stones.
I lean back, as the evening darkens and comes on.
A chicken hawk floats over, looking for home.
I have wasted my life.

The final line, of course, has attracted much attention. The source of the line, as well as its meaning, is disputed. A. Poulin, Jr., identifies the source as the last line of Rilke's "Archaic Torso of Apollo" ("Du musst dein Leben andern"),[40] while Alan Williamson claims Rimbaud's "Song of the Highest Tower" ("J'ai perdu ma vie").[41] The line's appropriateness and validity are also debated. It seems in place in the context of the whole book: its emotions ("frightened, empty and worthless") and attitude ("one of panicked and sterile self-regard") are certainly consistent with other poems of *Branch*.[42] But is the line appropriate at the end of *this* poem? Some find it a genuine conclusion for this series of images; others call it forced, "an intrusion of the ego into what should be an entirely objective poem."[43] I call it appropriate and remember what Frost described as "the figure a poem makes":

> It begins in delight and ends in widsom. . . . It begins in delight, it inclines to the impulse, it assumes direction with the first line laid down, it runs a course of lucky events, and ends in a clarification of life—not necessarily a great clarification, such as sects and cults are founded on, but in a momentary stay against confusion. . . . It finds its own name as it goes and discovers the best waiting for it in some final phrase at once wise and sad—the happy-sad blend of the drinking song.[44]

"Lying in a Hammock" is no drinking song, but the rest of Frost's quotation applies to the poem. The first line seems spontaneous, as if Wright, lying peacefully in a hammock, really did simply happen to look up and see a butterfly. He wants to delight in the insect's bronze beauty but cannot, for his mood ("his own separation from the glories of nature"[45]) takes the poem in another direction. The butterfly is asleep on a black trunk, as the poet is lying in the middle of a dark world. The butterfly's bronze color becomes mere heaviness and passivity as it blows in the wind, a victim of the elements rather than an active participant. The chicken hawk, too, is merely floating, gliding on the currents. Wright is trapped in the hammock, off the earth but not of it, separate from nature, in limbo—even the farm is not his, but William Duffy's. He is an intruder everywhere, "looking for home," lost, searching, and suspended.

The tone is passive, heavy, and calm, the calm resulting from a sense of total futility, not from an inner peace. The cows follow one another down the ravine, the narrow track of time, their bells announcing the inexorable passing of life. Wright looks "Over," "down," "to [his] right," and then "lean[s] back" to look as dispassionately at himself. He reports his predicament as honestly as he has reported the other facts in his field of vision: "I have wasted my life." As Breslin says, it is precisely "the fullness of this moment," the fact that Wright has so objectively concentrated upon the natural world surrounding him, "that allows him to leap to [his] realization."[46] The "intrusion" of Wright in the final line, then, does not violate the objectivity of the rest of the poem but is prepared for by that careful presentation of data. As Frost prescribes, Wright follows the poem's impulse to its logical conclusion, finding himself uttering a "final phrase" that is "at once wise and sad." The "clarification" he discovers is not "a great clarification," but it does provide a "momentary stay against confusion" by summing up and fixing the heaviness in time, the way one stops bleeding by applying pressure to the wound.

There is even a cautious hope held out to us in lines 7 through 10. The horses' droppings, reminiscent of the waste we have already seen, is the only hopeful image in the poem. The "golden stones" promise new life and beauty out of the waste of past days, another sort of "stay against confusion." (This hopeful image, I think, justifies Peter Stitt's contention that, in the poem's final line, Wright "is not condemning himself . . . ; instead, the line should be read as expressing desire, a vow taken for the future."[47]) This magical, alchemical transformation of droppings into gold is almost lost in the poem and in the first half of *Branch*. It remains as a germ of happiness in the poet's consciousness that blossoms, but only much later in "A Blessing," one of the last poems in this volume. Like "Lying in a Hammock," "A Blessing" has a forceful ending and, perhaps because of this, is also often anthologized. (Or perhaps these three poems are favorites of anthologizers because, as my discussion here illustrates, they are accessible to logical interpretation, beg to be victims of the "heresy of paraphrase," as many other poems in *Branch* do not.) Here is the whole of "A Blessing":

Just off the highway to Rochester, Minnesota,
Twilight bounds softly forth on the grass.
And the eyes of those two Indian ponies
Darken with kindness.
They have come gladly out of the willows
To welcome my friend and me.
We step over the barbed wire into the pasture
Where they have been grazing all day, alone.
They ripple tensely, they can hardly contain their happiness
That we have come.
They bow shyly as wet swans. They love each other.
There is no loneliness like theirs.
At home once more,
They begin munching the young tufts of spring in the darkness.
I would like to hold the slenderer one in my arms,
For she has walked over to me
And nuzzled my left hand.
She is black and white,
Her mane falls wild on her forehead,
And the light breeze moves me to caress her long ear
That is delicate as the skin over a girl's wrist.
Suddenly I realize

> That if I stepped out of my body I would break
> Into blossom.

The poet, like the hound of *The Green Wall*, steps over a boundary (the barbed wire fence) preparatory to breaking through to real life. He enters the horses' more vital, and more innocent, realm, the fenced pasture that is distinct from the "empty house" of man's world. The horses' struggle to "contain" themselves also foreshadows the final "breaking" through boundaries that concludes the poem. We are prepared by the tone, certainly joyous and anticipatory, for some event, which turns out to be more like a state of mind, "an intuited confidence in the surrounding environment," as Breslin says.[48] The poet constructs a dome of calm that shuts out all tension, clears away a clean circle in which he and nature meet but do not quite merge, as the "if" makes clear. The conclusion is "a leap of visionary insight" and "a kind of mystical union"[49] but not a genuine metamorphosis, although the boundary between "vision," "union," and "metamorphosis" is, I think, deliberately kept vague. The fact that Wright does not really "break" makes the conclusion more hopeful and magical than if he had, for he manages this "visionary insight" "without annihilating the physical,"[50] implying that such joy is possible even though we are trapped in our humanness, limited by natural, unbreakable boundaries. As Peter Stitt remarks, the poem holds out the possibility of "an ultimate spiritual union beyond the bounds of physical limitation,"[51] even as, or "if," we retain our physical selves.

Despite the "if" in the penultimate line that makes the transcendence "only" imaginary, then, "the power of this poem lies," as John Martone sees, "in the speaker's imagining of ecstasy as *possible*" (emphasis added).[52] Therefore, even with the "if," even though there is no supernatural metamorphosis of human to animal, no Ovidian transformation, there is the kind of "metamorphosis in which a limited, partial, human self is abandoned and a larger, natural world is embraced as a source of meaning."[53] As Williamson notes, for Wright's generation, "the truly important educative experiences become . . . experiences of unlearning," including "empathy with animals."[54] Wright here tries to "unlearn" what separates him from the horses.

The horses' droppings of "Lying in a Hammock," those veiled images of possibility, here finally "blossom" in an ecstasy that Wright declares is possible despite human limitations and bodily limits. The horse's muzzle is the alchemist's stone. Wright has to "break," leave behind his human ego if not his human body, before he can "blossom." He does not die to find salvation, but the imagery is a modern translation of the imagery a religious poet would use to picture the casting off of vanity, pride, and human flesh (which Wright keeps) that necessarily precedes redemption. We hear an unexpected echo in Donne's famous "Holy Sonnet":

> Batter my heart, three person'd God; for you
> As yet but knocke, breathe, shine, and seeke to mend;
> That I may rise, and stand, o'erthrow mee, 'and bend
> Your force, to breake, blowe, burn and make me new.

The tone, of course, is different. Donne acknowledges his sin and need for God's touch, which both destroys and saves. Wright's imagery is less violent—he substitutes a nuzzling for a battering—but he, too, believes himself past mending. He wants a new beginning and admits himself incapable of self-regeneration. His hope, though, is that such a reseeding is possible on earth in this lifetime. The brevity of life, and the absence of any intimation of an afterlife, makes the quest an urgent one. For the poet without Donne's religious convictions, every hour is the eleventh one, every day may be his last chance to live, every bed is a deathbed. Wright needs to find whatever brand of salvation he can find, and quickly. Hence the pressure, that we noticed as early as *The Green Wall*, on everyday reality to be meaningful, to give the poet access to realms of significance that expose the lies of the slag heaps, thickets, and dead mulberry trees. Wright wants to be able to declare with Thoreau, in a passage the poet uses as an epigraph for *Saint Judas*, that "news had come that IT was well." In "A Blessing," that news seems to have arrived, but where did it come from? Who delivered it? How can the poet trust the message? Can we trust the poet's optimism? How has Wright moved from "I have wasted my life" to "I would break / Into blossom"? How has he apparently found the "home" that he seeks?

The transition from despair to hope has been made possible by the poet's new voice, the topic I began this chapter with. The curser of "At the Executed Murderer's Grave" and "In Shame and Humiliation," who occasionally tried to bully himself and his readers into believing what he could not quite accept—that his voice was authentic—has become the confident, or more confident, or temporarily more confident, "poet of immanence," who is convinced that his experience and his voice are valid because they are his sincere utterances emerging from his deepest self. As poem piles upon poem in *Branch*, Wright hears his own voice becoming stronger, sounding perfectly valid and adequate to its subjects. We noticed that in *The Green Wall* he occasionally lets his "dark" diction carry his poems toward predictably "dark" conclusions. Here I think his own voice affects him in a more fortunate way. He fears himself "lost" in the early poems but then discovers—or hears—that he has survived. Nothing is broken, as he feared when the book began in such despair. *Branch* almost seems to surprise the poet as more and more successful poems emerge. I earlier alluded to Kafka's "The Metamorphosis." Readers of that story often note that Gregor's transformation into an insect is an instance of the truth, long buried, rising into horrible view from some great depth, through a fissure in the family's carefully maintained facade of decorum. The poems in *The Branch Will Not Break* often sound like just that eruption of truth into the light:

> I am frightened by the sorrow
> Of escaping animals.
> ("In the Face of Hatred")

> Many animals that our fathers killed in America
> Had quick eyes.
> ("Fear Is What Quickens Me")

> Women are dancing around a fire
> By a pond of creosote and waste water from the river

In the dank fog of Ohio.
They are dead.
> ("A Message Hidden in an Empty Wine Bottle
> That I Threw into a Gully of Maple Trees
> One Night at an Indecent Hour")

I began in Ohio.
I still dream of home.
> ("Stages on a Journey Westward")

The lines are the openings of four consecutive poems typical of those in *Branch*. The lines all announce a revelation, an awakening to a fact or an announcement of a fact the poet has recently discovered. The revelations are personal, sometimes painful, but are always the starting point for an unfolding of the emotion inherent in the awakening. The announcements are never hysterical themselves or even particularly emotional—they are the calmly faced facts the poet has found residing inside himself. The fact that a poem is autobiographical, of course, does not make it confessional. David Kalstone, in *Five Temperaments*, distinguishes autobiographical poetry from the verse M. L. Rosenthal called Confessional in *The New Poets*.[55] The confessional poet, as Kalstone says, can never be detached or humorous about his own sufferings. Wright is rarely humorous—we wish at times he were—yet he is here detached. We cannot say of Wright what Bly says of "the confessional poet": "anything less than an abortion or a cancer operation really doesn't justify the machinery. A poem becomes a tank that can't maneuver on soft ground without destroying it."[56] (Bly has a sense of humor even if Wright sometimes seems not to.) Wright does not simply prick himself to see if he will bleed, nor does he remain sealed within his own ego. He begins with himself, with what he has dredged up from the "river" that runs through his psyche, but he is not merely speaking for himself. He is speaking as the seer whose visions are germane for all. His hatred is our hatred; his fear, our fear. His salvation, then, will also mean ours. The quest is more serious than a search for a new scar to expose to the gaping reader. Wright is not simply making personal narratives of his latest breakdown, breakup, or breakout: he hopes to save us as he saves himself, to lead us to the "city of isolated men beyond mountains." But he first needs to climb those mountains himself, or, a more accurate metaphor, to dig beneath those mountains.

We hear him searching for the right images in "In the Face of Hatred." He walks just along the edge between heightened realism and surrealism, maintaining an uncanny balance until the end of the poem:

> I am frightened by the sorrow
> Of escaping animals.
> The snake moves slowly
> Beyond his horizon of yellow stone.
> A great harvest of convicts has shaken loose
> And hurries across the wall of your eyes.
> Most of them, all moving alike,
> Are gone already along the river.
> Only two boys,
> Trailed by shadows of rooted police,
> Turn aimlessly in the lashing elderberries.
> One cries for his father's death,
> And the other, the silent one,
> Listens into the hallway
> Of a dark leaf.

"The wall of your eyes" strikes me as a particularly good metaphor for the retina. It allows Wright to impart the image of the eye as a screen without using that hackneyed comparison. But as we come to the line break after "hallway," we have no way of expecting "Of a dark leaf." Nor, even after a second or third effort, can we visualize what is meant. Wright tantalizes us with "harvest of convicts" and "rooted police," makes us struggle to keep pace with his imagery, builds up a tension between the rational and irrational, and only defies our sense in the final lines. Plus, the individual images have no obvious logical link one to the next. Yet they manage a coherence despite their apparent disjointedness. The poem is dark, like a nightmare of escape in which your legs grow heavy and the "snake," as

slowly as it moves, still gains ground. The picture the reader re-
ceives is not necessarily composed of any of the individual images of
the poem but is, instead, a feeling that the reader must make pic-
torial himself, building from his own memories, which somehow
connect with the memories Wright has put into the poems. Eliz-
abeth Bishop draws precise pictures to define the limits of her own
self; Randall Jarrell, in such poems as "A Hunt in the Black Forest"
and "The House in the Wood," paints a mood that we feel as much as
see. Wright here is more like Jarrell in that he is also painting a
mood. The point is, first, as I said earlier, that Wright requires our
emotional and imaginative participation if we are to "get" the poems
and, second, that although Wright begins with himself he does not
end there. The images, drawn from some "cave / In the air behind
[the poet's] body" ("The Jewel"), are perhaps incomprehensible by
themselves, but when they work, they combine with an emotional
force that is difficult to account for by simply rereading the poem.
His fear *is* our fear.

As the poems proceed in *Branch*, Wright sounds stronger, more
confident that he can overcome the weeds that surround him. We
see this clearly in "Two Hangovers,"[57] the poem that contains the
book's title line. The poem is divided into two numbered sections.
In section 1, the speaker lists images of death and drunkenness,
which all elaborate the rather heavy, self-hateful, self-pitying, and
pessimistic mood that accompanies a hangover. The mood provides
the coherence, for the images are not related grammatically by sub-
ordination or any method to indicate causal or temporal rela-
tionships. The poet looks around, as he did in "Lying in a
Hammock" but refuses to impose any interpretation on the data:

> I slouch in bed.
> Beyond the streaked trees of my window,
> All groves are bare.
> Locusts and poplars change to unmarried women
> Sorting slate from anthracite
> Between railroad ties:
> The yellow-bearded winter of the depression
> Is still alive somewhere, an old man

Counting his collection of bottle caps
In a tarpaper shack under the cold trees
Of my grave.

The poet concludes section 1 in darkness:

The filaments of cold light bulbs tremble
In music like delicate birds.
Ah, turn it off.

There is a causality in section 2 that was absent in section 1:

In a pine tree,
A few yards away from my window sill,
A brilliant blue jay is springing up and down, up and down,
On a branch.
I laugh, as I see him abandon himself
To entire delight, for he knows as well as I do
That the branch will not break.

Wright concludes that the blue jay he sees "springing" (an appropriate verb to imply a new life) is happy *because* he (the bird) knows that the branch will not break. We are meant to believe, of course, that the poet is bringing what Bly calls "news of the universe,"[58] rather than news of his own ego, but we are forced to notice that Wright not only provides the cause of the bird's delight, he also defines the bird's reaction as "delight." Passive observance is probably impossible—the very selecting and ordering of the images of part one are acts of interpretation—and certainly will not provide the poet with the hope he needs "to waken and greet the world once again." But does Wright discover "delight" and unity, or does he impose it? Is this poem an instance of what psychoanalyst Georg Groddeck calls *Gott-natur*, "the holy nature,"[59] breaking through the poet's consciousness, a revelation of the world's interdependence, or is it an example of the poet's imposing a meaningful form on a formless world? Is Wright the explorer who happens onto a world alive and well, or is he the projector of the delight he needs to believe exists? We remember the same dull, heavy passive tone of "Lying in a Hammock." There the poet concludes that he has wasted his life. Are things "dead" in section 1 and in "Lying in a Hammock" because the poet refuses his role as vivifier, as life-giver, or do they only seem enervated because he simply does not see their vitality? Does passive viewing reveal only death, while active enjoyment reveals meaning that can sustain the poet? Where, then, does meaning reside? Is the speaker's mood the most important datum in the poem, or is the mood created by what he sees? I suppose the next question should be do we believe that *Esse es percipi,* or do we believe that a meaningful universe exists independently of our perceptions? I am not presumptuous enough to try to answer these questions, and I trust the reader would not be foolish enough to take my word over Berkeley's or Plato's. What we can do is acknowledge that Wright has faith (the necessary component in any philosophy that finds values in facts) "that the branch will not break," that there is a meaningful ground of being that underlies all life. Or, as James E. B. Breslin phrases it, Wright maintains "the integrity of both self and object" while establishing "a ground of resemblance between them." This is possible because Wright believes the "external world offers not a merciless threat but a supportive context: the branch will *not* break."[60] Whether this is a supreme fiction or a religious intuition or a discovery of fact cannot be resolved here. The poet believes he has discovered *Gott-natur,* and that belief not only informs the rest of the poems in *The Branch Will Not Break* but also provides the verses their power, coherence, and confidence.

Not all poets, of course, are in tune with *Gott-natur,* and Wright not only voluntarily separates himself from "them," the leaden, unimaginative residents of *The Green Wall,* but also from bad poets, perhaps of the sort Bly accused of being "locked inside the ego":

> Relieved, I let the book fall behind a stone.
> I climb a slight rise of grass.
> I do not want to disturb the ants
> Who are walking single file up the fence post,
> Carrying small white petals,
> Casting shadows so frail that I can see through them.

In the poem, rather ungainly titled "Depressed by a Book of Bad Poetry, I Walk toward an Unused Pasture and Invite the Insects to Join Me," Wright, the true poet, experiences harmony with nature only after discarding the burden of bad poetry. We can think of this as an act of discarding his past and starting fresh, as he does to some extent in this book. He can now "see through" to the peace of nature that has eluded him. In past books, he had insisted on enforcing a poet's harmony on the world that he now claims to be internally harmonized. The poem continues:

> I close my eyes for a moment, and listen.
> The old grasshoppers
> Are tired, they leap heavily now,
> Their thighs are burdened.
> I want to hear them, they have clear sounds to make.
> Then lovely, far off, a dark cricket begins
> In the maple trees.

The only message is the sound of belonging. Wright "climbs" (note how often "climbing" and "digging" move one in the same direction) to a new relationship with the world around him. He neither stands above it, as in the first section of "The Morality of Poetry," nor forces his mental forms onto it. Rather, "relieved" now of the false statements of the bad poet, including his own false statements, he listens quietly. He clears his senses to hear the crickets. However, as before, we cannot be certain that this is a passive hearing rather than a willed projection. Notice Wright says, "I want to hear them" and "I do not want to disturb the ants." These are conscious decisions. The poet is not only shedding his old formalist skin but is also consciously growing a new, more permeable covering that, he hopes, is less a barrier to the outside than an invitation to the ants, grasshoppers, and crickets. Whether we believe him or not, the poet wants us to conclude that the era of willful projection is past in his work. The old active ethic of *The Green Wall* has gone the way of rhyme and meter. We are no longer urged to jump or fly but to sit and listen or, at most, walk softly. As the "wheat leans," so the poet leans, imitating not imposing. Wright is like "the moon's young, trying / Their wings," terrified at his fragile freedom and skeptical of his power of flight. He sounds like the conductor or stager of some grand event, telling us "Now" to direct our attention to what might be neglected. He is the poet as guide, pointer to truth, revealer of nature's secrets that are now impinging on his own consciousness in a new way. His is the enthusiasm of the convert.

Many of the poems that follow indicate this new mood: "March," "Two Spring Charms," "Spring Images," "Arriving in the Country Again," "Today I Was Happy, So I Made This Poem." We are urged to replace understanding and interpretation with perception, although, as is clear from the poems and from earlier discussion, the line between interpretation that is imposed willfully and aggressively and perception that interprets without violating the object's integrity is a very difficult one to draw. The poet experiments more and more with being an unjudging eye:

> Cribs loaded with roughage huddle together
> Before the north clouds.
> The wind tiptoes between poplars.
> The silver maple leaves squint
> Toward the ground.
> An old farmer, his scarlet face
> Apologetic with whiskey, swings back a barn door
> And calls a hundred black-and-white Holsteins
> From the clover field.

The title, too, is merely descriptive: "From a Bus Window in Central Ohio, Just before a Thunder Shower." Choosing to record simple folk and country scenes is itself a judgment, of course, especially when the recording is done as reverently as it is here. But Wright makes every effort in some of the poems to be nothing more than the conduit for the world's message:

> I stand still in the late afternoon.
> My face is turned away from the sun.
> A horse grazes in my long shadow.
>   ("Arriving in the Country Again")

I slept a few minutes ago,
Even though the stove has been out for hours.
I am growing old.
A bird cries in the bare elder trees.
        ("In the Cold House")

The images are bare (which is fitting here for bare trees or a blank stare, while "spare" imagery was not fitting for a description of the "anarchic" sea in "The Morality of Poetry"—we must judge each poem individually rather than construct rules with which to evaluate them all) and are juxtaposed without comment. Most clauses are coordinated; logical relationships are only implied or are absent altogether. The poems rely on the reader's participation (and, when good, compel that participation) and often deny by their very artlessness the poet's importance (even though, as I have said, the poet obviously selects those elements that best suit his rhetorical goal of convincing us and himself that he truly has arrived "in the country again"). This archetypal wanderer is straining through the desert—occasionally snow-covered—for his promised land, from which thorns and slag heaps have been banished and where horses, Chippewas, Norwegians, and poets can rise above "the beautiful white ruins / Of America" ("Having Lost My Sons, I Confront the Wreckage of the Moon: Christmas, 1960"). He searches, in other words, for "the branch that will not break."

I have tried to establish that the poems of *Branch* evolve from thematic and formal tensions present in Wright's work from the beginning of his career. Even so, the poems sound like the sort of beginning that James Dickey calls a "Second Birth," a renewal that

> does not, of course, reside in a complete originality, which does not and could not exist. It dwells, rather, in the development of the personality, with its unique weight of experience and memory, as a writing instrument, and in the ability to give literary influence a new dimension which has the quality of this personality as informing principle. The Second Birth is largely a matter of self-criticism and endless experiment, presided over by an unwavering effort to ascertain what is most satisfying to the poet's self as it develops, or as it remains more clearly what it has always been.[61]

As we have seen, Wright's personality is more fully *in* the poems. He is his own persona now, not simply writing about his experience to satisfy some egotistical need to see his life in print, but letting that experience become his personality as the poem and the persona develop simultaneously. We get the impression of spontaneity, even though the poems are not spontaneous outpourings.[62] Every new poem seems a new beginning:

> The moon drops one or two feathers into the field.
> The dark wheat listens.
> Be still.
> Now.
> There they are, the moon's young, trying
> Their wings.
> ("Beginning")

The fact that Wright is now experimenting "to ascertain what is most satisfying to the poet's self as it develops" does not mean he will always write in this mood, but that he now finds it helpful, as he replaces his old memories and habits with new ones, to record images of emergence. He has "left my body behind me, crying / In its dark thorns" to find the "good things in this world" ("Trying to Pray"). Like the bear in "March," he is emerging from his hibernation:

> A bear under the snow
> Turns over to yawn.
> It's been a long, hard rest.

We do not normally think of a rest as being long and hard, but Wright's quiescence has not been normal. It has been, as he looks back on it now, more of a spiritual death than a time for recuperation, a "tight grave" from which he has escaped by roaring, like the bear, until the "roof breaks" and he delivers himself from the tomb, womb, or prison of his enslavement to others' voices and forms. He must almost literally reintroduce himself to the world:

I touch leaves.
I close my eyes, and think of water.
    ("Trying to Pray")

As the reader can hear, these later poems in *The Branch Will Not Break* are often chants of rejuvenation. The repetitive sentence structure reminds one of liturgical readings, as Wright establishes rituals of acceptance and perception to replace the rituals (see, for example, "Autumn Begins in Martins Ferry, Ohio") of stylized violence and passive impotence that he feels he has inherited:

Two athletes
Are dancing in the cathedral
Of the wind.

A butterfly lights on the branch
Of your green voice.

Small antelopes
Fall asleep in the ashes
Of the moon.

This is what I earlier called his religious, as opposed to his prayerful, tone. He is quiet and reverent, placing himself into a posture of acceptance (not subservience), in which he will be able to receive the "news of the universe" should he be so lucky to have it descend upon him. The simple sentences of "Spring Images," always arranged in basic subject/verb/object order and ending with a prepositional phrase headed by "Of," set up and then fulfill the reader's expectation for a logically complete and rounded image. The pattern reassures us, and we almost find ourselves back in the world of rhyme and meter, a world where we are made comfortable by the ability of the poet to order diverse and potentially threatening phenomena. Here it is not the artist's formal skill, however, that reassures us, but his simple presence: the poet, deity of this universe, is in his heaven and all's right with the world. Everythng is neatly tied together in the end, spring returns, and peace prevails after all. The "black snow," reminiscent of the slag heaps,

Like a strange sea creature,
Draws back into itself,
Restoring grass to earth.
　　("Two Spring Charms")

The quest of *Branch* has been, as Peter Stitt notes, "pastoral." The poet "turns from the city to the country, from society to nature, from human beings to animals, from a fear of the finality of death to a trust in immortality."[63]

The climax of *The Branch Will Not Break* is "A Blessing," quoted earlier. The transition from "I have wasted my life" early in the book to "I would break / Into blossom" near the end has been effected by the poet's voice and style (a calmly confident, apparently artless, respectful recording of nature in lines cut to the dimensions of the objects perceived) and by his attitude (like Whitman, he has lain down with the animals). Wright reaches the heights of his power in *Branch* when he believes himself capable of populating the barren land with his images:

. . . At a touch of my hand,
The air fills with delicate creatures
From the other world.
　　("Milkweed")

In this, the penultimate poem of the book, his happiness is, for a moment, complete. He has imagined ecstasy, the horses' droppings have become golden, and the water has returned to the Midwest. The "tight grave" of *The Green Wall* and *Saint Judas*, from which he tried to send the world lessons about how to live written on other men's stationery, has been replaced by a faith in his own magical— that is, poetical—ability to turn dead air into "delicate creatures." We are aware that such moods cannot last long but are happy to have been present for this rare flowering.

4

"And you bear it"

The final poems of *The Branch Will Not Break* left us with such a sense of the poet's power and confidence that we are shocked to turn to *Shall We Gather at the River* (1968),[1] Wright's fourth book, and be greeted with suicidal dreams, unmasked agony, and a darkness so black it almost overwhelms the poet. Everyone who reads *River* notices, as Peter Stitt says, that, at least in the early poems, "the speaker's mood has changed significantly,"[2] and, in Mazzaro's words, we hear "a return to the pessimism that dominated *Saint Judas*."[3] In fact, a death wish hovers over many of the poems:

> Well, I still have a train ticket valid.
> I can get out.
> ("The Poor Washed up by the Chicago River")

> Morgan the lonely,
> Morgan the dead,
> Has followed his only
> Child into a vast
> Desolation.
> When I heard he was going
> I tried to blossom

Into the boat beside him,
But I had no money.
        ("An Elegy for the Poet Morgan Blum")

The morbidity that underlies much of the poet's earlier, hopeful imagery is revealed in *River*. The joyful tone with which Wright imagined blossoming at the end of *Branch* hid the fact that to bloom is to die as a human, an implication that now becomes explicit. The longing for innocence that permeates *The Green Wall* is Freud's lure of Thanatos, the common enough wish for a return to the state of the inorganic, free of responsibilities, duties, choices, human demands, and tensions of any kind. The earlier imagery of breaking down or climbing over walls is not only a depiction of innocent play or liberation but also a reminder that the poet can only imagine salvation in terms of escape, the final escape of course being death. The deathly implications of his imagery that had been shielded from us now crowd forward. In particular, we notice that Wright has always paradoxically depicted "darkness" as an image of illumination. To dig to one's dark depths is to come into touch with the true sources of one's culturally untainted vitality and purity and to discover the true self beneath the encrustations of one's cultural definition. This is an act of liberation and a source of new life in Wright's work. But that darkness begins as a rejection of all that is inherited, a renunciation that threatens to become an end in itself, a truly "Everlasting No." And while the darkness discovered through introspection and painfully honest observation can promise liberation, it can also produce a loneliness, the result of severing one's ties to "home and love," as Wright says in "Sappho," which is at first invigorating but later onerous. The poet has so cherished and sought out his loneliness and darkness, his symbols of strength and defiance, and painted them so alluringly for himself and for us, that the truly dark implications of his quest—that loneliness is also isolation, that darkness can become a self-generating and consuming despair, and that the quest for innocence easily turns into stasis or fear of any action or engagement—have been obscured. Those implications blossom in *River*. As he says in "Before a Cashier's Window in a Department Store," in words that ring of Lowell's anguished "I myself am hell" ("Skunk Hour"), "I am the dark. I am the dark / Bone I was born to be."

Renato Poggioli, in *The Theory of the Avant-Garde*, notes that "many romantic artists and other hardy pioneers in subsequent generations conceived of [alienation] as a source of pride, a chance to hurl a haughty defiance, titanic and promethean, against man, history, and God."[4] In his first two books, Wright was a "hardy pioneer," stepping beyond the bounds of man's society. He consciously set himself apart from the "light" world of "them" and assumed the role of proud outcast, the hero-victim in search of his darkness. Being apart meant being pure, and only the "chicken" or the culpable walked lockstep in their assigned roles. The "it" of the epigraph to *Saint Judas*, however ("news had come that IT was well," Thoreau), has become the "it" of *River*, the wintry isolation that holds no promise of new spring life:

> I am hungry. In two more days
> It will be spring. So this
> Is what it feels like.
> ("Before a Cashier's Window in a Department Store")

The final "it" is the loneliness the poet has been unwittingly pursuing. By insisting so adamantly on being the uncompromising "dark / Bone I was born to be," Wright has imposed a sentence of exile on himself. Now, with spring only two days away, "IT" is far from being "well." He realized in *Branch* that the compensation he derived from the "heroic doom" of alienation was insufficient by itself and sought a substitute for society in nature. That solution was temporarily satisfying, but, as Stitt notes, in *River*, "even nature" is "empty of consolation for him."[5] *River* is a complement to *Branch* because here Wright discovers, as Poggioli would have predicted, that "later, alienation came to be felt as pathetic and tragic rather than heroic and dionysian. By virtue of that feeling, the artist was driven to turn against himself the weapons of his own antagonism and the nihilism he had previously directed against society and the outside world."[6]

In *River*, Wright is led for the first time to "turn against himself the weapons of his own antagonism" and consider suicide as an escape, not only from "them" but from the "pathetic and tragic" prison of alienation he has constructed for himself. As I have said, his themes of sleep, darkness, and stasis, although employed by Wright as positive alternatives to the culture's work ethic, materialism, and aggression, if used in the name of escape rather than reform, tend logically toward death, or at least a cessation of all action that we recognize as life. Here the poet follows his poetry's momentum to that end himself and looks frequently at suicide as a way out, a final escape that cannot be found by merely moving back to the country, as he did in *Branch*. One of the controlling image clusters of the book, that of river, water, boats, and shores, is meant to evoke ideas of death and the passage to an afterlife. Even the title of the volume, *Shall We Gather at the River*, in addition to reminding us of the Protestant hymn of the same name, reminds us of the host of lost souls gathered at the edge of the river Styx as they await the arrival of Charon to ferry them to the other side. The odor of death permeates the early poems in *River*, as it had the poems in *The Green Wall*. The important difference is that there the odor was of others' death-in-life, while the poet stood by, confident of his invulnerability; here the poet fears for himself.

The central conflict of *River*, then, is between the determination to live and the desire to die. The neat parallelism of the conflict is complicated by the fact that the desire to live is not always positive (sometimes it is imagined as a noble effort, sometimes as a pointless and impossible mockery of true life), while the desire to die is not always negative (at times it is imagined as a shameless reneging of life's promise, at times as an enlightened renunciation). The river (or occasionally the sea) is a perfectly chosen central image for this conflict because it can be an image of both life and death, and of either as positive or negative: shall we gather at the river to be reborn or to drown unredeemed? Shall we stay and do anything, even "beg coins," to live, or shall we give up, walk "outside / To wade in the sea, drowsing, and soothed"? The river's waters, when turbulent, can represent the turmoil created in the one who must discover how to live, and, when calm, the tranquillity of the one who chooses to avoid himself in a state of death-in-life. The waters both rejuvenate and erode, and the river can symbolize the hope for meaningful existence as well as the grave for those who have given up. It is both baptismal font and drowning pool. The river is Styx, separating earth from hell, life from death, and also the Ohio, whose dark waters separate Wright from his home. If he crosses, he risks death, either the real death of the suicide he contemplates occasionally in this volume or the spiritual death that might result from the freezing of his soul by returning home, the clipping of his wings in cold Ohio. However, if he crosses, the other shore might also be the resurrection he longs for, the reintegration into the community of family or country. He is trapped in an approach-avoidance conflict in which his choices present him with possibilities he desires and fears at the same time. Death, the other side, home, Ohio are all attractive because they promise company, security, and a rest. For that reason, they are also repulsive, because they could mean a loss of individual self. Yet death—either suicide or simply reneging on his quest and returning "home"—might be preferable to a life of lonely pain. And, still another possibility, this metaphorical or real death might be a rebirth, a way finally to unite his darkness with his light, the ordered, stable world of "home and love." Underlying the large conflict is the poet's fear that his need to belong is stronger than his need or ability to be an artist and will cause him to compromise his artistic self or to quiet it, as it is the source of his conflict with society.

As confusing as this sounds, there is an order to the poet's struggles in *River.* Mazzaro, Stitt, and Wright himself have outlined the structure of the book, which begins in despair but does not end there. If I may combine Mazzaro's and Stitt's words, the book breaks down into roughly three sections: (1) Wright "trapped in a hostile environment,"[7] "an outsider living close to the bottom";[8] (2) the poet's "efforts to escape his situation and supply in the process a summary of those events which brought him to where he is";[9] and (3) his partial solution, a return to "what he thinks of as home, . . . the Ohio,"[10] a stage in which "some of the threat has subsided."[11] Wright has said, in an interview with Stitt, "I was trying to move

from death to resurrection and death again, and challenge death fi-
nally."[12] The book, then, moves from a very dark beginning to a
guardedly hopeful ending, with plenty of vacillation, backsliding,
and trying out of possibilities in between. The second and third
stages of the book are sometimes hard to distinguish, for in Wright's
"efforts to escape his situation," he draws on sources of inner
strength that cause "the threat" to "subside" gradually throughout
the final two-thirds of the book. In fact, Stitt identifies only two
stages in *River*.

The first poem, "A Christmas Greeting," written in italics, serves
as an extended epigraph for the whole book, introducing the themes
of loneliness, despair, disillusionment, and confusion that we have
come to expect in Wright's poems in general, but also introducing
"the main theme of death by suicide in the river, and also the sec-
ondary theme of pain and self-pity"[13] that we will learn to expect
from this volume's early poems in particular. Regardless of our ex-
pectations based on Wright's other verse, however, we are all too
conditioned by modernist irony to expect a conventional "Christ-
mas greeting" of peace and love and are hardly surprised to find that
Charlie, the ghost the speaker addresses in the poem, is an alcoholic
suicide. What other character would we find in a Wright poem with
this title? Charlie's body finally rebelled against the bootleg whiskey
it had been fed for years, but Wright, in a tone characteristic of the
hard-edged voice of some poems in *The Green Wall*, sympathizes
with the man while treating his body's aches with a clinical detach-
ment:

> . . . A child, I saw you hunch your spine,
> Wrench your left elbow round, to hold in line
> The left-hand hollow of your back, as though
> The kidney prayed for mercy. Years ago.
> The kidneys do not pray, the kidneys drip.
> Urine stains at the liver.

The naturalistic and unsentimental treatment of the kidneys is a
device to distance the speaker from Charlie's, and hence his own,
pain, a device we saw in the opening poems of *Saint Judas*. It fails

the poet here, as it did there, for several reasons. First, by trying to use neutral terms, the speaker only reinforces his sense of loss. As a child, he perhaps believed in prayer, but now the world is completely material, even vulgar. By trying to "unload" a term like "pray" of its connotations, the speaker has only written a testament to his loss of faith, particularly noticeable in a poem ostensibly about Christmas. Also, the speaker, almost despite himself, repeats the verbs "drip," "hunch," and "stain," ultimately dragging himself into the shadow of Charlie's agony. The poet in him seeks verbal unity, but in so doing, he reminds us and himself that the moon is no longer for him a locus of romantic images, a symbol of love, beauty, or hope. What could be less romantic or hopeful than an image of moonbeams "dripping" from the sky?

> Charlie, the moon drips slowly in the dark,
> The mill smoke stains the snow, the gray whores walk,
> The left-hand hollow fills up, like the tide
> Drowning the moon, skillful with suicide.
> Charlie, don't ask me. Charlie go away,
> I feel my own spine hunching.

The poet cannot evade his role as observer and namer who assumes his subject's pain as his own. He is hopelessly vulnerable because insatiably verbal. He has to speak, has to remember, has to make poems, which means creating coherent image structures that pull him into the suffering, which, at this point, is all his eyes land on. If he could resign his job, he would, but in the meantime, he will go on filling the world with words, even empty ones that merely temporarily hold the accusing suffering at bay:

> . . . I'm afraid to die,
> It hurts to die, although the lucky do.
> Charlie, I don't know what to say to you
> Except Good Evening, Greetings, and Good Night,
> God Bless Us Every One.

This sounds like a false attempt to force the happy ending of *A Christmas Carol* onto an unresolved obituary for a drunk who jumped from a bridge (and we remember that Dickens was the subject of Wright's doctoral dissertation at the University of Washington in 1959). The poet throws out excerpts snatched desperately from his memory to shut up Charlie's insistent questioning, all in the speaker's mind, of course, about the reason for living. The final line of the poem ("What are you doing here?"), the only line not part of a rhymed couplet, cuts two ways. It is Wright's question addressed to Charlie, and it is Charlie's question addressed to Wright. From attempting to deny any relationship with Charlie, Wright has led himself, by the pull of "drip," "stain," and "hunch," to speak simultaneously with the doomed man. The demons that were once external harpies—slag heaps and steel mills—are now internal and inseparable from the speaker and the poet. The "pain" of the poem, as Edward Lense notes, is thus "both physical and metaphysical: life is terrible, Wright insists, because there can be no escape from suffering, no comforting visions of the other world."[14]

The river returns immediately in the next poem, "The Minneapolis Poem," a long production by Wright's standards, sixty-nine lines divided into seven numbered sections. We should note that Wright increasingly uses numbered sections as an organizing device in his poetry. There is only one poem employing numbered sections in *The Green Wall*, three in *Saint Judas*, six in *Branch*, and eight in *River*. As his sense of the discontinuity of experience increases, his attempts to create "seamless webs" and to make smooth, logical transitions inside poems decrease. However, there is frequently a smooth transition between poems, as here the river, specifically the Mississippi, and the theme of suicide are introduced straightaway, connecting nicely to Charlie:

> I wonder how many old men last winter
> Hungry and frightened by namelessness prowled
> The Mississippi shore
> Lashed blind by the wind, dreaming
> Of suicide in the river.

The water is "dark," "warm," and "beautifully slow," and the imagined suicides are "my brothers," so there is no doubt with whom the speaker identifies. Rather than freeing the waters to rejuvenate a dry land, the quester contemplates freeing himself by plunging into the "warm grave" of the Mississippi, which must really be bitterly cold in Minneapolis in the middle of winter. Despite this longing for death and escape, however, the poet still sees himself as a sort of hero to the rightful inheritors of the land, "us," "my brothers," the nameless old men whose drownings strike us as desperate escapes but which are acts of purification to Wright. Wright is here to save "us":

> Tall Negro girls from Chicago
> Listen to light songs.
> They know when the supposed patron
> Is a plainclothesman.
> A cop's palm
> Is a roach dangling down the scorched fangs
> Of a light bulb.

He employs poetic sisters of golden-thighed Betty from *The Green Wall* to accompany his "legless beggars," "Chippewa young men," and "split-lipped homosexuals" in a caravan of the feeble and outcast whom he, the speaker and poet who is their savior, will lead through the desert of Minneapolis to the fertile promised land, whose precise location is unknown and perhaps is not even on this earth or in this life:

> I want to be lifted up
> By some great white bird unknown to the police,
> And soar for a thousand miles and be carefully hidden
> Modest and golden as one last corn grain,
> Stored with the secrets of the wheat and the mysterious lives
> Of the unnamed poor.

His plea sounds like Job's to God: "Oh, that you would hide me in the nether world and keep me sheltered till your wrath is past; would fix a time for me, and then remember me!" (Job 15:13–14). His burying is not a death but a postponement of the fulfillment of

God's promise to will the world to the meek. God is left out of the picture, but the idea is essentially the same in this collage of secularized echoes of Job and the Sermon on the Mount: the time will come when those now poor will be rich, those legless will be powerful, those unnamed will be named. The "dry groins" of this sterile land will perform their procreative function once more, but until that time, I, the poet-hero-victim, will keep alive "the secrets" of those who have been passed over. The corn and wheat imagery, as Maud Bodkin attests in *Archetypal Patterns in Poetry*, suggests "the sequence of rain, flood, and spring corn [that] constitutes a holy rebirth."[15] The final stanza lifts us from contemporary Minneapolis to "a world whose less discriminating mode of thought has upon us the power of an inchoate or unconscious poetry."[16] Thus, whether we recognize the exact meaning of the imagery or not, we do hear the oracular tone and feel the "aura of significance" that together convey a hope not otherwise inferable from the preceding threatening, almost apocalyptic, imagery.

Wright shrinks our notion of the hero from one capable of bold and decisive action to one who wants to be "carefully hidden / Modest and golden," but he maintains a vision of the artist as someone noble, transcendent, able to stand more than most. The hero is not the strong-armed vanquisher who relies on brute force, but the recorder and bearer of the unbearable. Wright's heroism has a particularly twentieth-century flavor: he must face and enumerate his own Furies, resist the temptation to shut out or run from the world, and continue the cathartic talk, talk, talk that will deliver himself and the silent sufferers, like his father, whose "song remains secret" until the poet can sing it. His personality, not his sword, will deliver him. The quotation is from M. L. Rosenthal:

> Ultimately, wherever you have an insight into the unheroic
> loneliness of human consciousness in an impersonally hostile
> universe, . . . you have a related motivation, however undeveloped.
> It is the insistence on the transforming and liberating capacity of
> personality—the personality behind artistic sensibility—through its
> power to size up "things as they are" that restores heroism of
> attitude if not of a more effectively worldly kind.[17]

This "insistence on the transforming and liberating capacity of personality," then, is a kind of defeat, the product of the poet's recognition that "poetry makes nothing happen," as Auden says. Yet it is not total defeat or unconditional surrender. This quester faces his internal demons and talks the rest of us through ours. He does not slay dragons or rescue damsels, true, but he gives names, and hence power and identity, to the faceless. The poet is, then, a true hero, a quester who will, by the power of his magic words, in his role as chronicler of the weak's trials, bring new life, new harvests of justice, to the land now desiccated and "scorched" like the cop's palm in "The Minneapolis Poem." His quest is in some ways a contemporary analogue of the medieval hero's holy mission to restore the land's fertility. Wright knows the secrets; he is the shaman of the tribe, and the poet's words will blossom with the secrets whose time has come. There has always been a part of Wright, even in his darkest moments, as in these opening poems of *River*, that has thought of the poet as the culture's savior, the visionary being stranded in a wasteland but endowed with the power to speak the names of the gods that will cause spring to return or, in the prevalent imagery of the book, will bring freshening water to the parched earth. As Emerson knew, "Words are also actions, and actions are a kind of words."[18] The poet is "the Namer or Language-maker,"[19] but his naming does more than rejoice the intellect. Naming returns to the object named its true identity, which the culture has stripped clean, preferring faceless men who have no reason to value their lives or to fight for them. Like Wordsworth's or Emerson's poet, Wright's speaker is a representative human who is simply more sensitive than other men. He wanders the land and listens for the truth, which all people value but only the true poet can hear. Through the aesthetic process, he has hoped, he can call together his own fragmented being and thus show others the way to unity and completeness. In Wright's wasteland, the quester-poet-seer has always been the central figure whose charge is not to purify the tribe's language but to speak it clearly, to voice those secrets that will show the tribe the way to harmony, peace, fellowship, and cooperation, and away from the egotism and competitiveness that now sow only division and hostility. What he reports, then, is not just for other poets' ears, not elitist rumblings from the land of poesy, but the facts of his fellow beings' lives, facts that will return the listeners to themselves. As Emerson says, "The poets are thus liberating gods."[20]

The most dangerous fact, to "us" and to "them," is the importance of one's life. The person who feels in his bones that his life is valuable cannot accept its degradation (at his own hands or others'), cannot be complacent, and, perhaps most frightening, cannot escape himself:

> My life was never so precious
> To me as now.
> I gape unbelieving at those two lines
> Of my words, caught and frisked naked.

Thus begins "Inscription for the Tank," immediately after "The Minneapolis Poem." The reluctant savior has trapped himself, again by his propensity to talk and to verbalize his life. If one talks enough, one may accidentally say something so real, honest, and true that it will change one's life. Wright is trapped by his own words. It is as if, again like Emerson's poet, he sees through the form of his life to its essence with "that better preception"[21] that characterizes the true poet. His autonomous words come to remind him that, complain as he might, he must never forget the "secret" that he does prefer life to death. He has let himself be carried so far toward a romantic longing for death by the momentum of his own images that his psyche must call out to him the "secret" that is so obvious it is almost overlooked: "My life was never so precious / To me as now."

This expression of a determination to live, however, is not a free gift. Recognizing it obligates the poet to formulate more responsible resolutions to his despair than suicide. It would be easier, he says, not to have seen his secret: "I wish I had copied some words from Isaiah, / Kabir, Ansari, oh Whitman, oh anyone, anyone." However, "I wrote down mine, and now / I must read them forever." His words make demands of him, demands for life that will not allow him the

self-pity and maudlin flirtations with death or escape that have en-
ticed him thus far. "Even / When the wings in my shoulders cringe
up / At the cold's fangs," even when he is most miserable, most con-
fined, and least like the free soaring bird he would like to be, he
must still remember his resolution to live. He has created a di-
lemma for himself by admitting his desire to live, for now he must
figure out how to live, must face the same problem he announced on
the cover of *Saint Judas*: how does one live a good and humane life?
And who can help him? No one: "Let the dead pray for their own
dead. / What is their pity to me?" He is on his own, with no help
from the dead or the living they have left behind to mourn them.

The next poem, "In Terror of Hospital Bills," proves again that the
poet cannot deny what he has seen:

> My throat is open, insane,
> Tempting pneumonia.
> But my life was never so precious
> To me as now.
> I will have to beg coins
> After dark.

Wright, having seen as if in a vision his determination to live, will
not give in to this desire to escape:

> I will learn to scent the police,
> And sit or go blind, stay mute, be taken for dead
> For your sake, oh my secret,
> My life.

His confessions are somewhat like Whitman's: they acknowledge
his identity with the reader and admit that the reader is as good as
the poet but just does not recognize his beauty. "Our worst weakness
is the strongest bond of our humanity,"[22] as Larzer Ziff says when
discussing Whitman. Wright's "weakness" is that he wants to live,
and it is this "shared vulnerability,"[23] again using Ziff's phrase, that
connects him with his audience.

At this point the reader may think this is really the same role

Wright assumed in *The Green Wall.* In many ways it is, and one of the most striking things about reading Wright's entire output is the consistency of his theme. Nonetheless, this is not precisely the same attitude as in that first book. Subtle changes have taken place. Wright began thinking primarily, almost entirely, of himself and his identity in his tight poems of suppressed protest. The "us" and "them" early in his work are not so much communities of opposed people as they are labels for opposed ideas. They are clashing abstractions, and in Wright's first two books, he is the only real person around—even then he usually speaks from behind a mask or persona or through other poets' forms and voices. At the end of *Saint Judas,* he can still think of himself as both Saint Judas (a paradoxical self-aggrandizement through identification with the arch-villain and outcast, an almost adolescent thumbing of the nose at the powers that be) and as James A. Wright of Martins Ferry, Ohio, a real person neither more nor less than himself. The contradiction is really a transition between the impersonal, modernist voice of the first two books and the personal voice that follows. He intellectually acknowledges that, yes, we are all united by the "branch that will not break," but even in the breaking of vessels of *Branch,* Wright still seems surrounded by shadow people. In the title poem of *Branch,* the speaker has to shut off the lights in his room and thus blot out the suffering he has depicted for us before he can make his affirmation that "the branch will not break." He claims community by closing his eyes. It is not until *River* that the "simple, separate Person," to use Whitman's term, really recognizes himself also as part of the "En-Masse" at some point deep in his being, in his musculature, as the images of the early poems in this fourth book suggest. The "we" in the title of this book is as important as the "river," for Wright finally recognizes himself as truly a part of a community, a group to which he has some responsibility. His commitment is not only to his life, but to others' as well. "The existential decision not to commit suicide," as Mazzaro notes, leads to "a strengthening responsibility for his own and others' individuality."[24] His personal needs become commitments; his talents become common wealth. The savior's work is finally social.

There is one more way in which this quest differs from the quest of *The Green Wall* and *Saint Judas*. When discussing those early poems, I contended that the reader could hear Wright's youth in the poems. In *River*, one can hear his aging, especially in such a poem as "Speak." He is past the passion of "In Shame and Humiliation" (*Saint Judas*), in which man's angry curse is the weapon he needs to bring him to his own humanity. There Wright was willing to shout himself back to his humanity; here he sounds drained, worn-out, and worn-down. There can be no angry cursing, for man's defeat is unworthy of histrionics or tragic tone:

> To speak in a flat voice
> Is all that I can do. . . .
> I speak of flat defeat
> In a flat voice.

These poems are clearly written after the speaker has made his initial efforts to live. He says he has made sacrifices, accepted loneliness, and still, "I returned rebuffed

> And saw under the sun
> The race not to the swift
> Nor the battle won.

He has found neither the peace nor the assurance he has sought. How much longer can he continue to struggle? He has loved the outcasts ("Thy cursed"), worshiped the beauty of nature ("Thy house"), and still, like Job, cannot find salvation. He is the abandoned son, one who has not deserved the rough treatment he has received. As a forsaken son, he is like Christ in His days of doubt, but wandering instead in the desert of America. Wright addresses God directly in "Speak," an uncharacteristic technique for a poet who frequently mentions deities but has little faith in them. Mazzaro, using "Speak" as one example, says that in *River*, "despite" the volume's "overall pessimism," Wright "makes several inroads into positing and accepting deity."[25] I would change "despite" to "because of," for Wright's appeal to God seems a mid-life grasping at straws when all else has failed him.

The longing to die that begins *River* is a warming-up on the poet's part. We have to recognize the dynamics that underlie this book's early poems: the poet wants to live but has to deny that urge until he is ready to commit himself to life and the living. In that, he is only normal. The dominant image of the river as the river of death in the book's opening poems can surely be no accident, nor can the fact that, as the volume continues, the river begins to take on the look of the river of life. As early as the volume's fifth poem, "I Am a Sioux Brave, He Said in Minneapolis," Wright can no longer even envy the dead: "How lonely the dead must be." He will take his stance firmly in this world; however, unfortunately for the author, after fronting what Camus called "the only truly philosophical problem,"[26] the problem of suicide, the poet is left with little more than his resolution to live as the book continues. He is without "company," in a hostile land, and his terrible need is exposed to everyone, even the cashier in a local department store: "Beneath her terrible blaze, my skeleton / Glitters out." He is left naked, with only his darkness, "in the sea alone." His frequent unanswered questions ("Am I dead? And, if not, why not?") and his obvious vulnerability make us wonder what the poet can do to live in this world of cashiers, department store managers, and police officers. He is placed here with "one candle" ("Old Age Compensation") or "a worthless agate / In my pocket" ("Gambling in Stateline, Nevada"), clothed in a "frayed coat" and "pinned down / By debt" ("Before a Cashier's Window in a Department Store"). He has no talents to beat the system, no hope of justice ("I . . . saw under the sun / The race not to the swift / Nor the battle won"), and fails pathetically when he tries to win. The "old woman" in "Gambling in Stateline, Nevada" is Wright's double:

Here, across from the keno board,
An old woman
Has been beating a strange machine
In its face all day.

The enjambment in the third line makes us believe momentarily that the woman is actually winning, but our hopes are broken. What Wright does possess, we must remember, is his ability to speak, if only "of flat defeat / In a flat voice." It was that ability, that poetic habit, that committed him to live, in "Inscription for the Tank," and it will have to be his ability to speak, to be the poet and language-maker, that will keep him alive. Suited to this world or not, he will be true to his determination to stay and live, as he muddles through the middle and final sections of *River* attempting to return himself to life, now sounding resolute, now sounding defeated, but moving toward a reaffirmation of his desire to live and of his role as poet.

However slowly, in the final two-thirds of the book, the poet attempts to return to his "native land." The return is spiritual, of course, since he was only exiled in spirit. "Rip," the tale of a contemporary Rip Van Winkle after he awakens from a long sleep during which he had "lost" his land, announces the poet's intention to return to the land. The speaker is watching the effects of a sunset, perhaps, on the river:

> It can't be the passing of time that casts
> That white shadow across the waters
> Just offshore.
> I shiver a little, with the evening.
> I turn down the steep path to find
> What's left of the river gold.

Is there something other than "the passing of time" that has caused the river to look so attractive this night? Perhaps a change in the viewer's heart has cast the "white shadow" across the water? Is it really "the evening" that makes the poet shiver, or a realization somewhere in his nervous system that a transformation is taking place within him?

> Close by a big river, I am alive in my own country,
> I am home again.

He looks around as Rip Van Winkle did, remarking the spots he can remember from his past:

Yes: I lived here, and here, and my name,
That I carved young, with a girl's, is healed over, now,
And lies sleeping beneath the inward sky
Of a tree's skin, close to the quick.

The wounds he inflicted on the life around him, the renunciations of
the splenetic poems of his unforgiving youth, have healed. His tone
is conciliatory here because he is now attempting to consolidate his
gains. The "river gold" he imagines is the salvageable part of the
culture earlier rejected as wholly evil by the young poet eager to
carve his name into the poetry anthologies and histories. The vio-
lent assertions of his own identity are not necessary anymore, he
says, because he knows who he is and carries that name "close to the
quick," at his core.

One way Wright manages to take heart and declare himself "home
again" after the opening despair of *River* is by realizing the impor-
tance of his role in the culture. The self-proclaimed exile, as I have
said, does have a social role, that of the voice of the dispossessed. He
begins to feel the power and importance of that role in the middle of
River. For example, his worst doubts but also his greatest hope in-
form the short "Living by the Red River":

Blood flows in me, but what does it have to do
With the rain that is falling?
In me, scarlet-jacketed armies march into the rain
Across dark fields. My blood lies still,
Indifferent to cannons on the ships of imperialists
Drifting offshore.
Sometimes I have to sleep
In dangerous places, on cliffs underground,
Walls that still hold the whole prints
Of ancient ferns.

What is the relationship, if any, between his system, his blood, and
the system of the world around him? Is he in any way relevant to the
world of imperialists' cannons, or is he an *isolato*, an irrelevant tic
on the face of the "real" world, living in "the valley of [his] own

making where executives / Would never wish to tamper," to quote Auden again? The rain freshens the land, but is the poet part of that renewal process? What role has he in bringing new life to anything or anyone? Can he be the rain?

The concluding image of ferns is important. The "whole prints / Of ancient ferns" would, I think, be incomprehensible if we could not refer to the rest of Wright's work as a context, a key to his imagery. His earlier poetry is the glossary that tells us how to understand an individual poem's images. The underground cave is another in the cluster of images of the unconscious. Wright retreats to his deepest self and finds there ancient memories, a collective unconscious ripe with venerable signs of life. The ferns, though dead, live on in fossilized forms, as the poet's words, his "prints," are immortal on the page. The record of the ferns' presence lifts the poet's spirit, as his own records may, possibly, lift the spirit of others. Ferns also, of course, rely on the rain to survive, but here the poet, by recording his observation of the fossilized ferns, brings them back to life and, in a sense, becomes their rain, quietly asserting his rejuvenating power. Yes, he says, I am relevant. The connection between the poet's work, the ferns, the rain, the rejuvenation of the land, and the possible uplifting of other lost souls by the power of the word is made in an encrusting of images and their various connotations one on top of the other. In ten lines, Wright depicts his doubt and his hope, avoids any facile resolution, and hints of more than he actually says. The poem rewards rereading and makes us realize the density of these short, apparently offhand lyrics that abound in *River*.

"Listening to the Mourners" is another of Wright's compact lyrics and is also typical of the combined despair and hope of the middle poems in *River*. He begins the poem on the edge of civilization, in the wilderness (like Christ) huddled in a fetal position against the cold that is part of this "endless American winter";

> Crouched down by a roadside windbreak
> At the edge of the prairie,
> I flinch under the baleful jangling of the wind
> Through the telephone wires, a wilderness of voices

Blown for a thousand miles, for a hundred years.
They all have the same name, and the name is lost.

He hears what the Emersonian poet can but the normal person cannot: the long voices carried across miles, trying to raise other voices through the culture's technology, which supposedly makes communication easier, but which here seems to exile the human sound to the edge of the world, to cast it out to a land where it will never be heard. But Wright, the poet, is there, listening, recording, recovering the voices that would otherwise be lost. He is like Whitman in *Song of Myself,* section 24:

Through me many long dumb voices,
Voices of the interminable generations of slaves,
Voices of prostitutes and of deformed persons,
Voices of the diseased and despairing, and of thieves and dwarfs. . . .

The speakers' names become identities only if they are heard by other ears, if the connection goes through. If not, the names are "lost," in the sense that they are misplaced and in the sense that "lost" identifies the callers. The poet is crouched in the wilderness to make sure that someone hears the call for communion. His job is to retrieve the name from the wind, to pluck what is real and meaningful from what is simply noise. His role is to be attentive, listen, and then speak honestly what he hears. It is an important role, and realizing that empowers the poet to continue speaking, to resist the temptation to "get out."

Wright finds other sources of strength in this section of *River.* One commentator, William V. Spanos, has defined "the archetypal myth of the existential imagination" as follows: "the flight from a dark, threatening agent who pursues the fugitive protagonist into an isolated corner (often, the underground), where he must confront his relentless pursuer, whereupon, in a blinding moment of illumination he discovers the paradoxically benevolent aspect of his persecutor."[27] The "dark, threatening agent" has been Wright's fear, grief, and despair as well as the personifications of those fears, for example, the police and other of "them." The "underground" has occasionally been the poet's own unconscious and at other times the country, frontier, or nature, either thought of as a wild jungle or a bucolic retreat. In either case, he has sought answers and escape from the "dark, threatening agent." Now, although the revelation "at the edge of the prairie" that "this field is the beginning of my native land" ("Listening to the Mourners") may not be precisely a "blinding moment of illumination," it is a discovery of the poet's ability to live because he can face the Furies he has been fleeing. His Furies, of course, are relentless pursuers because they are within him and inescapable. Disillusion and grief are difficult to run from, especially for one who cannot help being introspective. The "persecutor" is benevolent because only by facing his despair can Wright ever return home, to his native land, as poet and person. Embracing his "locusts of bitterness" ("In Shame and Humiliation," *Saint Judas*) will enable him to become the "bird" that will fulfill him as poet and man, as speaker of the tribe's truths in the act of uttering his own deepest secrets (specifically, that "my life was never so precious / To me as now").

For example, in "The Small Blue Heron," the speaker's friends somehow have a heron, perhaps one rescued from some disaster, in their kitchen wastebasket (I get an image of a bird bespattered with oil from a spill, but there is no real evidence in the poem for that):

> I stroked his long throat
> On the floor. I was glad to hear him
> Croaking with terror.

The heron's croak of terror at least announces that he is alive, and if Wright has only his grief, if his only voice can be the "baleful jangling of the wind" ("Listening to the Mourners"), then he will have to sing his grief—like the heron and bird, but not as a heron or bird. As a human. Or, more emphatically, in order to be human. If he is to be the "whole man" that he has hoped to be since *The Green Wall*, he must recover what William Barrett calls "the man underneath . . . who is born, suffers, and dies."[28] His weeping may be just the voice he needs, not the voice he must flee.

Spanos continues: "This symbolic pattern, of course, is the Greek myth of the Furies, in which the protagonist's (Orestes') face-to-face encounter with the pursuing Erinyes (the Angry Ones) activates their transfiguration into the Eumenides (the Kindly Ones)."[29] Facing the Furies is like being born again:

> Murdered, I went risen,
> Where the murderers are,
> That black ditch
> Of river.
> ("The Life")

He, the exiled son that the "ugly" tried to murder by denying him his own soul, is now "risen" from his anger and despair, reborn and confronting his assailants alongside the great river that they have polluted. He has come, as he says in "Rip," to see "What's left of the river gold" after the others have turned the waters black. The second stanza is directed to the reader:

> And if I come back to my only country
> With a white rose on my shoulder,
> What is that to you?
> It is the grave
> In blossom.

He cannot renounce the only home he has been given, but he cannot return without the "white rose," here a white flag of peace that was formed in the grave, the product of being so long dead and isolated. It is interesting to recall in this context the first time in this volume that Wright referred to "blossoming." In "An Elegy for the Poet Morgan Blum," he had longed "to blossom / Into the boat" beside the dead poet and thus end his own life. Now his venom "blossoms" into life after he has seen, by flirting with death, how much he really wants to live and after he has gained the strength, by facing his own Furies, to continue.

The "white rose," however, is more than a peace symbol. Stanzas 3 and 4 further define it as his emblem, the fruit of his darkness, in a way his scarlet letter. It is used as a symbol of all that his journey into the darkness has caused to blossom, as a symbol of the fact that, in Spanos's terms, he has converted his black Erinyes into white Eumenides, blossoms of his self-knowledge, almost his Holy grail:

> It is the trillium of darkness,
> It is hell, it is the beginning of winter,
> It is a ghost town of Etruscans who have no names
> Any more.

It is white because it has been purified by the "flame" of his passionate quest. It has been formed by "a flame that burns beyond the names / Of sludge and filth of which this world is made," as he said earlier in "Sappho" (*The Green Wall*). What he said there still applies:

> I light the fire and see the blossom dance
> On air alone; I will not douse that flame,
> That searing flower; I will burn in it.

In "The Life," then, Wright does not simply declare his intention to return home, but simultaneously to return home and to retain the "white rose," the pure flame of self that can save him from "the sludge and filth" of "that black ditch / Of river," the wasteland man has made. He makes it clear that his return is not that of a cowed supplicant come home to beg forgiveness. The rose is a true part of himself that he will not abandon, not a simple adornment. As he says repeatedly in the concluding stanza, "It is." (We should also note that Wright repeats "It is" seven times in "The Life," a poem of only seventeen lines. Six times "It is" begins a line. He is less confident than his tone indicates, repeatedly pinching himself with the assertive "It is" to convince himself that he is really awake. Coming back from the dead, as Nick Adams learned in Hemingway's "Big Two-Hearted River," is less a "blinding moment of illumination" than a slow recovery, a tedious process of feeling one's limbs working again.)

We can phrase this awakening and empowering in psychological as well as poetic and existential terms. Wright is saying that he has incorporated parts of his collective unconscious into his conscious self. He has dredged up parts of the darkness and made them light, a "white rose." In one sense, this is what Spanos defines as the existentialist's project, but we can also see it as the process Jung calls "individuation," by which one sees and assimilates, through introspection, the parts of one's unconscious psyche that have escaped conscious recognition.[30] Individuation is capturing those exiled pieces, even, or especially, the socially unacceptable ones, and developing spiritually in the process. Wright is declaring here that he has been at least partially successful and has no intention of refunding the spoils of his arduous struggle. He will move back to the "murderers'" soil, but he will not be their victim: "He will not deny, he will not deny his own" ("In Shame and Humiliation").

Is this spot at the figurative core of the poet, this residence of a darkness that must be retrieved before the culture's "river gold" can be mined and the poet returned to his land and home whole, the same locale as Yeats's "foul rag-and-bone shop of the heart"? Is Wright simply "carrying on where Yeats left off" as M. L. Rosenthal says of American "Confessional" poets in general?[31] Bearing in mind the dangers of disagreeing with Rosenthal, I will have to agree with John Bayley when he says, in a discussion of Berryman, that Lowell and Berryman differ from Auden and Yeats in that "to both Auden and Yeats it would make no sense to be in search of their own voices. They remain what they were from the beginning."[32] Yeats, Bayley claims, "had always affirmed the self; he took it for granted, he did not have to find it."[33] By contrast, Lowell and Berryman, Bayley says, continue "the significant American poetic journey—to discover the living ego as it has to be," in the process renouncing nothing, "not a hair of their heads,"[34] not a stain in their hearts. As I have said, though, Wright, and many of his contemporaries, are one more generation removed from Yeats and Auden. They seek not "the living ego" that we hear asserted in Lowell and Berryman, but that substratum of the psyche that lies below the ego, identified in the poems by "the branch" and other images of stable depth. They share with Lowell and Berryman, however, the problematic nature of their quest, which is truly a quest rather than an affirmation of what is already known, because the goal is only a vague longing for something better, a release from the bonds of their confident poetic forebears as well as the bonds of a philistine culture that both needs and denies them. His quest is informed by an uncertainty, and hence a perilousness and real possibility of failure, that earlier modernist poets did not know. Yeats knew where to find the "rag-and-bone shop." The road to Wright's grail, however, is obscure, the treasure may be guarded by monsters, the quester may be defenseless, the escape route is never guaranteed, but the poet cannot turn back and choose comfort, because his words will die before anyone can hear them if they are not informed by the demons. He cannot return home without the treasure, the "white rose," nor will he be able to trust his own voice if he fails to reach the frontier.

This quest to recover the lost portions of his psyche is related to his perception of himself as the poet-hero-savior. To probe to his own identity is to reach the truth that defines our humanness, that ground of being that he insists is real, not a supreme fiction or a convenient belief to be used for a while and then discarded. His road lies through himself to all of us. The belief that the poet can discover something meaningful for all his readers by digging as far into his being as possible, can discover something sacred at his core that will allow him to move outside himself to a communion with all others, is a common enough element in contemporary poetry. The movement is like the movement in Roethke's "Journey to the Interior," in which the speaker looks into himself in order to reach out of himself. Or it is like Adrienne Rich's "diving into the wreck" of herself:

> I stroke the beam of my lamp
> slowly along the flank
> of something more permanent
> than fish or weed
> the thing I came for:
> the wreck and not the story of the wreck
> the thing itself and not the myth
>   ("Diving into the Wreck")

Rich wants the truth that lies beneath the patriarchal myths of her identity. By going "down," she hopes to find a universal, androgynous self: "I am she: I am he." Wright is thus voicing a central hope of postmodern poetry: that the personal is not the merely personal but will prove to be universal if one dives deeply enough to get beneath "the damage that was done" to find "the treasures that prevail," again in Rich's words. It is the belief, or what Alan Williamson calls the "gamble," that "because the self seems to have an intuited order, the more candid [the poet] is, the more he surrenders to the accidents and nuances of experience, the more significant poetic order will emerge."[35] The homeless character we see in *River* is on the frontier, as the title of "The Frontier" tells us, braving the cold winds that others avoid as they pose before their domestic fires. He gives the impression that he is recording his experience immediately, as it happens ("I nod as I write good evening"), because he is recording *our* experience for us, the experience of praying in the desert that we lock ourselves away from, and he must therefore not overlook one moment. Any moment may be *the* moment that holds the key to our salvation. If he can record enough, he may speak himself sane and reveal what we need to hear. The act of recording is thus personally therapeutic and socially useful, he hopes. The poet must bear our pain for us and write it down, relying on two of his most powerful tools, startling enjambment and vivid, in this case chilling, description:

> How many scrawny children
> Lie dead and half-hidden among frozen ruts
> In my body, along my dark roads.
>   ("The Frontier")

The process of facing and recovering his dark underground, whether we use Spanos's or Jung's terminology, and thereby feeling strengthened, in himself and in his role as poet-hero, is chronicled in several other poems in this part of *River*. In "Listening to the Mourners," already mentioned, Wright, by listening to "the baleful jangling of the wind / Through the telephone wires," finds himself transformed:

Now I am speaking with the voice
Of a scarecrow that stands up
And suddenly turns into a bird.

He captures "the grief" and becomes, not weaker or more desperate, but stronger and more confident, transforming himself from the dead matter of the scarecrow to the living bird. He has become the thing (the bird) that he, as scarecrow, was supposed to frighten away. He has become what he was first afraid of, what was originally a threat. This is what Jung would call integrating the shadow, discovering that the darkness inside himself is not threatening, or only threatening as long as it is kept at bay by defensive devices designed to protect the fragile psyche. The paradox is that by trying to protect the psyche, one makes it more vulnerable, and that by exposing the psyche, one protects it, strengthens it with the darkness that is necessary for one's wholeness. The bird had been Wright's imagined means of escape in "The Minneapolis Poem" (the "great white bird unknown to the police"). Imagining himself as a bird now is not, as his earlier desires to be one with nature were, a hope to be dead. The bird is not a contemporary version of Keats's nightingale. Wright does not imagine himself a bird so that he may leave behind the baggage of human consciousness, but so that he may incorporate all of his psychic components. What Wright does here is use the dark bird of his psyche to strengthen himself, not escape to a safe hiding place.

The bird image returns. In "Three Sentences for a Dead Swan," the poet finds a black swan, apparently almost dead, "beginning to starve / Between two cold white shadows." He speaks of the swan as a part of himself, attributing it to his darkness and calling it "My black fire, / Ovoid of my darkness." He wants to save the dark bird *and* the white shadows, that is, wants to claim both "my only country" *and* his "white rose," wants to return to "my native land" whole. The swan's mistake, however, was to land on "the strange water" of the Ohio and then find himself unable to "rise." Will the same happen to Wright if he returns? If he crosses to the "other side" of the Ohio, will he find rebirth, a new peace, or will be find the same death he fled earlier? "Brush Fire," the next poem, is a companion piece of "Three Sentences." Again we are given a dark bird:

> I find only two gray stones,
> And, lying between them,
> A dead bird the color of slate.

The bird died in the title's brushfire, but not before it was able to call to the poet:

> It is a voice
> In burned weeds, saying
> I love you.

As in "Rip," the poet follows a bird's voice down to seek the "gold" of the river, the abiding values that the shores of his home still hold. Rather ominously, however, here the bird is not a free, soaring thing but a dead animal, as the black swan of "Three Sentences" was near death. The bird's cry of love is overwhelmed by the toxic fumes of this burned-out land. Despite his resolution to return to "my only country," and despite the more hopeful tone noted by myself and others in the volume's last poems, the poet still clearly fears being suffocated by returning to the atmosphere of repression he feels he has escaped. The "Ohio river," as he says, "is no tomb to / Rise from the dead / From."

The poet again plumbs his underground, his dark source of life, inspiration, and imagination, for strength in "Poems to a Brown Cricket." In the poem, the speaker has been asleep and awakens to find a brown cricket sunning itself "asleep / In the Secret Life of Jakob Boehme / Left open on the desk." In the fourth section, the key to the poem, the speaker addresses the cricket:

> As for you, I won't press you to tell me
> Where you have gone.
> I know. I know how you love to edge down
> The long trails of canyons.

> At the bottom, along willow shores, you stand, waiting for twilight,
> In the silence of deep grass.
> You are safe there, guarded, for you know how the dark faces
> Of the cliffs forbid easy plundering
> Of their beautiful pueblos:
> White cities concealed delicately in their chasms
> As the new eggs of the mourning dove
> In her ground nest,
> That only the spirit hunters
> Of the snow can find.

The speaker traces his paths back to the psyche's depths and silence. Both he and the cricket "know" these treacherous routes because both are "spirit hunters," rewarded for their sacrifices on the quest with "beautiful pueblos," "white cities," new life, and safety. No one can reach them when they are safely "underground," guarded by the confidence of self-knowledge. This may sound at first like the same desire for escape we heard at the end of "The Minneapolis Poem," but it is not. There the poet simply wanted to escape and wait for a more propitious time to return. Here he will return strengthened within himself, having changed his internal spiritual condition rather than waiting for external political, social, and cultural conditions to change and make "my only country" a more hospitable residence for "spirit hunters." In "The Minneapolis Poem," he imagined himself as the buried and dormant "last corn grain." Here he is the guardian of "new eggs," new life that will not wait to be born. He brings new life and jealously guards it; there is no hint of death here, as in the earlier poem. Life is "precious," as he says in "Inscription for the Tank," and needs to be nurtured, not abandoned temporarily or permanently to await a better world or heavenly reward. The cricket, birds, and rose are the "delicate creatures / From the other world"—the "other world" being not death now but the buried darkness of the poet's own psyche that must be recaptured, his Furies that must be faced, if he is to be the whole man or poet—with which the speaker filled the world in "Milkweed" at the end of *Branch*. That optimistic, confident tone that was lost in the opening poems of *River* returns as we near the volume's end.

I do not want to imply that the book reaches a resolution, for it does not. Turning his despair into hope, facing his Furies, integrating his shadow, or achieving individuation and thereby having the strength, confidence, and power to return "home," to continue the romantic poet's journey from the "Everlasting No" to the "Everlasting Yea," however one likes to talk of the process that the poet goes through in *River*, is the struggle of a lifetime. There is progress made in the book, but no resolution. If we look at two poems from near the end of *River*—"Lifting Illegal Nets by Flashlight" and "To the Muse"—we can see the ambivalence that remains.

"Lifting Illegal Nets by Flashlight" is a calmly meditative poem in which Wright seems to have succeeded in his desire to "challenge death finally." Through the poem's first eight lines the poet looks around at the darkened world of night fishing, or poaching, as he had quietly looked around himself in "Lying in a Hammock at William Duffy's Farm in Pine Island, Minnesota." As in that poem, his observation becomes a revelation, but of a different kind:

> The carp are secrets
> Of the creation: I do not
> Know if they are lonely.
> The poachers drift with an almost frightening
> Care under the bridge.
> Water is a luminous
> Mirror of swallows' nests. The stars
> Have gone down.
> What does my anguish
> Matter?

His anguish, which has been his only identity, is still present, can never be or should be escaped, but now does not matter, is completely insignificant in the world of "secrets of the creation." Thus he does not matter. The poachers and carp are recorded as equally significant: not as superior and inferior intelligence, not as intruder and natural resident, not as hunter and hunted, but just as two parts of a whole, a whole to which Wright belongs but over which he has no dominion. Instead of inspiring dread and its attendant defiance, as it did in the Promethean poet of "In Shame and Humiliation," the realization of his insignificance inspires relief. And as Wright realizes that he does not have to hold onto his anger in order to face his Furies, something large and dark rips through the fishermen's nets:

> . . . Something
> The color
> Of a puma has plunged through the net, and is gone.
> This is the firmest
> Net I ever saw, and yet something
> Is gone lonely
> Into the headwaters of the Minnesota.

We can feel the relief, like the collapse at the end of a terrible migraine. "Pull down thy vanity, Paquin, pull down," Pound says in "Canto LXXXI." Wright has let loose rather than pulled down, and the "something," intentionally kept vague, I suspect, so that it can function as both the object captured and the egotistical, assertive impulses to capture, has been released back to "the headwaters," those deepest parts of the psyche where toothed threats reside. The threat, again, is nullified not by capturing it or controlling it, but by releasing it, setting it free, when it becomes harmless. The poem records a purgation, a release of ego. When he relies on imagery and observation and eschews abstraction, Wright's sense of timing is impeccable. Details build to a climax, surface becomes depth, and the images become, like the river as it mirrors swallows' nests, more than what they seem to be.

Loss of ego, I feel compelled to reiterate, is not the same as denial of self. Wright's quest has been for an honest identity that he can own. To find that self, he first had to lose the impediments to self-awareness, including the intervening ego and insistent rationality that tend to appropriate the world to the human's ends and relate to the other as an object to be conquered or used. The nets of the poachers are the extensions of their egos and rational competencies, their mechanical and disruptive modes of being in the world. To set free the "something" is to release the poet from self-absorption but not from self-awareness. He is small but not irrelevant, for we are all small in the context of Creation. The poet's only way to feel his identity had been to keep pricking himself, to concentrate on his glaring need and anger, which are his ego's reactions to being denied its desired exalted place in the sum of things. To let that anger loose is to be empty, like the ripped net, but to be as much an integrated part of the larger river as any human can be. The net is not the river, but the river and its inhabitants flow freely through it now. Wright believes in "total immersion," as Elizabeth Bishop does ("At the Fish-houses"), without fooling himself that immersion and identity are the same. Immersed or not, he is different from the river. The difference is inevitable, but as long as Wright holds to the "something" and keeps his net taut, he will never connect with other fishermen (and the image of fishermen naturally brings us back not only to thoughts of the Fisher King but also to Christ's injunction that we all be fishers of men). He must empty himself to be himself, must let loose to touch others. Or, by emptying himself, he hopes both to be himself and to touch others, to some extent to save himself and others, to be his savior and others'. The fisher with the broken net will catch the real fish without seeking to catch it. To Wright, salvation is internal first, a change in consciousness being the beginning of a change in all the world's relationships. The salvation becomes more than personal when it is verbalized; hence, *River* is the poet's attempt to revivify the wasteland by renewing himself and passing on the news of that renewal in the hope that others will be changed. Wright thus seeks universality by penetrating his own depths and revealing to the reader what he has found there. Alan Williamson outlines the course by which personal poetry becomes universally significant: "It is through some combination of fullness or richness of rendering with this avoidance of false transcendence—of smugness, of embarrassment, of forced or pat conclusions—that the humbling yet liberating realization that 'I am that I am' takes place, and is shared by the reader, in personal poetry."[36] This quiet poem clearly avoids all the pitfalls of "false transcendence" that Williamson notes and makes a small circle of hope in which Wright and the reader meet, his personal "humbling" becoming a universal "liberating realization."

In the book's final poem, "To the Muse," Wright makes a less successful attempt to "challenge death finally," to brush off the dirt of the grave he was buried in in "The Minneapolis Poem." The poet attempts to resurrect Jenny, his muse and the person to whom the whole volume is dedicated. The triumph of "Lifting Illegal Nets by Flashlight" was a personal, psychological realization; resurrecting Jenny would signify a poetic triumph, the reintegration of the poet and his inspiration. The poem is placed last perhaps because this is the challenge the poet has been avoiding, or gathering his strength for. Again the river is the boundary between life and death, and again to cross it may mean either new life (Jenny raised "out of the suckhole") or a step into death (Jenny and the poet reunited, but back in "this world, this scurvy / And disastrous place"). This is only part of the ambivalence of the poem. As before, if to die is painful, to live is almost unbearable:

> It is all right. All they do
> Is go in by dividing
> One rib from another. I wouldn't
> Lie to you. It hurts
> Like nothing I know. All they do
> Is burn their way in with a wire.
> It forks in and out a little like the tongue
> Of that frightened garter snake we caught
> At Cloverfield, you and me, Jenny,
> So long ago.

That is only stanza 1. The images of physical suffering increase, and "the images become increasingly bizarre, until finally the speaker comes to recognize that his desperation is verging upon insanity."[37] We realize that although the poet had declared himself "home again," just as he had in *Branch*, that declaration was more a hope— the hope that dogs his entire career—than an accomplished fact. He is still "poised" on the banks, not sure whether it is wiser to call Jenny up or to join her below:

Come up to me, love,
Out of the river, or I will
Come down to you.

To "come down" could be interpreted as a suicidal step or as the reaching into one's own psyche that precedes resurrection or completion. The phrase as well as the tone are ambiguous. If one interprets Wright's tone as hopeful, then descent is always prelude to ascent; if one reads the tone as despondent, then descent is an end in itself, an escape through the dissolution of the self. The final lines, quoted above, can be read as a resolution or a resignation. They are, appropriately, the final lines of *River*. We are left hanging, toes over the edge of the river, looking down toward peaceful death but holding onto painful life. This does not mean that the poet's earlier contention that he had found "my native land" was false, nor does it mean that my contention that he had successfully faced his Furies and integrated his shadow was wrong. What it does mean is that we cannot expect any poet as intensely honest, sensitive, and intellectually rigorous as Wright is to be done with life's problems once and for all just because he has faced them, written of them, and declared them conquered. That itself would be a sort of death.

His journey is not completed, nor will it be until his actual death, but it is advanced. I think of a passage from Thomas Hardy's *The Return of the Native* that may be relevant here: "To have lost the godlike conceit that we may do what we will, and not to have acquired a homely zest for doing what we can, shows a grandeur of temper which cannot be objected to in the abstract, for it denotes a mind that, though disappointed, forswears compromise."[38] I believe Wright has "lost the godlike conceit that [he] may do what [he] will," but not yet "acquired a homely zest for doing what [he] can." He is not yet confident that he can make his "white rose" "blossom" in his "native land's" soil, yet he knows it will blossom nowhere else.

5

"That brutal and savage place whom I still love"

The poetry of Wright's final three books, beginning with *Two Citizens* (1973),[1] is "the poetry of a grown man," a frequently quoted phrase from "Many of Our Waters: Variations on a Poem by a Black Child" in the "New Poems" section of Wright's *Collected Poems*. The "poetry of a grown man" has two components, one aesthetic and one moral and ontological. (Wright always treats questions of being and of moral action as one and the same.) First, the moral and ontological issue: what sort of man is a "grown man"? Not only how does he act, what does he think, and what does he believe, but also what sort of man, in essence, is he? Wright earlier, on the cover of *Saint Judas*, asked what a "good and humane action" is. This new question is larger—what sort of man is the whole, mature, grown man? Next is the aesthetic component: what sort of poetry would such a man write? What would it look like, sound like, talk about? That Wright deals with all these questions simultaneously implies an attitude not altogether popular today: only a grown man can write a grown man's poetry. The poet's mature humanity is necessary before his words will be fully mature and humane.

We will discover that the key to all the above questions is love, or the act of loving. It is by loving another, and, equally important, understanding what loving means, that Wright is able to define both what a "grown man" is and what kind of poetry that man should write. I want to discuss all these issues—what a "grown man" is, what his poetry looks like, how loving makes one "grown"—in detail, and in conjunction with a discussion of the individual poems that are relevant to the ideas. To begin, then, I will look at "Many of Our Waters," where Wright uses the phrase "the poetry of a grown man." I will then move to a discussion of the opening poem in *Two Citizens*, "Ars Poetica: Some Recent Criticism" which continues the same theme while adding the key element, love of a woman, specifically of Annie, the poet's second wife. Finally, I will show how Wright relies heavily on images of women in *Two Citizens*, and how those images lead to the central act of "gathering," or embracing those people and elements of the culture the poet had earlier rejected, culminating in a self-recognition based on his understanding of his relationship to the other—a more profound self-recognition than that in "At the Executed Murderer's Grave," which is based on his understanding only of his isolated identity. The "grown man," it turns out, embraces the whole, rather than divides it against itself by sympathizing with some elements (the "beautiful") while rejecting others (the "ugly"). I am reminded of Arnold Bennett's definition of the novelist: "the essential characteristic of the really great novelist," Bennett wrote in his *Journal*, is "a Christlike, all-embracing compassion." In *Two Citizens*, Wright moves toward that compassion.

"Many of Our Waters" is set in New York City and written in seven sections. It begins with a transcription, with line breaks added, of Wright's journal entry for 8 March 1969, of an observation by Garnie Braxton, who appears in other "New Poems," most noticeably "A Poem by Garnie Braxton," and later in *Two Citizens*, as a noble savage, a semiliterate black youth, one of the Wordsworthian characters whose fresh insights into everyday reality Wright mines like gemstones. Most of section 1 is Garnie's reaction to a deep pit, dug in preparation for a skyscraper's foundation:

You know,
if a blind boy

ride his bicycle
down there
he might fall into that water
I think it's water
but I don't know
they call it acid
and if that poor boy
drive his poor blind bicycle
into that acid
he drown
he die
and then
they bury him
up

From sympathizing with outcasts, to identifying with them, to living with them, Wright now moves a step further and records Garnie's voice directly. Garnie enters as a voice from the outside, not simply as one critiquing America's myths but as their victim. I am reminded here of a quotation from Alan Williamson that I used in the preceding chapter: "The truly important educative experiences become . . . experiences of unlearning: empathy with animals, primitive and peasant cultures, the wilderness. . . ."[2] "Primitive," I think, would fit Garnie in the sense that his reaction is primordial and instinctive, and section 1 is the text from which Wright will learn. Wright incorporates Garnie's slang and his person, not his persona, directly into the poem as both an aesthetic and philosophical statement: he claims validity as art and status as prophetic utterance for Garnie's words and vision. This transcription is Wright's way of carrying out the romantic project of getting into verse the speech of real people, not tampered with but received and cherished.

Section 1 is something more, too. Dave Smith correctly notes that *Two Citizens* is characterized by "blunt and garrulous simplicity" and "undressed language."[3] The "primitive" slang or colloquial diction we hear so much of in *Two Citizens*, and with which this poem begins, is not an end in itself, or Wright could simply have made his entire poem a transcription of Garnie's observations. The "undressed language" is first a battering ram to get through the reader's polite expectations that protect one from the insight that is necessary to produce, or understand, "the poetry of a grown man." As Wright says, "If great poetry means anything, anything at all, it means disturbance."[4] One of the first things a poet must "disturb" is his reader's language, which, among other things, helps to create the myths that shelter us from self-recognition, as individuals and as a culture. As Laurence Lieberman says, in *Two Citizens*, Wright "repudiates all of the favorite myths": "Our freedom of religion, our canonizing of the common man, our permissiveness in child-rearing and our epidemic hero-worshipping of the untutored juvenile mentality, our pretense that animals—wild or domestic—suffer less brutality here than in other countries."[5] He also, as in "Many of Our Waters," rebels against the stereotypical thinking that would assume that one who, like Garnie, has to rely on "undressed language," must be incapable of intelligent observation and therefore not worth listening to, thus eliminating from the nation's debate over its direction and values entire segments of the population, "outcast" groups, while cleansing the actions of others with innocuous phrases. For example, the giggling sadists of "Ars Poetica: Some Recent Criticism" who stone a runaway goat in an alley (explicitly identified as "my country . . . America") are converted into "charming Tom Sawyers" and their actions thereby trivialized by our language that routinely designates fair-skinned rock throwers as just boys being boys. The poet chooses occasionally to use an informal diction and even a subliterate phrasing to dissociate himself from the debased language that, he suggests, legitimizes the country's brutality and savagery, in particular its hostility to the unusual, "broken," or "scrawny" among us, such as the beleaguered goat. Merwin's words in "The Port" could be Wright's:

it is true that in
our language deaths are to be heard
at any moment through the talk
pacing their wooden rooms jarring
the dried flowers.

"We had a lovely language," Wright tells us in "Ars Poetica," but "We would not listen." So he will sometimes use a "blunt and garrulous" language, a character's unedited insight, usually a cry for love or a demand for dignity, to jar us into listening and to "disturb" our preconceptions.

What we do hear when we listen to Garnie's response to the deep pit being dug for a skyscraper is a cultural criticism much more complex than we would have anticipated had we simply judged the speaker by his ungrammatical language. Garnie imagines the water collecting in the pit as acid, perceives the death underlying all of our monuments to ourselves and waiting for the unsuspecting, poor "blind boy" on his "poor blind bicycle" to unwittingly become its victim. He sees the bones of the laborers and the displaced upon which man's cities and cultures are constructed, just as Wright has seen and warned us of. Garnie's vision unites, apparently effortlessly and intuitively, the pyramids of Egypt, the Metropolis of Fritz Lang's film, and the Minneapolis of Wright's *River*. Garnie's is a spontaneous recognition of life's acid pits into which we all, no matter how intelligent or sophisticated we think we are, wander blindly, especially if we happen to wander while looking up toward the heavens. The conclusion of the stanza, "he die / and then / they bury him / up," draws our attention not "up" to hope but down to those buried. The natural cycle, in which one generation dies and fertilizes the soil for the next, is mocked, as one generation is buried under concrete and simply sacrificed. For what the next generation needs, apparently, is not the former as fertilizer but simply more inorganic concrete to carry it farther and farther from the soil. We scrape the sky, but at what cost is the implicit question. The acid bath obliterates any trace of one's existence, whereas a pool of water would signify a slow, beneficial return to nature and the pool of resources that keep the world going. The men digging become almost like mad scientists taking part in their own destruction, while they seem to believe they are doing the opposite. The skyscraper builders, then, are digging deep into the earth not to find depth or truth—the truth that, as we saw in the last chapter, Wright believes resides right next to the blackness at man's core—and to humble themselves before its mystery, but to conquer the earth, subdue it, and extend their dominion over it. Garnie sees what they do not, and out of the mouth of this babe, Wright records the basic facts of life and death, seeing directly and intuitively to first things. It is a complex vision made simple and almost childlike by Garnie's diction and the complete absence of self-consciousness in his phrasing. It is, in other words, the foundation for "the poetry of a grown man." "Many of Our Waters" is a watershed poem, like "At the Executed Murderer's Grave." As in that earlier poem, Wright begins with a pure expression, Garnie's this time rather than Wright's bald announcement of his identity in "At the Executed Murderer's Grave," and then for several painful sections wrestles with the demons loosed by that pure harmonizing of expression, emotion, and insight.

In sections 3 and 4, Wright moves to his present and makes explicit what was implicit in section 1, that he seeks the purity of line that Garnie automatically achieves. Section 3 begins with the statement already quoted ("The kind of poetry I want to write is / The poetry of a grown man") and introduces the aesthetic element. The kind of poetry the "grown man" would write, at least at this stage of the poem, is Garnie's speech, the poetry of "the pure clear word," an example of which is section 1. The "grown man plows down," as Garnie did when observing the construction workers, and does not waste his time on the trivial or superficial. The "grown man" does not bother "explaining . . . / The difference between a nutmeg and a squirrel," not only because such difference is obvious and trivial. He eschews mere description also because, as Alan Williamson notes of the middle generation of contemporary American poets, the generation that includes Wright, he is suspicious of "the whole aesthetic of 'rendering,'" whose "necessarily overburdened descriptions seem cold and predictable, its theory a rejection of the spontaneity and subjective validity of feelings."[6] Spontaneous, subjective, and in some sense "primitive," then, but the "grown man" is no innocent— he has loved and he "has got his guts kicked in." He simply sees and speaks with purity and immediacy.

In section 5, we are placed at the corner of 84th and Amsterdam, a testing ground, almost a Colosseum or arena, where you had better

"Be proud and true to yourself" or be in trouble. A group of charac-
ters, more like a family, composed of Wright, Garnie, "the baby
Gemela," Kinny, and "the lithe white girl," are attempting to cross
the street. It is a small band linked against chaos, here in the form of
the traffic and the rain. The street is like the river of *River*, a dan-
gerous passage, with Wright now standing on one side shouting in-
structions ("Garnie / The light's changing. / Get the HELL over
here"), having assumed Garnie's role as guide and mentor, the one
knowledgeable in the ways of the world who leads the others. This is
important, for the poem is the tale of Wright's movement from stu-
dent (listening attentively to Garnie) to leader (the others listening
to him) and from recorder of Garnie's words to speaker himself of
"the pure clear word." Wright is literally the "grown man" in section
5, keeping an eye on his young charges, uniting the family, and guid-
ing them safely home. He is now the poet as clear perceiver and
organizing consciousness uniting all the different generations and
perspectives. In other words, his vision now surpasses Garnie's. He
sees more than his own point of view. He projects himself into
others' lives. Garnie's reaction in section 1 seemed almost an ac-
cident—Wright's response (clear, honest, purposive) to danger in sec-
tion 5 is calculated, an instance of the poet assuming his chosen role
as leader and guide. He leads as well as sees, guides as well as ex-
poses, and points the direction to safety as well as draws our atten-
tion to danger. This largeness of vision (the moral aspect) is as
important a component of the "poetry of a grown man" as is Gar-
nie's intuitively clean line (the aesthetic aspect) of section 1.

The tentative declaration of poetic independence of section 3
("The kind of poetry I want to write is / The poetry of a grown man")
is completed in the poem's seventh and final section:

> All this time I've been slicking into my own words
> The beautiful language of my friends.
> I have to use my own, now.

"My friends" refers to the likes of Trakl, Neruda, and Vallejo. James
Seay has rather tentatively extended this same idea. In "Many of Our

Waters," Seay contends, "It is possible that . . . Wright is, in part at least, expressing an intention to free himself from the foreign influences. . . ."[7] In "At the Executed Murderer's Grave," he had admitted "Leaning for language on a dead man's voice" and declared himself independent. Now he distances himself from those poets who were so influential in his evolution from the style of *The Green Wall* to the style of *Branch* and also from the newer poets *he* has influenced by his earlier translations and recent verse:

> The young poets of New York come to me with
> Their mangled figures of speech,
> But they have little pity
> For the pure clear word.

He wants the "pure" word, not "mangled," but also the "clear" word, not the false surrealism of those "new poets [who] have devoted their attention to the art of typewriting" and whose poems "sound like bad prose hacked into arbitrary linelengths."[8] This poem is his second declaration of independence, from those who influenced him and from those he has influenced in turn. Even Garnie's words, which Wright used in section 1, cannot be Wright's. To make that clear, he "translates" Garnie's sentiment of section 5 ("I ain't got nothing but my brother") into his own words of section 7 ("I don't have anything / Except my brother"). But he maintains the "primitive" state of Garnie. He and his love "went swimming naked one afternoon," vulnerable and exposed, but also reduced to their essential human condition, without encumbrances or appurtenances that define them as anything except members of the all-inclusive human race or family. They float naked in the water, almost an image of a return to the womb.

The "grown man," then, at this point, is secure enough to learn from those more "primitive," wise enough to listen to the world's raw data, and strong enough to expose himself to life's chaos. His poetry is founded in his intuitive responses to the world and may incorporate those inchoate, irrational, and prerational reactions, but it may not simply be inarticulate rumblings. For his own words, the poet must "translate" those instinctive, raw phrases, without losing their power, by filtering them through his vision, which incorporates multiple perspectives, not just his own reaction.

In "Ars Poetica: Some Recent Criticism," the opening poem in *Two Citizens*, Wright continues to formulate the terms of his poetics, but not as explicitly as we might desire. He begins not with a statement about his poetry, but instead with a statement about love of country, and in the past tense: "I loved my country, / When I was a little boy." The reader, or at least the one unfamiliar with Wright, wonders why the speaker no longer loves his country and what that fact has to do with an ars poetica. More confusing is the shift, in the next lines, to an apparently unrelated topic:

> Agnes is my aunt,
> And she doesn't even know
> If I love any thing
> On this God's
> Green little apple.

Somehow, we infer, America, Agnes, and poetry are related.

Uncle Sherman next enters, as an alter ego to Wright, we discover, for Sherman is a singer who "fell in with" Agnes and managed to love her despite her being sloppy, nuts, and repulsive. Wright is connected to Sherman because, like his uncle, he is a singer who has "fallen in / With a luminous woman." All these pieces are in section 1, and section 1 is not done yet. We also discover that Agnes did one "bright thing" in her life: she "g[o]t hurt and angry." This is truly a jigsaw puzzle of a poem, and we need to ask how the pieces fit together. We discover that Sherman and Agnes are models and analogues for Wright and his "luminous woman," who is Annie, Wright's second wife, but not yet named. Garnie served as Wright's model in "Many of Our Waters"; Sherman will here. The important addition is Agnes, for her presence implies Wright's relationship with Annie, who is the symbol of relationship, a relationship of love that will eventually include the country he loved as a boy but has since rejected (as we are told in section 1), and the symbol of the end of loneliness for the speaker. Annie's love, then, foreshadowed by

Agnes's presence, will lead Wright back to his country and to "the poetry of a grown man," a mature poetry that will embrace not only those souls cast out by society but also that society itself that Wright has sought to cast out.

James Seay has noted about the "New Poems" that "Wright seems to have found a new source of spirituality within the human realm—in a woman, to be exact—and there is an indication that this discovery has somewhat diminished, or at least made bearable, the anguish that informs so much of his work."[9] The woman's influence is even more noticeable in *Two Citizens* as "an intermediary between two states of being,"[10] specifically the states of anguish and hope, or death and resurrection. How? Finding love fully initiates the poet into the social world. No longer alone, he is implicitly part of a system of relations that extend beyond his closed ego. The speaker steps out into a net of cultural relations, a world larger than his own sufferings, needs, dreams, and fears. Once he makes contact on this level with another individual, he is part of a social structure that includes not only the specific person loved, but that person's past and other lovers' pasts and futures. Psychologist Harry Stack Sullivan sums up the process by which love eases the person into the society:

> As soon as one finds that all this vast autistic and somewhat validated structure to which one refers as one's mind, one's thoughts, one's personality, is really open to some comparing of notes, to some checking and counter-checking, one begins to feel human in a sense in which one has not previously felt human. One becomes more fully human in that one begins to appreciate the common humanity of people—there comes a new sympathy for the other fellow. . . .[11]

Thus Annie and other women, including Aunt Agnes, as objects of various forms of love, are important as catalysts for the poet's continuing recovery of the "river gold" that he sought in *River* and for his increasing "sympathy for the other fellow," or *all* other fellows. This enlarged sympathy is a central component of "the poetry of a grown man."

Mature love, of course, is also an act of self-completion, a way for the man, in this case, to become aware of and integrate those forces within his own psyche typically associated, in this case, with the "feminine"—fecund, sensual, nonpurposive, nourishing, and protecting forces—and in that way achieve wholeness. The result, ideally, is increased tolerance for others' complexities, greater empathy for a wider range of humanity, and an escape from the limited realm of the narrow, individual self by, paradoxically, discovering the depths within oneself that are shared by all people, and which therefore make one a part of all humanity. This is another important aspect of being a "grown man," the only man who can write "the poetry of a grown man." Wright's outline of the book's movement, carried on the back cover, confirms the role that love or self-completion has in his own reconciliation with life's imperfections and disappointments: "*Two Citizens* is an expression of my patriotism, of my love and discovery of my native place. I never knew or loved my America so well, and I began with a savage attack on it. Then I discovered it. It took the shape of a beautiful woman who loved me and who led me through France and Italy. I discovered my America there. That is why this is most of all a book of love poems. The two citizens are Annie and I." Wright tells us that Annie replaces Jenny of *River*, who has represented, as Kevin Stein notes, "the pure life of the soul, unsullied by the human condition. . . ."[12] Wright, so eager to avoid the guilt associated with living, especially with living in this culture, as I showed in earlier chapters, has been attracted to Jenny's "Neoplatonic world of ideals."[13] As I have noted, though, to join Jenny, the poet "must accept a release from the body that is also its death."[14] Finally, beginning in *Two Citizens*, the poet can accept a sullied love associated with the world's body, and the fecundity and hope of Eros triumph over the sterility and despair of Thanatos. The book is an important step in the poet's movement from the young rebel, now disenchanted with his rebellion, to the middle-aged and mature poet coming to terms with his poetry and allegiance to a land he both loves and hates. On the book's cover, the poet provides us clues to the book's place in his evolution: "There are some savage poems about Ohio, my home, in that book, poems that I could not have written if I hadn't found Annie. She gave me the strength to come to terms with things which I loved and hated at the same time. . . . Even though I don't love that book, I love what lies behind it, because it grew out of my new life, my life with Annie." "Things which I loved and hated at the same time" will turn out to be the theme of *Two Citizens*. The "things" themselves are America, Americans, Americans' inability to love, the culture's philistinism—in short, all those "things" we have seen before. Wright is still disappointed with his fellow human beings because he expects more, but he suspects that their failings are his, too. The "terms" he "comes to" with respect to those "things [he] loved and hated at the same time" are, in order, resignation, recognition, and reluctant acceptance. He has to learn to accept those "things" he is profoundly ambivalent about, and it is only the act of falling in love that effects that acceptance. He chooses a life-producing love over the comfort of the grave. The "dark woman" he has been searching for since *The Green Wall* takes the shape of a woman who "gathers" the light around her, rather than the shape of a doomed singer of lost causes, the form Wright had flirted with for so long. And this lover, who is also a muse, eases the poet back into the world and helps him realize his place in "my America," rather than lures the writer to the "far shores" of alienation and death. To transcend the hatred expressed in section 7 of "Ars Poetica" ("Ah, you bastards, / How I hate you," what Dave Smith calls "sword-rattling"),[15] Wright will have to gather a real lover, Annie, not merely a symbol of love, such as Agnes. "To love," Wright says, "is to effect an overwhelmingly difficult act of self-knowledge."[16] When the speaker of *Two Citizens* finally poetically gathers or loves Annie, the "luminous woman," he will find that "something" that will enable him to understand himself, make his guarded peace with his native land, and become the "grown man" who alone is capable of writing mature poetry.

Two Citizens, and Wright's poetry in general, is a long lesson in acceptance, what the poet here calls "gathering." A reading of Wright's first four books would confirm, I believe, that the poet has been generous with his hatred and niggardly with his love: the outcasts deserved and got his sympathy, but so many others got only his venom. Yet what of those many unaccounted for, those who deserve neither love nor hatred, in other words, the vast majority of the human race? His sympathy has ignored most of humanity, all those who deserve neither heaven nor hell. Like God, then, Wright has to choose to offer his grace even if it is not, perhaps cannot be, deserved. He must make what Alan Williamson calls "a commitment prior to judgment."[17] Hence Aunt Agnes must be as repulsive as Wright portrays her. We might think that making Agnes a "slob," "fat and stupid," "crazy," and "lonely" is piling too many liabilities onto the aunt. We might also first believe that Wright is making Aunt Agnes as uncouth and foul as possible with the sole, transparent intent of then loving her to show that he can in fact embrace outcasts. But we would be wrong; Wright does not need to prove his love of the outcast. He has amply illustrated his ability to love the unlovable, from Judas to Charlie, with various bums, drunks, and poor women in between. He makes Agnes so repulsive (even "her house stank") because if she were attractive, loving her would be no miracle, and it is precisely the miracle of undeserved love that moves Wright from hatred for America and "them" to love of country and all its residents. He feels undeserving of Annie's love. Yet she offers it. All of Wright's "muse-women, from the prostitute in all his books to his wife Annie" offer their love "gratuitously."[18] Can he do any less? He finally chooses acceptance, while recognizing that both loves—of a single woman, of an entire culture—are partial hells: "human love is a hell,"[19] he writes. Once Wright realizes, as he begins to in this book, that his self is his only self, his love his only love, and his country his only country, he can return to that self, love, and country in peace, accepting, if not necessarily satisfied with, what he is and what he has. "What thou lovest well remains," Pound says, "the rest is dross." Wright returns finally to what he loves well after sifting through years of bitterness and disillusion. This attitude of acceptance, gathering, and sympathy defines for Wright the "grown man" and is therefore one more of the bases of "the poetry of a grown man."

To offer miraculous love to those who cannot deserve it will be his program, his new "morality of poetry." It is a program based in

Wright's recognition of his own sin and sense of shame. Like Judas, he can offer love, "for nothing," because he sees his own unlovely face so clearly. Sometimes this sense of shame verges on self-hatred, but always with a purpose. The worst cursing and self-hatred occur in the first section of "A Secret Gratitude," from "New Poems," where we are told, among other unpleasant things, that

> Man's heart is the rotten yolk of a blacksnake egg
> Corroding, as it is just born, in a pile of dead
> Horse dung.

Such vituperation, however, is not without its role. "We are men," he says in the same poem—only men and nothing more, not deserving grace or mercy or even beauty:

> Why should any mere multitude of the angels care
> To lay one blind white plume down
> On this outermost limit of something that is probably no more
> Than an aphid.

The answer to the above question is, implicitly, "I don't know," a common refrain in "New Poems" and *Two Citizens*. There is no good reason why any angel or deer, "those fleet lights," should deign to look on our pitifully wretched selves. Yet we are occasionally allowed into the presence of beauty and that is the wonder, that we, "chemical accidents of horror," may sometimes approach beauty. Behind the wonder—and the unprecedented cursing of the human creature—is the seed of a hope: perhaps, if we can occasionally stumble upon such beauty as Wright does in this poem when five deer in the woods momentarily do not flee, although they must know that the men they meet are murderers "capable of anything," perhaps we are not so terrible as we seem. This is a religious idea—if God can love us and cause good things to happen to us despite our wickedness, then perhaps we are lovable and should offer our love to other undeserving souls. It is also the opposite of the "logic" of the young man, who assumes, in his vitality, his own godlike potential, in light of which any failure is a catastrophe and any flaw is a blatant contradiction of his self-image. Wright now realizes that it is our nature to be flawed, so that whatever we do achieve is miraculous and wonderful.

As I said earlier, love effects the transition from youthful poet to grown man, so it should not be surprising that the dominant image in *Two Citizens* is that of a woman. The female characters take many forms here—from nameless, mysterious forces in the poet's life, to identifiable women as diverse as Aunt Agnes, Annie, and Mary Magdalene—but they invariably inspire tenderness and acceptance in the poet. We meet the women in America and Europe as flesh-and-blood females and as little more than ghostly images. They seem vaguely familiar, for they are often images we have met before. For example, the girl of "A Little Girl on her Way to School" (*The Green Wall*) returns in this volume in "The Old WPA Swimming Pool in Martins Ferry, Ohio," where she allows the poet a brief glimpse into his own soul to the foundation of love and harmony that too often escapes his apprehension. In the poem, the Ohio River, which was "supposed to be some holiness," was dying, and the town's "fierce husbands" made "a long gouge in the ground," a swimming pool, which Wright interprets as a substitute for the river's holiness, a way of preserving something sacred, the husbands' attempt at a poem. The pool, however, is only the setting for the "thing" that Wright says he was "almost afraid to write down."

The climactic moment comes when the boy "rose from that water," emerging as it were from a concrete baptismal font, and receives the blessing of a spectral girl:

> A little girl who belonged to somebody else,
> A face thin and haunted appeared
> Over my left shoulder, and whispered, take care now,
> Be patient, and live.

The girl is hardly human. She appears as an angel might, or as if she is straight from the boy's unconscious, an otherwordly figure pausing just long enough to chant her magic words and produce the "thing," a radiant, charged moment of awareness that appears unannounced. It is significant that this "thing" is a resolution to live, that it appears after Wright has so roundly denounced the United States in the previous poem ("I Wish I May Never Hear of the United States Again"), and that it occurs in his hometown. Precisely when he feels life, in America and in general, has nothing for him, he proclaims life's possibilities. The sequence of events is just like that in "Inscription for the Tank," in which the poet, caught in a hostile environment and just after announcing hostility for his country in the previous poem, declares "My life was never so precious / To me as now." In both poems, he is afraid of his own words: in "Inscription," he writes, "I gape unbelieving at those two lines," while he begins this poem with, "I am almost afriad to write down / This thing."

The muse-lover figure is usually associated with sunlight and hope, as in "Bologna: A Poem about Gold," which begins,

> Give me this time, my first and severe
> Italian, a poem about gold,
> The left corners of eyes, and the heavy
> Night of the locomotives that brought me here,
> And the heavy wine in the old green body,
> The glass that so many have drunk from.

The poem's beginning is reminiscent of the Lord's Prayer ("Give us this day our daily bread"), except that the poet is asking for a particular type of sustenance, inspiration for a poem.

In the second stanza, Wright addresses Mary Magdalene as she is captured in a painting by Raphael, *The St. Cecilia Altarpiece* (1513–14), hanging in Pinacoteca, Bologna:

> White wine of Bologna,
> And the knowing golden shadows
> At the left corners of Mary Magdalene's eyes,
> While St. Cecilia stands
> Smirking in the center of a blank wall,
> The saint letting her silly pipes wilt down,
> Adoring

Herself, while the lowly and the richest of all women eyes
Me the beholder, with a knowing sympathy, her love
For the golden body of the earth, she knows me,
Her halo faintly askew,
And no despair in her gold
That drags thrones down
And then makes them pay for it.

Saint Cecilia is in the center of the painting, looking heavenward at a group of singing angels. On her extreme right is Saint Paul, looking at the cracked viola da gamba on the ground at Cecilia's feet. Next to Paul, and behind Cecilia's right elbow, is Saint John the Evangelist, looking behind Cecilia's back at Saint Augustine, who is behind Cecilia's left elbow. On the extreme left is Mary Magdalene, gazing boldly forward at the viewer.[20] The "smirking" Saint Cecilia contrasts, in a way familiar to readers of Wright's poetry, with Mary Magdalene, the "lowly" yet more sympathetic character because her thoughts seem more of this earth than of a distant heaven. She is sensuous as well as spiritual, "the prototypic complete woman,"[21] as she peers straight at the viewer with eyes open and head level. She is "the poem about gold" that inspired Wright's "A Poem about Gold":

Mary in Bologna, sunlight I gathered all morning
And pressed in my arms all afternoon
And drank all day with my golden-breasted

Love in my arms.

Mary Magdalene in Raphael's painting is unapproachable in reality, even though her stare beckons one; the woman with the poet, however, is approachable, and Wright drinks in Mary Magdalene's "sunlight" as he holds his lover, Annie, we assume, in his arms. The woman of the present is identified with the woman of the past through the gold imagery. "Gold" is used six times in association with Mary Magdalene, and now Wright's lover is "golden-breasted." She is another poem about gold, and that realization reminds us that finding love, gathering this flesh-and-blood "golden" woman, is not only symbolic of, but also essential for, finding one's "grown" poetic self, or writing this "Poem about Gold."

Occasionally, the women are the "browned" or silent women of the type we also first saw in *The Green Wall*:

> In Yugoslavia I am learning the words
> For greeting and goodbye.
> Everything else is the language
> Of the silent woman who walks beside me.
>   ("I Wish I May Never Hear of the United States Again")

These women still counsel, by their presence, a silent acceptance of the world:

> Well,
> For the first time in my life,
> I shut up and listened.
>   ("Afternoon and Evening at Ohrid")

The male character in the poem learns to replace his egotistical need to name and thereby to catalog and control the phenomena of his world, with the desire to hold, embrace, or gather the world even before he rationally understands it:

> How could I tell her about their clear names?
> I did not know them. I had to hold her.
> That was all I had.
>   ("Afternoon and Evening at Ohrid")

The poet's "clear names" are replaced by the woman's loving presence:

> . . . She spoke the best language.
> And it spins her face.

The woman's identity is not her name, but her ability to love:

> . . . What is your name,
> I said.
> I love you,
> She said.

While the poet Wright never can—and never does—stop speaking, he is learning from the silence of the "browned woman" that the Adamic act of filling the world with words is only one step in the process of understanding and accepting that world, as a "grown man" must. In "the vastness of that place" in which we live, it is as necessary to recognize "love's clear name" as it is to know the mountains' "clear names." For after all, Wright says, it is the clear face of love that finally enables one to live.

The most important woman we meet, however, the "beautiful woman who loved me," is Annie, mentioned by name only once in this volume, in "Voices between Waking and Sleeping in the Mountains." In the poem, Annie goes walking in the mountains, but the poet decides to stay where he is:

> I was trying to find something in that mountain snow,
> And I couldn't find it by walking,
> So I lay asleep
> For three good hours.

We are reminded of the "something" the poet claimed "there must be" ("Ars Poetica: Some Recent Criticism"). What is that "something?"

> There is something in you that is able to discover the crystal.
> Somewhere in me there is a crystal that I cannot find
> Alone, the wing that I used to think was a poor
> Blindness I had to live with with the dead.

The "something" is the core of himself that he can only find with the help of his lover and muse. What he finds by himself frightens him:

> There was something I was trying to find
> In that dream. When I finally fought my way

> Down to the bottom of the stairs
> I got trapped, I kept yelling
> Help, help, the savage woman
> With two heads loaded me, the one
> Face broken and savage, the other,
> The face dead.

Wright discovers "the horror" in his own unconscious, much like what Emily Dickinson called "That Cooler Host" that inhabits the brain's "Corridors" ("One need not be a Chamber—to be Haunted"). The poet is rescued by Annie: "Two hands gathered my two." She is his Beatrice, the "luminous woman" whose presence makes things light. The poet finally understands, through experience, the simplest lesson, which is really nothing more than a tautology, that his life is his own life:

> Annie, it has taken me a long time to live.
> And to take a long time to live it to take a long time
> To understand that your life is your own life.

For four books, he has been trying to define himself negatively, as not like the others, as different from the ugly. Now he defines himself positively: I am myself, a definition he attempted in *Saint Judas* ("My name is James A. Wright") but without lasting success. Defined as himself, confident of his identity, fulfilled by his love, "a grown man," Wright need not fear being associated with the "ugly Americans" whom he has been trying to distinguish himself from for so long. Now he can claim them as his vulgar brothers, for he no longer depends on being different from them as the basis of his identity.

Love here is broader than the specific love of Annie, however. It often takes the form of "gathering," the poet's attempt to capture and surround the love that will bring him to himself, to the "self-knowledge" that he claims results from loving. "Gathering" is the poet's "Christlike, all-embracing compassion" that brings him to himself by gathering others to him. Sometimes gathering is a physical act:

And my Aunt Agnes,
Who stank and lied,
Threw stones back at the boys
And gathered the goat,
Nuts as she was,
Into her sloppy arms.
　　("Ars Poetica: Some Recent Criticism")

One afternoon in northern California,
Which is a Jack London nut house,
I almost found my own country.
At the edge of a field
I gathered the neck of a buckskin into
My arms and whispered: Where were you
All this time?
　　("I Wish I May Never Hear of the United States Again")

Sometimes gathering is an imaginative act of affection or love:

I gather my Aunt Agnes
Into my veins.
　　("Ars Poetica: Some Recent Criticism")

Even if gathering is not the act of love itself, it is always associated with affectionate acts:

Mary in Bologna, sunlight I gathered all morning
And pressed in my hands all afternoon
And drank all day with my golden-breasted

Love in my arms.
　　("Bologna: A Poem about Gold")

Those little birds ate singing
In a language that is strange to you and me.
So our love for them is a silly
Love, a smooth gathering and ringing
In a coil of snail shells.
　　("Afternoon and Evening at Ohrid")

I was too much of a small boy to love
The cold trees you know.

Forgive and gather
My man's broken arms
Beneath them.
    ("On the Liberation of Women")

As Dave Smith has pointed out, "Wright insists that the most funda-
mental nature of poetry is its affirmation of *possibility,* exactly the
root characteristic of the American dream. His new poetry [i.e., *Two
Citizens*] is an aggressive reaching for and embracing of that pos-
sibility."[22] The "reaching for and embracing of" that Smith remarks
is Wright's "gathering," a sympathetic extending beyond himself, a
side effect of loving and a characteristic of the "grown man." In *Two
Citizens,* Wright achieves a fragile cease-fire that is only occasion-
ally marred by brief skirmishes, like the "savage attack" mentioned
earlier, against various representatives of the "ugly" camp, and he
finds within himself a love large enough to gather "my America,"
despite what he still considers to be the country's physical and
metaphysical ugliness, precisely because he realizes that love by its
nature is also a mixed blessing:

Though love can be scarcely imaginable Hell,
By God, it is not a lie.
    ("The Art of the Fugue: A Prayer")

His country is a frustratingly complex place, one that he now recog-
nizes as neither completely good nor bad: ". . . in the middle of
America / (That brutal and savage place whom I still love)" ("Paul").
By reading these poems we understand what Wright means when he
says that Annie helped him find his patriotism: the personal act of
falling in love and the patriotic act of discovering "my native place"
are analogous forms of gathering the other, who is at times as repug-
nant as she (or it) is alluring. When he does recognize himself as one
with all Americans and all humanity, not with his audience alone,
and truly believes, almost in spite of himself still, that *everyone*

resides on "the branch" that "will not break," then these poems of hate become poems of love, as he contends they do. The personal, poetic, and cultural levels of meaning intersect in the artist's creation, and we have the mature poems of *Two Citizens*.

A sure test of the poet's maturity is the way he responds to the "ugly." His response to the beautiful, vulnerable, hopeless, and defenseless victim is the same as it was in his first volume: "Be kind" ("Well, What Are You Going to Do?"). But his response to the ugly has changed, and that change is the measure of his poetry's maturity. We can see this new reluctant acceptance of himself as an American and of his ugly American heritage in "Names Scarred at the Entrance to Chartres," six poems after "Voices." The poem begins with the names of two other Americans: "P. Dolan and A. Doyle / Have scrawled their names here." We expect Wright to castigate Dolan and Doyle as "two stupid harley-charlies" and to pretend to have nothing in common with them. But he does more:

> This cracking blossom is my second America.
> And though my first
> Shatters itself cold with hatred, though
> I might have given my leaves here
> A long time ago,
>
> P. Dolan and A. Doyle are the faint names
> I enter with.

This is the poet's "second America" because here, just as in America, he has to face the "stupid angels" who seem to enjoy defacing the beauty in the world. Scratching one's name at the entrance to Chartres is the sort of arrogant, irreverent, and appropriative act that Wright earlier, "A long time ago," would have categorically denounced, just as he denounced the presence of Hanna's strip mines on the Ohio countryside. Yet he has "no home among the local strawberry leaves" because he comes from a land far removed from the harmony he sees among the French laborers, cathedral stones, wild peas, and strawberry leaves. He is not really part of this "second America"; he belongs elsewhere. Though he would perhaps prefer to enter Chartres more reverently, he must bear as his identity the "faint names" of the heritage he inherits, whether he wants that heritage or not:

> I have no way to go in
> Except only
> In the company of two vulgars.

We see Wright does not wholeheartedly embrace Dolan, Doyle, and the America they represent. He makes it clear that their way of expressing themselves, by scratching their names on the cathedral, is not his:

> I remember the names Doyle and Dolan,
> Who had their own ugly way to hack
> Their names on this prayer.

And he makes it clear that their way of living is not his:

> These hideous wanderers hate life, they
> Love, sullen, bitter, sitting
> Up all night waking beside women, waking
> With leaves in their hands.

Even so, he cannot, and now need not, deny that he is one of them, an American: "All three Americans, drunk on our lonely women." As Lieberman notes, "he cannot repudiate the burden of his countrymen's disreputable acts" without also "forfeiting his American heritage,"[23] which he does not now want or need to do.

Confronted with the facts of death, evil, and his own powerlessness, Hemingway's "bright boy" in "The Killers," quoted in the epigraph to *Two Citizens*, has to admit his ignorance and abandon his hope for pat solutions, just as Wright in *Branch* and *River* had to abandon his hope for simple solutions to the complex problems of living that he had posed in *The Green Wall* and *Saint Judas*. "I don't know," "bright boy's" answer to Max's challenge, "What do you think?", becomes a theme of this volume. Wright frequently states his bewilderment:

> I don't know why,
> One evening in August something illuminated my body
> And I got sick of laying my cold
> Hands on myself.
> ("The Young Good Man")

> . . . I didn't know what in hell
> Was happening to me.
> ("Paul")

> All afternoon you went walking,
> Just you, all alone,
> And what you went wondering about
> I still don't know.
> ("Voices between Waking and Sleeping in the Mountains")

The struggle to discover what one knows and does not know, and to determine whether or not that limited knowledge will suffice as the foundation for the life and poetry of a "grown man" lies behind *Two Citizens.* Wright slowly leaves behind the simple division of the world into white and black, good and bad, beautiful and ugly, us and them, which he had clung to through his first four volumes. In that sense, too, the book chronicles a loss of innocence, as does "The Killers." Now the poet finds himself

> . . . hovering between the dead sycamore,
> That tree I made my secret love to,
> And the edge of a wound I paid for by God,
> I have bought your world.
> ("Son of Judas")

The sycamore, the tree he had once risen "out of my body so high into" in *Branch,* is one refuge. The wound of a despoiled America is the other possibility. He wonders if his failure to live alone in his "sycamore," to be the pristine self he had hoped was possible back in *The Green Wall*, means he has sold out, "bought" the world of Mark Hanna's strip mines. "Between" is the key word in this passage and one of the key ideas in all of Wright's poetry since we first saw him caught between earth and air in *The Green Wall*: is "between" nowhere or is it his true home; is it a compromised position or an honest compromise? Is "between" where life is produced, as Muriel Rukeyser tells us in "The Speed of Darkness," or is it another wasteland? Can he live in this world of Hanna's strip mines without being tainted by them? Where can he live the "new life" referred to on the book's cover if not in this culture? Wright, from the beginning of his poetic career, has had no desire to live "between." His has not been the attitude or temperament of the compromiser, but he forces himself to come to terms with moral ambiguity by coming to terms with the fact that his country, his love, and his self are all composed of both beauty and ugliness. He loses his moral purity and superiority, but he gains, or gathers, his imperfect self, love, and country. Though not proud of his American heritage, he accepts it, and he also accepts the fact that his native language, no matter how unfavorably it compares to the silence of the leaves or the "affectionate sounds" he has encountered in Europe, is still the tongue he must use:

> No, I ain't much.
> The one tongue I can write in
> Is my Ohioan.
> ("To the Creature of the Creation")

Berryman's Henry says, "I am a monoglot of English / (American version") ("Dream Song #48"). Wright, too, must use what he knows, his "American verison," to try to understand what seems beyond comprehension. He "ain't much"; he is not "beautiful"; his country "ain't much"; even his Ohioan "ain't much." But they are all he has, and out of them he sees that he must, and can, produce "the poetry of a grown man":

> Emerson Buchanan, gun on his arm.
> Uncle Willy, the lone, Shorty the drunk.

> All I wanted to do. That was the wrong
> Place to be dead. All that we have,
> Death, is Ohio. Franklin Pierce will scan.
> Nobody else will scan, Allen the love,
> Allen the lovely song, these are my friends.
> Reader, alone, die. Die in the cold.
> Publius Vergilius Maro scans.
> ("Emerson Buchanan")

Can he use a language that does not scan, the language that he cursed in "Ars Poetica," to make poetry? Can he use a heritage of death to make a "lovely song"? Does he have a choice?

> Emerson Buchanan, who talked too much,
> Shut up, and now he is one half-hendecasyllabic,
>
> And almost an amphibrach.
>
> I try and try to hear them, and all I get
>
> Is a blind dial tone.
> ("Emerson Buchanan")

He must try, in spite of the difficulty of the task, to make his song from the materials he has been given, including Emerson, Willy, Shorty, and Ohio, even if "Shorty is puke on the ground" and Emerson Buchanan not quite metrical.

Two of the volume's finest poems, those in which the poet allows himself to be lyrical and take on the large issues of love, death, or country indirectly, show how successful Wright can be at writing "the poetry of a grown man." In these humble moments, he contributes more to his humanitarian vision than when stridently attacking Barbra Streisand (as in "To You, Out There (Mars? Jupiter?)" or Mark Hanna's coal company. One of the poems is "You and I Saw Hawks Exchanging Prey":

> They did the deed of darkness
> In their own mid-light.

He plucked a gray field mouse
Suddenly in the wind.

The small dead fly alive
Helplessly in his beak,

His cold pride, helpless.
All she receives is life.

They are terrified. They touch.
Life is too much.

She flies away sorrowing.
Sorrowing, she goes alone.

Then her small falcon, gone,
Will not rise here again.

Smaller than she, he goes
Claw beneath claw beneath
Needles and leaning boughs,

While she, the lovelier
Of these brief differing two,
Floats away sorrowing,

Tall as my love for you,
And almost lonelier.

Delighted in the delighting.
I love you in mid-air,
I love myself the ground.

The great wings sing nothing.
Lightly. Lightly fall.

We are shown, rather than told, that life is hazardous, especially for lovers, and that death fuels all life. The humble, restrained tone and the understatement ("All she receives is life") are uncharacteristic of this volume and convince us, more powerfully than Wright's occasional virulences, that love, though brutal and perhaps even futile, is still the only reasonable solution to the problem of living. The essential difference between the two partners, the vio-

lence and danger of their meeting, the life they both receive, and the
subdued tone are all reminiscent of Whitman's "The Dalliance of
Eagles" and might also echo line 30 of Whitman's "From Pent-up
Aching Rivers": "Two hawks in the air, two fishes swimming in the
sea not more lawless than we."

Another successful poem is "A Poem of Towers":

> I am becoming one
> Of the old men.
> I wonder about them,
> And how they became
> So happy. Tonight
> The trees in Carl Schurz
> Park by the East River
> Had no need of electricity
> To light their boughs, for the moon
> And my love were enough.
> More than enough the garbage
> Scow plunging, the front hoof
> Of a mule gone so wild through the water,
> No need to flee. Who pities
> You tonight, white-haired
> Lu Yu? Wise and foolish
> Both are gone, and my love
> Leans on my shoulder precise
> As the flute notes
> Of the snow, with songs
> And poems scattered
> Over Shu, over the East River
> That loves them and drowns them.

In this poem, Wright achieves the vision of wholeness that some of
this volume's poems miss. Love and garbage mix in the air like
sounds or odors, ineffable qualities that really do complement each
other, as the poet has been telling us but not always convincingly
showing us they do. He speaks here from his heart, rather than
solely from his head. We may believe he has a heartfelt antipathy to
Mark Hanna, but too often in *Two Citizens*, we see only the for-

mulations of his brain. Here the East River, garbage scow and all, quietly becomes a symbol of rejuvenation and hope, even as it "drowns" the snowflakes that are emblematic of the speaker's love and lover. His vision is deceptively simple. In this quiet moment, he feels, and successfully conveys, not only the intermingling of beauty and ugliness, but also the identity of love and poetry. His lover's presence is as "precise / As the flute notes / Of the snow," which are also poems. When Wright feels love, the world sings to him, and he to us, and it makes no difference that the river is polluted, for that garbage is redeemed by the poet's love, just as the poet is, and we see what he means when he speaks of coming to terms with "things" he both loves and hates.

One final word about *Two Citizens*. In "The Art of the Fugue: A Prayer," the poet climbs a hill in Fiesole, Italy, the same hill on which "the dark happy Florentine" Dante once stood. His ascension is symbolic and announces a desire to live. He is now "As far away as I will ever get from dying," standing in this rarefied atmosphere "waiting to begin," waiting to start a new life. There is one significant line that he repeats in the poem. First, he says, "Me, there, alone, at last . . . ," slowly enumerating what he knows. He has finally ("at last") achieved an identity ("Me") and a place ("there"), yet he is still "alone." When he repeats the line, he omits the commas. The separate facts are integrated into a smooth sentence, due to the added presence of "my only love": "And me there alone at last with my only love, / Waiting to begin." He is "alone" now in the sense that he feels completed within himself. Whether or not "my only love" is physically present is irrelevant, for now that he has understood love, that "scarcely imaginable Hell" that "By God, . . . is not a lie," his love, in the form of a woman or of his own fulfillment, is always with him. To be "alone," then, is different from being lonely. Now that she is there, finally gathered to him, either with him or within him, he can begin his life. As he says later in "The Snail's Road," "Too late be damned." It is never "too late" to "begin," never too late to be the "grown man" writing his proper poetry.

6

"I call it beauty"

any reviewers would have agreed with Wright's judgment that *To a Blossoming Pear Tree* (1977),[1] the last book he published during his lifetime, was "the best book that I have ever published. It is the best written and, whatever it says, whatever the value of the book, it is the book I wanted to write."[2] Peter Serchuk's remarks are typical of the nearly unanimous critical approval the book earned when first published: "What perhaps most distinguishes Wright's voice in this book from that of his previous collections is its authority of middle-age, its active acceptance of a tottering world along with the well-seasoned understanding that among the rubbled debris there is always some sustaining beauty to be found, however difficult it may be to recognize."[3] If one has followed the argument of this study's first five chapters, it should be clear that this "active acceptance of a tottering world" has been the goal and natural end of Wright's poetry from his first book. "His central project," as Randall Stiffler has noted, "was to move toward a synthesis of the opposition of affirmation and negation, toward a reconciliation of the possibility of epiphany with the reality of despair."[4] We have seen the poet struggle through five volumes of verse to earn the right to compose poems in which "the brutal and the beautiful mysteriously illuminate each other,"[5] that is, in which the darkness and the light balance and respect each other. While before he could often only "note the daylight gone," now there is a new light in his work, and he fears only his own timidity: as we turn the pages, we continually run into images of light (secret light, dazzles, brilliances, candlelight, sunlight, light of every variety) and images of the poet "facing" everything, keeping nothing hidden. By my count, Wright returns ten times in the book to the necessity of looking onself or another person or animal in the face. One has to turn to oneself, or to one's image reflected in another's face, rather than turn away from oneself.

This does not mean that the darkness is gone from the poems. Much pain remains and has to if the poet is to produce poems of fulfillment, balanced poems from a balanced perspective. But the presence of pain does not mean its dominance. "Sorrow" does not "prevail after all," as Hayden Carruth concludes of this volume.[6] What prevails is "beauty," the book's last word. We should remember Wright's emphatic statement, in a 1975 interview, that he structured and ordered the poems in his books "every time."[7] Then we will realize that the theme of the book is its movement from the old bitterness at Ohio in the opening poems to the resolution in "beauty" in "Beautiful Ohio," the volume's last poem. Serchuk was correct when he wrote that *Pear Tree* is in many ways a continuation of *Two Citizens*, but that "it moves beyond the other"[8] by consolidating the gains the poet made in that earlier book. In *Two Citizens*, motivated by a personal love that eases him beyond his egocentric boundaries, the poet resignedly accepts what he cannot avoid—his humanity, his country, and his heritage. In *Pear Tree*, motivated by a charity, humility, faith, and courage that transcend personal love, he takes an active joy in what before had the power to daunt him, his identity as singer, American, and simple fallen human being.

Joseph Campbell tells us that once the "mythological hero" has completed his dark and tortuous journey into the self, "into depths where obscure resistances are overcome, and long lost, forgotten powers are reinforced . . . ," life no longer suffers hopelessly under the terrible mutilations of ubiquitous disaster, battered by time, hideous throughout space; but with its horror visible still, its cries of anguish still tumultuous, it becomes penetrated by an all-suffusing, all-sustaining love, and a knowledge of its own unconquered power. Something of the light that blazes invisible within the abysses of its normally opaque materiality breaks forth, with an increasing uproar.[9]

Like Campbell's "mythological hero," Wright has made the lonely journey into the depths of his psyche and become intimate with "disaster." He has suffered the lovelessness of *Saint Judas*, the slag heaps of *The Branch Will Not Break*, and the personal and universal loneliness of *Shall We Gather at the River*. We saw the poet begin his ascent toward the light, toward an "active acceptance of a tottering world," toward a recognition of the world's love and power, which redeem its ugliness, in *Two Citizens*. He completes that ascent in *Pear Tree*, whose quiet poems are the "uproar" of the poet's vision, which manages to reconcile "horror," "anguish," "love," and "power" within its "light."

Campbell reminds us, however, that the hero must always pay dearly for his victory if it is to be meaningful, and that anyone who returns to the world with his "boon" too easily or swiftly won is likely to be "blasted from within and without—crucified, like Prometheus, on the rock of his own violated unconscious."[10] Consequently, we start *Pear Tree* in a ditch. Indecisive and ignorant, like the young Nick Adams we heard in the epigraph to *Two Citizens*, Wright stands on a bridge above the ditch, unable to move shoreward. The opening three poems form a triptych, what Campbell would call Wright's "initiatory tests,"[11] answered in time by the concluding three. We begin with Wright suspended over the darkness, as he was in "Lying in a Hammock at William Duffy's Farm in Pine Island, Minnesota," unable to move from the facts he describes to a value system that he can believe in and that will allow him to live. He observes, almost compulsively, animals and plants and things, all manner of nonhuman nouns, trying to move from observation to realization to resolution. By the middle of the book, he realizes—and where these realizations are made we cannot know; perhaps the poet himself did not know—that he will never be able to, nor does he need or any longer want to, "blossom" into an immaculate, because mute and unself-conscious, horse or grain of wheat. The desire to release his own and his subjects' "secret light" replaces the futile earlier desires to "blossom" into some nonhuman realm "Free of the body's work of twisted iron" ("Sappho"), as human subjects noticeably replace nonhuman ones in the second half of the book. Images of emergence, arrival, or appearance, of animals, objects, and people answering the challenge of life, dominate the middle of the book. A crab, a bee, a spider, a "secret angel," the poet's wife, earth itself—all are uncovered, revealed, celebrated between the opening and closing triptychs. Wright uses these presences, not so much muses as they are models and images of possibility, to move to the book's joyful conclusion. In *The Green Wall*, things fell and rotted. Here they appear unexpectedly, surrounded by light, either the light of the sun or the light of revelation and recognition or both. And, what might seem odd in another poet but what is characteristic of Wright, these items that emerge from shadow into light carry their darkness with them, for, as we saw clearly in "The Life" and "Three Sentences for a Dead Swan" (*River*), to return from "that black ditch / Of river" without the "ovoid of my darkness" intact would be capitulation rather than victory, resignation rather than resolution. As Campbell says, the "tree of life, i.e., the universe itself . . . is rooted in the supporting darkness,"[12] and for Wright to bring the fuit of that tree to us without its darkness would be to fulfill only half his mission. Finally, we are led to the concluding triptych of poems, a perfect balance to the opening three, in which the "ditch" that began the book, a sewer main in the poet's hometown, becomes "beauty." The book is, then, Wright's career in miniature, moving from "waste" to "beauty," from despair and doubt to faith and hope.

Let us begin by looking at the first three poems: "Redwings," "One Last Look at the Adige: Verona in the Rain," and "Hell." "Redwings" presents us with what looks like a straightforward romantic opposition between the scientist (Wright's nephew) and the poet. The scientist is all rationality and no feeling, manipulation without identification. The fact that "you can kill them," the troublesome redwings, is presented as if "can" equals "may," as if the possibility of an action justifies that action. Because a human being "can" do something, has the expertise to do it, he or she "may" do it with impunity. Wright correctly defines this as irresponsible but refuses to condemn the nephew-scientist alone. Instead, in a line separated on the page as a complete stanza, he turns to the reader and makes us all responsible: "Can you hear me?"[13] The question effectively divides the poem into two parts, although it is not at the poem's middle, if one counts lines. It separates the "scientific report" of Wright's nephew on the efficient killing of a pest species (the first eleven lines) from the poet's own account of his affinity with the birds (the final twenty-eight lines).

Were this a typical scientist/poet theme, however, we would expect the scientist, the materialist, to be guilty of dissociating fact from value, of pretending that the birds' extermination would be a value-free fact. But he does attach a value to the contemplated act, and Wright updates the traditional theme for contemporary readers used to pesticides and Corps of Engineers' projects. To "kill them" would be to "make the earth absolutely clean." That is, it would have its own value because it would be practical (I assume the birds eat crops) but also tidy, just as eradicating any pest is functional and aesthetically pleasing to some (all those green fields of perfectly straight rows without a single vermin in sight), and just as "channeling" once great rivers such as the Missouri not only makes river traffic and "recreational opportunities" practicable but also gives the engineer straight banks and uniform widths to admire. When one is "absolutely clean," however, spontaneity, randomness, and vitality are replaced by the "gray" scar Wright shows us. The scar is not only the river or the field or the air vacant of redwings—it is "on the small / Of your spine," our spine, in our central nervous system and core, part of us because we live in, are inured to, and learn to value as the "modern way" a sanitized world where the possibility of life appearing unexpectedly—the very sort of life that emerges so frequently in the middle of this volume—has been taken from us. We are reminded that purity (being "absolutely clean") is death, as we are told in many earlier poems. To cleanse is to defile, for it is to intervene destructively in processes that do not require our intervention. Yet this is not simply Wright claiming superiority again: the planned, or proposed, extermination is a family affair, including Wright's older brother, younger brother, nephew, and himself, as well as the reader. We are all responsible and all affected. Instead of the mark of Adam's sin, we carry the mark of modern man's transgressions, the mark, as Serchuk calls it, of "an America so beautiful yet seemingly so bent on destroying its own beauty."[14]

The possibility of an act does not justify the act, and power does not create value, as the high-flying scientist seems to have overlooked while in awe at his own power. Wright's awe is directed toward the blackbirds, and rather than fly above the earth in an airplane, as the nephew had done while delivering his disquisition, Wright sits on the earth and sees directly the implications of such a detached and aloof relationship to the objects of the world. The birds now only feel safe coming out at night:

> It was only in the evening I saw a few redwings
> Come out and rip their brilliant yellow
> Bills in their scarlet shoulders.
> Ohio was already going to hell.

We detect a note of the poet's former despair in that last line, but this poem strikes a subtle first note that will be echoed in "Beautiful Ohio," the volume's concluding poem. Here, as in "Beautiful Ohio," the poet sits next to a sewer, which is more than a mere waste pipe:

> One afternoon, along the Ohio, where the sewer
> Poured out, I found a nest,
> The way they build their nests in the reeds,
> So beautiful,
> Redwings and solitaries.

Just as the birds had earlier perched on and tolerated the unclean "creosote / Soaked pasture fence posts," so too at the poem's end the "beautiful" redwings and solitaries build their nests near the sewer, live near the ugliness, and redeem that ugliness, in part, by their presence. They do not require the earth to be "clean" in order to live on it. We recall that Wright had once insisted on leaving behind the "slag heaps" and "long gouge" of the Ohio, seeking a personal purity. He had been misguided, cutting off an essential part of himself, and now learns from these threatened birds. Even at the very entrance of the waste of man's culture into their once pristine river, the red-wings build their nest, raise their young, and create new life out of life's remains. They are like the skunk and her "column of kittens" in Lowell's "Skunk Hour," jabbing their wedge-heads into the garbage dump and swilling an existence. The birds, like the poet, wrest existence out of a hostile land, and Wright identifies with them:

> Somebody is on the wing, somebody
> Is wondering right at this moment
> How to get rid of us, while we sleep.

We sense a bit of the paranoia of earlier poems, particularly "The Minneapolis Poem," but the point seems to be not that someone is actively pursuing the poet, but that even if we do not notice the destruction, we will be scarred. We cannot remain aloof, asleep, or passive, as Wright had hoped in earlier work: stasis, dreaming, and sleep are not solutions. Rather than propose escape, as he had in *Branch*, the poet imagines in the next stanza a scene of retaliation that might be right out of Hitchcock's *The Birds*:

> Together among the dead gorges
> Of highway construction, we flare
> Across highways and drive
> Motorists crazy, we fly
> Down home to the river.

He "gathers at the river" with the redwings. The buried last grain of corn that he had dreamed of being in "The Minneapolis Poem" is dug up here, not by the simple passage of time, as he had there imagined, but by an act of will. Wright had been very wary of acts of will because they are too often aggressive acts of destruction, like his nephew's proposed extermination of the redwings. An act of will, however, can be an act of love and preservation, as he sees. The poet began his last book, *Two Citizens*, with an ars poetica. He begins this one with a declaration of determination, something short of war, that action and intervention can be constructive. Passivity and bitterness will not suffice.

The poem ends puzzlingly. The final stanza, set at the river, immediately follows the one quoted in the paragraph above and introduces a man we have never seen before in this poem:

> There, one summer evening, a dirty man
> Gave me a nickel and a potato
> And fell asleep by a fire.

The man reminds us of the bums and outcasts of earlier poems, and his presence balances the presence of the young scientist in the poem's opening stanzas, just as the redwings' "scarlet shoulders" balance the metal wings of the scientist's airplane, and the birds' "beautiful," living nest counters the sewer's constant stream of filth. In one sense, then, the old man is simply ballast to counter the scientist who begins the poem. He has a more important role, however, for he is also an incarnation of Saint Judas, giving "for nothing," committing an act of human charity. Wright may identify with, be inspired by, and learn from the birds, but he can only get help from the human.

Like Dante in his *Divine Comedy*, Wright begins "One Last Look at the Adige" "in the middle of my own life / . . . dying," but "still alive." Although the Ohio is dead, he still has the Adige, "my moving jewel," to sustain him temporarily, but he has no Virgil to guide him. He stands "out on the stone bridge" over the Adige, thinking of Ohio and the Ohio River, "alone,"

> A dark city on one shore,
> And, on the other,
> A dark forest.

The domesticated city or the wild forest? The realm of human will and consciousness or the uncharted land of prehuman darkness? Can he stretch to touch both shores? This state of suspension recurs often enough in Wright's poetry to attract our attention. He is suspended between life and death throughout *The Green Wall*. He finds himself suspended in "Lying in a Hammock." He concludes *River* with "To the Muse," in which he hovers just above the abyss. Unless one of his muses—Betty, Jenny, Annie—shows up to lead him to darkness or light, he has been unable to guide himself out of the dark woods of his own self-doubt. He has already tentatively put forward two potential guides in *Pear Tree*—the blackbirds and the old man with the potato in "Redwings." He will in this book find suitable guides to lead him to the faith and charity within his own soul, which will enable him, finally, to guide himself to the light. Now, however, the light that will be central to the book's later poems is extinguished ("The lights / Have gone out"), for, as I said, the poet must always begin in conflict and earn his way to resolution if that resolution is to be valuable. These opening poems are Wright's way of earning his later, joyful conclusion and of earning the right to deliver that message to us. They also point to the fact that without maintaining his darkness, the light that he later reveals would be incomplete, unsupported by its counterpart, anguish.

The third poem, "Hell," begins with Wright again suspended in darkness ("I had no idea / How far down I was. / I stood there, nothing") but also answers "Redwings" and finally moves us forward. The speaker is in a psychological hell and fears his death:

> Then I heard the tiny
> Rustling, the wings.
> Here they come,
> I thought.

We cannot avoid connecting "they" and their "wings" to the people of "Redwings," who were also "on the wing" and coming "to get rid of us." He calls himself "a dead fact," which makes me think of the birds in "Redwings." His "bones," however, cast an "emerald shadow." There is still a hard, crystalline, green, and living core left, the same protected and sacrosanct core he celebrated in "The Jewel" (*Branch*):

> There is this cave
> In the air behind my body
> That nobody is going to touch:
> A cloister, a silence
> Closing around a blossom of fire.
> When I stand upright in the wind,
> My bones turn to dark emeralds.

This is the same "crystal that I cannot find / Alone" that Annie helped him discover in "Voices between Waking and Sleeping in the Mountains" (*Two Citizens*). It is, as Stiffler notes, "the irreducible element of himself."[15] When Wright is pushed to the wall, as "far down" as he can go without giving up entirely, he remarkably summons strength and continues his journey. Now fortified, he writes a concluding stanza to "Hell," which sounds very much like a self-mocking answer to the short-lived paranoia of the book's opening poem:

> But nobody came
> Except a delicate little mosquito.
> And I gave him all I had left
> To drink, to live.

The final line is intentionally ambiguous—both the speaker and the mosquito are given life by the speaker's offer. This again reminds us of course of Wright's Saint Judas, but more to the point, it echoes the act of the old man in "Redwings" who gave the poet all he had and nourished both giver and receiver by the act of charity as much as by the "nickel and a potato." Acts of charity, then, acts in which one gives all one has to another rather than hoards it for oneself, significantly frame acts of destruction in these first three poems. Wright guides and is guided, gives as well as receives, and the act nourishes both giver and receiver. The poet shows the reader images of himself and others making the effort to live and finding that effort worthwhile. This charity, an extension of the love discovered in *Two Cit-izens*, will prove to be the antidote to the fear, anger, and self-doubt that have been Wright's reactions to destruction. Another act of charity, in "Hook," one of the final three poems in *Pear Tree*, will begin our exit from the book.

Between the opening triptych and the closing one, however, we cover a lot of territory, much of it European. In the middle section of the book, Wright has three main topics: how to see, recognize, or acknowledge the light that is at the heart of all things; how to re-lease that light; and how to give form to that light. The first of these projects involves Wright primarily as an observer. His mode is de-scription, which does not mean that he simply looks at things. Richard Howard tells us Wright's message is that there "is nothing to do but sit still and look very carefully at what is in front of your eyes, his eyes."[16] Yet in "Piccolini," for example, the poet is surely more than a passive observer. We are aware of the distance between the perceiver (Wright) and the perceived ("an easy thousand" dimin-utive fish). The piccolini tickle his skin, their skin against his, and he is not tempted to contend that the gap between himself and his objects is illusory. He observes in order to reflect, not just to "look very carefully," even though the reflection often remains only im-plicit in the imagery. The ground between poet and subject is now more fertile than it ever has been. It is the land where reflections grow, ideas take root, resolutions and recognitions are sown. When the goal of the poetry was to narrow or obliterate that ground, there was little room for the poet's mind to work, and indeed the poet, by wishing to eliminate the gap, was trying to avoid the workings of his own mind. He can now fill up the picture more completely because he stands back a bit. I suspect that he had believed that to admit a distance between subject and object would make the poem thinner and would exile him from nature's world where value resides. But by admitting, for example, that he is not the piccolini, he makes the poem richer by accepting his own humanness. In *Pear Tree*, then, description for Wright is a technique of self-identification: it locates him with respect to those around him, shows him what they know and he does not, and allows him to learn from them. Description also is a technique of epistemology, as it was for Elizabeth Bishop, a way to define what he knows and can know by looking closely at his subjects and selectively enumerating their relevant points. The animals he describes, not being burdened by human consciousness and self-consciousness, can only act naturally, something he aspires to do. The paradox is that one has to "aspire" to act "naturally." Perhaps rather than "naturally" we should think of "preculturally," that is, in a manner unencumbered by specific cultural biases or attitudes. Picasso said it took him his whole life to learn to draw again like a child. Wright's journey is similar—toward a universal expression of being, the sort of expression he finds in the animals he describes.

The second project—to release the light observed and described— finds Wright following the lead of, or collaborating with, several guides or mentors, who themselves release light for the poet and thereby hint at how he can perform the act himself. Giving form to the light, Wright's third theme in the central section of the book, is the act of making poetry, and Wright becomes an even more active participant than in the other poems when observing or following another character's lead. He understands, as Stein says, that "the act of composing a poem" requires "both attention and action."[17] The poet has to release the light himself and, more importantly, give it some shape or form that we recognize as the product of a creative act. He knows that, to the extent that he has to release the light that would otherwise go unnoticed, he makes, or is partially responsible for, the truths he lives by, but—and here is where faith comes in—he insists that those truths are real, that he has discovered and recorded them, not made them up to satisfy his own needs for significance. That is, he does not only imply that language constitutes reality for him independent of the extraliterary world, but that language works in conjunction with what really exists independent of man's signs to convert those nonverbal portions of the world into meanings for the verbal poet. The "secret light" *is* in the world's objects; the poet's language ties him to the light across the ground that separates the perceiver and the perceived. His language drags out that light and carries it across the subject-object divide to the poet's life, where it becomes part of him, too. He is not radically suggesting that meanings exist only in his words, but that his words allow him access to meanings and, inasmuch as they make those meanings clear, aesthetically pleasing, and relevant to him, constitute those meanings, too.

Most of the poems dealing with seeing, releasing, and giving form to the secret light of things are set in Europe, which Wright has often, in the habit of many American authors before him, portrayed as his true spiritual home. We get the impression that the poet believes that if he had been born in the shadow of Chartres rather than in the shadow of the Hazel-Atlas glass factory, he would never have been at odds with his native culture and would be free of America's sins and crassness. In these poems, light is often associated with the present moment in Europe, the sun, and occasionally the moon. Dark is often associated with the past moments remembered in America, ditches, graves, and gouges. In *Pear Tree*, however, unlike in Wright's earlier work, the light bathes all and tends to blend all into a single luminous picture of hope, so that light and dark, Europe and America, past and present fulfill, rather than battle, each other. In fact, as I said earlier, Wright shows that darkness is really a dark core from which the light emanates, a vital source of illumination. Releasing that darkness is essential if the light is also to be released. We should not be surprised, then, that the poet, after discovering the secrets of seeing in his European poems, writes several poems set in America that have a distinctly different tone from that of many of his earlier American poems: they are confident, optimistic, witty, and accepting. So that we might deal with these poems in some order, I would like to follow the poet through several poems as he discovers how to see, release, and form light; then I would like to look at several of the American poems to see how they differ from earlier American poems and are informed by the light Wright managed to uncover and give form to in the European poems.

"A Lament for the Shadows in the Ditches" has the poet sipping "cappuccino at a wobbly sidewalk table" in the brilliance of the Roman noon. His first memory is of "that black ditch of horror," the Ohio River, "where a strange boy drowned." His thoughts shift to the floor of the Colosseum, "across the street," with its "intricate and intelligent series of ditches." The ditches of the Colosseum—

here in Europe, in the sun—would seem to be a contrast to the ditch of the Ohio—back there, in the darkness—but "the sun cannot reach" these Roman ditches, either. Instead, they remind Wright of the Christians whose blood ran through them, then of the Jews and mass graves in World War II, and all the while of the drowned boy in the Ohio "ditch." The martyrs of all ages pass before him as he sips his cappuccino in the Roman sun. There is no way to erase the images of the tortured; neither can he deny the warmth of the sun. The light does not eradicate or lessen or compensate for the darkness but reveals its horror as the sun's equal, and the two forces in human nature and history exist as equals, then as complements: "Even the noon sunlight in the Colosseum is the golden shadow of a starved lion, the most beautiful of God's creatures except maybe horses." The brilliant sunlight of the present and the ancient instruments of torture simply cannot be separated; the wonderful architecture of the Colosseum and the purposes it was used for will not be pried apart; the beautiful Ohio and the drowned boy are one. Those who had the Colosseum built are those who ordered its use. The world's darkness and light complement rather than conflict.

In "Piccolini," Wright at first appears to turn his back on Europe's solid, past grandeur in favor of the perishable, vegetable fecundity of the "present moment." He stands with his back to "the summer villa of the poet, the Grotte di Catullo," preferring to concentrate on the "easy thousand of silver, almost transparent piccolini" swimming around his ankles. These small, present fish—and we are quickly reminded by contrast of the monumental Grotte and Colosseum—are the mutable, insignificant reality to which he is limited. At Catullus's touch, the fish "would have dissolved altogether," but at Wright's poetic touch, they are preserved as the "tiny and happy" lives that skim his ankles. His comparison is not presumption, but humility, for Wright is "small" enough to write of the fish without crushing or overwhelming them.

By looking at the silver fish, the poet places himself in time and space and forces himself to ask if he is where he should be or wants to be. Am I more a part of the swimming piccolini, the world of nature, or of the Grotte, the world of humans? The poem creates a tension between the present life at the speaker's feet and the art of the past, implying that one can attend to either life or art, present or past, but not both simultaneously. The form, in which stanzas concerning the past alternate with those about the present, also implies that past and present are separate blocks of experience that cannot be blended, just as attending to Catullus's villa would mean ignoring the piccolini that "tickle the skin" of the poet's ankle. The dead past and static art seem incompatible with the living present and swimming fish. But perhaps the opposition is not that simple, not that complete. By making the Grotte di Catullo "Looming and almost molten and slowly moving its gold downhill," Wright gives it life in the present. The Grotte's animation ("moving") and radiance ("its gold") echo the movement of the "silver" piccolini. The fish are fragile, Wright says, implying that we had better not try to capture them with words lest we "dissolve" them "altogether." Yet their smallness is used to connect them with the Latin language that Catullus used to make art, almost to contain them within that language, for they are "diminutive," even "smaller than Latin diminutives." He can, and does here, reside in both worlds.

"The Fruits of the Season" could be a companion piece to "Piccolini," although the two are separated by a dozen other poems. Once again the poet has to choose between the timeless past ("a huge exhibit of paintings" at the Palazzo della Ragione) and the fleeting present (the "commonplace, ordinary" life in the square at Padua). The "enduring fruits of five hundred years" compete with the "grapes, melons, peaches, nectarines, and the other fruits that will soon fill [the] vast square." He chooses, again, the latter fruit, the poetry of the present moment. The fruit's mutability does not induce lamentation but a renewed desire to live, for "I would rather live my life than not live it," despite transience and imperfection. Again, though, the choice between the two possibilities he shows us is not so clear-cut, and the poem seems a bit disingenuous, for Wright must surely be as aware as the reader is that he creates, in his poem, an "enduring fruit." His poem is, in effect, a still life, richly colored and hung up with the others. His sympathies might lie with the vendors in the street, but his art will take its place with the rest on the second floor of the palazzo.

These vignettes of radiance and life are sprinkled throughout the middle poems of *Pear Tree* and serve two purposes: they show the character Wright, and they are used by the poet Wright to show us that the world is, in Campbell's phrase again, "penetrated by an all-suffusing, all-sustaining love,"[18] here imaged as an all-suffusing light. "The Silent Angel," for example, is pure light, again with the subject (an anonymous Veronese) framed by an enduring work of art ("the pink marble arches at the base of the great Roman Arena"). The man offers Wright a smile, "a gesture of the utmost sweetness," gratuitously, as the fruits and piccolini were simply there, as if the world had decided to make its bounty available to the poet. The tone in these poems is lighter than in "Saint Judas," but the phrase from that poem, "for nothing," keeps coming to mind. This is a continuation of a theme from *Two Citizens*: all is offered "for nothing," without expectation of payment, without consideration of merit, exemplifying a generosity and "gathering" that Wright is reaching for, a way to embrace all without asking for anything in return and without first testing to see if the others deserve to be embraced. The "silent angel" in this poem simply "emerges" into the sunlight from out of his shadowy resting place, light emerging from darkness, almost like the benevolent presence of the city itself, waving the poet "out of Verona as kindly as he could."

The poet's method of loving and gathering, of asserting his faith, is to describe carefully what he sees, the data of his life, and make cautious leaps (of faith) from those data to their meaning or meanings. Many of the poems move from observation to realization and sometimes to resolution, first describing a subject and then imaginatively appropriating it to the poet's life, like so many romantic poems and always on the scale of the short lyric, Wright's métier. In "With the Shell of a Hermit Crab," Wright is looking at a crab:

> This lovely little life whose toes
> Touched the white sand from side to side,

How delicately no one knows,
Crept from his loneliness, and died.

The facts are commonplace and true (if one thinks of crabs as having
"toes"), but their meaning for Wright is implicit. He, too, is lonely,
his proud defiance having become, in *River*, his anguish. The crab,
after coming out of his shell, found not "his name" but "A quick life
and a candle flame." Will Wright also find he is too vulnerable if he
leaves his "shell"? The idea is trite if stated baldly like that, but the
poem's indirection, as well as its interesting return to Wright's for-
mer iambic tetrameter and discernible rhyme scheme, saves its con-
tent. The speaker "flick[s] out the light," and we remember that in
"Two Hangovers" (*Branch*) he had also turned off the light so that, in
the darkness, where he could not see the poverty and degradation he
had shown us in the first half of the poem, he could feel buoyed:
"The branch will not break." Here he does not use the darkness to
ignore what he cannot bear, but to meditate upon it more intensely:

I reach out and flick out the light.
Darkly I touch his fragile scars,
So far away, so delicate,
Stars in a wilderness of stars.

The scars are his, and the leap of faith from "scars" to "stars" is facili-
tated by the rhyme but not accounted for wholly by it. His scars are
his stars; his pain is not simply his identity but his salvation as well.
Here a knowledge of Wright's whole body of work makes the poem
more meaningful. This conversion of "scars" to "stars," the implica-
tion that one's pains are one's shining moments, the careful inser-
tion of light in the middle of darkness, would not have been as
convincing before *River*, where we saw so many of the poet's scars,
or without the rest of Wright's work, in which so much is made of
the need to recover our essential "darkness."

This is not a return to the earlier desire to be like nature, to be like
the horse and hound, a desire I have claimed to be bankrupt and
unproductive, one of the chief errors in logic and desire that underlie

the turn toward morbidity and suicidal imagery in *River*, where the
desire to blossom into a horse became the desire to blossom into the
boat with Morgan Blum and be carried to the underworld. Here
Wright does not seek *identification* to *deny* his humanness but de-
sires *communion* to learn how to *live with* his humanness. He
"faces" things and others, and the very verb implies a consciousness
of the other rather than an identification with the other. He observes
with and is separated by his face, the edge of his human boundary,
his corporeal and spiritual limit. His descriptions become, in a way,
less inclusive: he no longer claims to be one with nature. But he is
moving toward claiming to be one with humans, with all their ex-
cesses and excrescences. In that sense, the descriptions move toward
a larger inclusiveness by, paradoxically, defining precisely the poet's
boundaries. He narrows to enlarge; he restricts to find his rightful
place.

After observing and describing the light, the poet's next project is
to learn how to release it. Several anonymous beings emerge in *Pear
Tree* to serve as Wright's composite mentor for this task. The main
event in "The Secret of Light," set in Verona, is the appearance of "a
startling woman" directly in front of the poet. She rises from her
park bench and walks away, but not before Wright can describe her
hair as being

> as black as the inmost secret of light in a perfectly cut diamond, a
> perilous black, a secret light that must have been studied for many
> years before the anxious and disciplined craftsman could achieve
> the necessary balance between courage and skill to stroke the
> strange stone and take the one chance he would ever have to bring
> that secret to light.

The "secret" is both the blackness and the light, as Wright plays
with the word "secret," making it serve here as adjective, there as
noun, modifying the light, standing for the blackness, and finally
symbolizing the union of darkness and light, all in the same sen-
tence. Wright is obviously an "anxious and disciplined craftsman"
himself, revealing to us the same "secret" that the woman's lover
revealed to the world. He exhibits the "skill" he alludes to and in the

next stanza reveals that he has the "courage" needed to pursue such difficult quarry as a darkness that is also light: "I am startled to discover that I am not afraid. I am free to give a blessing out of my silence into that woman's black hair." In other words, although he admits earlier to being afraid ("I am afraid her secret might never come to light in my lifetime"), his is not Pound's "diffidence that faltered" but a fear that he overcomes, balancing "courage and skill" to "stroke" the present moment into light and life.

Wright's goal has always been to bring light out of darkness, to create or release knowledge and art out of the darkest raw materials, to determine whether or not the dark heart of the individual and the country contains "a secret light" that is redeemable and good. He has always asked this of the poet but has never been confident that such an impossible-sounding task was feasible. Now he believes it to be within his grasp. One could not ask for a more succinct allegory for the acts of personal revelation and poetic creation than the prose poem "The Secret of Light." How can the poet take the black materials of this world—the slag heaps and strip mines of Ohio, the brutality of George Doty, the "scarcely imaginable Hell" that is love—and wring from them their beauty without romanticizing, idealizing, or sentimentalizing them? How can one turn to the blackness and, by releasing its darkness in song, also release light and beauty? No matter how one phrases the act, it sounds like a hopeless paradox, a logical contradiction. Yet this is what the poet has to do. The woman inspires the poet, who crafts the sentence that re-creates her "secret light," which describes the poet's own long struggle with his art and his soul. The person, with hard work, thought, and love, releases what is most basic in himself, just as the poet, with careful attention and loving craftsmanship, releases what is "secret" in his subject.

He imagines the release in sensual and sexual terms:

> Surely two careful and accurate hands, total strangers to me, measure the invisible idea of the secret vein in her hair. They are waiting patiently until they know what they alone can ever know: that time when her life will pause in mid-flight for a split second.

The hands will touch her black hair very gently. A wind off the
river Adige will flutter past her.

This imagery connects with the imagery used to describe Annie, the
releaser of Wright's "secret light," in *Two Citizens*, especially in
"Voices between Waking and Sleeping in the Mountains" ("Two
hands gathered my two") and "Bologna: A Poem about Gold" ("Mary
in Bologna, sunlight I gathered all morning / And pressed in
my hands all afternoon / And drank all day with my golden-
breasted / Love in my arms"). Just as Annie delivered Wright from
his personal, dark hell, so this woman delivers "a flawless and fully
formed Italian daybreak into the hands" of her lover. Both women
are sources of light, secrets of light, and revealers of the dark light in
their lovers, who themselves become craftsmen to release the secret
light of their "golden" and dark lovers. Wright admits the com-
parison of this woman to Annie: "I hope she brings some other
man's secret face to light, as somebody brought mine." He uses the
image of a woman as he had in *Two Citizens*. The muse-lover who
combines saintly light and earthly darkness, like Mary Magdalene
in "Bologna: A Poem about Gold," the woman in this poem, and
especially Annie, is the fulfillment of the image of woman, which
has been central to Wright's poetry from its beginnings. The earliest
women were either all sensuality and darkness (like Betty in "Morn-
ing Hymn to a Dark Girl") or all innocence and light (like the child
in "A Little Girl on Her Way to School"). Later, that darkness, once
celebrated as a liberating and rebellious sensuality and unconven-
tional morality, became morbidity, death, and the lure of disintegra-
tion (most clearly in the figure of Jenny throughout the middle of
Wright's career) or simply repulsiveness unredeemed by any light
except that supplied by the poet (as in Aunt Agnes in "Ars Poetica:
Some Recent Criticism"). The women in Wright's most mature po-
etry are whole, both dark and light, and, as I remarked in the preced-
ing chapter, initiate the poet into the mystery that any life, and any
culture, is composed of paradoxical elements, evil and good, profane
and sublime, the one feeding and sustaining the other.

The time of "The Secret of Light" is "early autumn," but the poem is no conventional autumnal lament. It is instead a celebration of the passing of time, because only in time can the secret light be released—it is the painstaking process of a lifetime. The poet does not worry that he is mortal and aging. The autumn winds off the river Adige blow only good news of new life:

> I am happy enough to sit in this park alone now. I turn my own
> face toward the river Adige. A little wind flutters off the water and
> brushes past me and returns.

Annie herself appears in the next poem, "A Small Grove in Torri del Benaco," a perfect companion to "The Secret of Light" because the poet's wife fulfills the promise of that earlier poem by emerging as the source of light, shining forth at the poet and bringing the world to life. The poet begins by simply observing: "Outside our window we have a small willow, and a little beyond it a fig tree, and then a stone shed." The "Outside" becomes "beyond," and there is already a natural movement toward integration: "the separate trees suddenly become a grove." It is up to Annie, however, to provide a focus and center for the grove: "She is the eye of the grove, the eye of mimosa and willow." Annie is not named but achieves greater status by being simply "she," a universal, almost mythical presence around which everything "blossoms" and "catches fire" as pure light. (We notice that Annie herself does not blossom, but "everything that *can* blossom" does. It is a subtle shift from "A Blessing," but a shift nonetheless from a desire to transcend one's boundaries to a desire to celebrate those boundaries and what they contain.)

There is a movement from scattered data ("separate trees") to integrated data (the "grove") to the "eye" of the whole, its ordering and vivifying center. The experience becomes more intense as we move closer to the center, almost as if we were moving closer to the densest part of a star, until the grove not only comes alive, it "catches fire," the heat of "her" presence being too great to resist. I think of the Calvinist notion of irresistible grace: the cypresses cannot resist Annie's presence and are forced into sudden life almost despite themselves. The "candle[s] of darkness," as the cypresses are called in paragraph 1, burst into fire and become symbolic of the poet, both "dark" and "light." "She," too, is dark—"Her skin is darker gold than the olives in the morning sun." She is so dark, in other words, that she is light, like the woman in "The Secret of Light." She not only embodies unity but also endows it on all those in proximity and allows the poet, through this vision, to create another vision of wholeness and unity, the poem itself. She does not simply shine her light onto the subjects around her but causes them to release their own inner light. This is the poet's task of creation, releasing what is light and latent in his subjects.

We meet two more unlikely poets and mentors in "The Best Days." Two Veronese workmen, with steel claw, steel pipe, and chisel, lift a quarter-ton marble floorstone. Through grace and skill, they turn manhandling into an aesthetic act, an act of balance, delicacy, and power:

> Balancing the great weight of this enormous
> And beautiful floorstone laid by the Romans,
> Holding a quarter ton of stone lightly
> Between earth and air,
> The tall man with the gray hair reaches
> Around the corner of stone
> And most delicately eases
> A steel pipe beneath.

Underneath the stone, where Wright perhaps expects to find something sinister, he sees instead, "It is just under the stone." This is emphatically not the sort of ditch we saw in "A Lament for the Shadows in the Ditches": "It does not look like a grave / Of anybody, anybody at all." We hear an echo of "The Old WPA Swimming Pool in Martins Ferry, Ohio": ". . . my father / And my uncles dug a hole in the ground, / No grave for once." We can hear an echo of another poem, too. "The earth smells fresh, like the breath / Of a calf just born in Ohio /With me" alludes to "Well, What Are You Going to Do?" from *Two Citizens*, in which the young Wright watches as Marian the calf is born. The allusion tells us that this dark earth underneath the floorstone is not only not the image of death that the poet feared but is instead an image of new life. The graceful act of lifting the stone released a great weight, which revealed a darkness that is life, not death, not a grave, not a "suckhole," as we might have discovered following the same action in an earlier Wright poem. In addition, the allusion to Marian and Martins Ferry ("this town / So like my own") connect America and the past to Italy and the present, making us suspect that these moments of light are transferable, that the "poetry of the present moment" produces a brilliance that can illuminate the past and future.

The real problem for the poet, however, is not just seeing the light or watching others release it, but learning how to release it oneself in a form suitable to it. This is the final project in the middle poems of *Pear Tree*. In "Two Moments in Rome," Wright observes as the Colosseum shapes light without destroying the light's integrity:

> At noon on a horizon the Colosseum poises in mid-flight, a crumbling moon of gibbous gold. It catches an ancient light, and gives form to that light. Gazing at the Colosseum from a spot two miles away, I feel as though I had just caught a quick glimpse of a girl's face.

The "crumbling" Colosseum radiates hope, not decay, by giving form to the light without distorting it more than necessary but without self-effacement, either. The light, a natural phenomenon, and the Colosseum, a phenomenon made by human beings, each remains what it is, but each complements the other. They are like poet and subject. The author has a moral obligation not to force himself on his subject but to seek instead a form that will allow the subject's life to breathe through the stanza. What the poet needs is the "necessary balance" between form and chaos. The poet wants to give form to beauty, just as the Colosseum in "Two Moments in Rome" gives form to the light. The Colosseum's form affords the light's radiance a chance to display itself, as Wright wants his poetic forms to give the beauty of his subjects an opportunity to display itself to the eye and mind of the reader.

The best example of the poet releasing light himself, rather than just observing others, as in "The Secret of Light," is in "The First Days." Wright tells us that the first thing he saw one morning was "a huge golden bee ploughing / His burly shoulder into the belly / Of a sleek yellow pear / Low on a bough." The bee was after the "sudden black honey" at the pear's core. The honey—black, at the core, life-giving—is the familiar, by now, source of life (for the bee) and light (of the yellow pear). When the bee's weight is too much for the bough and both he (embedded in the pear) and the pear fall, the poet has to make a decision. The bee "would have died" if Wright had not "sliced the pear gently / A little more open" to release him. The act—gentle slicing—reminds one of a cesarean delivery, which in a sense it is, but also of the smooth stroking that we were told in "The Secret of Light" is necessary to release the subject's light. The poet's active intervention releases life, and Wright now assumes Annie's role as deliverer and revealer. When earlier confronted with a similar predicament, the birth of Marian the calf, the poet was dumb-founded: "I don't know anything about the problem / Of beautiful women." Here he knows more, acts more calmly (that is, with "courage and skill"), and becomes an active participant in creation. The bee, "drowning in his own delight," may have been content to stay put. There may be no clear sign from life that beauty is present to be released. The poet has to make that decision and take the first step himself, hence "courage." And he must also apply just the right touch, trusting in his activity, hence "skill."

Beauty can die if not released "gently." The poet must be able to see the potential of the moment and understand that he is needed to release it, but he also must realize that any intervention on his part is necessarily a distortion of nature. To intervene, to write the poem that releases the beauty, is a moral act and requires a moral decision: "Maybe I should have left him alone there, / Drowning in his own delight." The danger in intervening is that one may not have the correct poetic touch and may destroy what one handles: "I let the bee go / Among the gasworks at the edge of Mantua." Writing a poem is an act of the human will and ego, as is building the gas-works. It takes the touch of the poet—whether the poet works with pen and paper or bricks and mortar or steel pipe and claw—to release beauty rather than create ugliness. What Wright implies, though, is that people, by the very act of living, have to intervene in the world around them. They cannot be passive, as the poet had hoped in *Branch* and *River*. One cannot simply turn one's back when faced with the decision of whether or not to release the bee in the pear or build the gasworks at Mantua. Or more accurately, to turn one's back is a decision in itself. Decisions must be made; passivity will not release us from that burden.

Wright thus moves from observer of things emerging spontaneously or being aided in their release by others, to one who does the releasing, making a conscious choice to offer his aid and eschew the passivity that was always so attractive because it was pure and uncommitted. The poet is more than a vessel, that metaphor occasionally used to describe the artist; he is an obstetrician, more actively involved and taking more risk in this most difficult operation of releasing beauty. I believe the poet has been tempted by passivity in part because his view of life is essentialist, rather than existentialist. Action does not precede existence, he tells us; existence, rather, begets action. Before one can act with anything like certainty, and Wright has sought certainty as surely as he has known that it is impossible to have, one must know who one is. Yet, as we recall the preponderance of questions and the confessions of ignorance in all of Wright's poetry after *Saint Judas*, we realize that "for all I know" is a major theme of all his later work, and certainty about his identity has been precisely what he has not had. Defining oneself negatively, as "different-from-them," only helps one see who one is not and what one should not do, as I said in chapter five. If he could be satisfied with a pluralism of values, he could turn to a defensive irony that plays with its own insecurity. If he could be happy working in an uncentered world, he could substitute verbal texture for meaning. Yet he does not want, will not be content, to stand in the middle, on the bridge between shores, and from that perch sing his songs. Finally recognizing his true essence, as a loving, vulnerable, American poet, frees him to act, and act responsibly, that is, to put his full moral weight behind his actions, including his poems.

As I said, the new light and enlarged vision of the poems set in

Europe illuminate those poems set in America. He does not curse those Americans he meets or remembers but speaks fondly and agrees to learn. In "The Wheeling Gospel Tabernacle," for example, the setting is a church in Wheeling, West Virginia, in 1925, just prior to the depression, which enters the poem ominously but fails to dampen its high spirits. The police are here also, pursuing Homer Rhodeheaver, "the evangelist Billy Sunday's psalmodist and shill at the offeratory," on a paternity charge. Homer becomes "one of the heroes / Of love," like Uncle Sherman in "Ars Poetica," and the police chase him as if eros were a crime. We expect the police to be drawn in as they were in "The Minneapolis Poem" (*River*), where they also persecuted love, in the form of prostitutes, "Tall Negro girls from Chicago." But just as Wright goes easy on the depression, mentioning it in passing rather than making it symbolic of a national malaise, so he treats the police with humor, as if they were Keystone Kops, "hurtling down the West Virginia Route 40 in their Prohibition-style armored Cord cars," rather than with hostility. The criminalization of love is played as a comedy, not made tragic or denounced. Wright also treats Billy Sunday mildly, whereas once he might have seriously decried the man's con game. The poem's first three paragraphs, with their mixture of levels of diction and breathless, long sentences, gently mock the reverend's hell-fire sermon. Wright, in other words, is having fun with the event, which one time would have provided him so much raw material for serious protest. Sunday was amusing; Homer spread love; the police were bumblers—who can judge them, the poem asks. In such poems as "The Wheeling Gospel Tabernacle," we get the human side, the everyday view, of America's past, as opposed to the view Wright had focused on earlier, the institutionalized destruction and careless (in the simple sense of not caring) waste of the culture's potential.

Another American poem, "The Flying Eagles of Troop 62," set in Wright's youth and featuring Ralph Neal, the scoutmaster, another hero of love, is also witty in places, especially Wright's Southern Ohio version of the Scout Law ("Ay scout is trusswortha, loll, hailpful, frenly, curtchuss, kand, abaydent, chairful, thrifta, dapraved, clane, and letcherass."), but it carries what might be the most important theme of Wright's final books: "and he loved us anyway." Despite the boys' "scrawniness, . . . acne, . . . fear," Neal loved them anyway. Like Uncle Sherman, again, who loved Aunt Agnes despite the fact that she was sloppy and stank, Neal accepted the boys for what they were. And he "was not a fool," which means he did not delude himself about their great potential. He knew they would face failure and frustration, which they did: Dickey Beck was in jail for the third time, Dale Headley drove a milk truck that "rattle[d] his spine over jagged street-bricks," Mike Kottelos "was making book in Wheeling," and Hub Snodgrass was trapped in the steel mills. Yet, "he loved us anyway." Wright has been touring European art museums. Now he constructs his own small portrait gallery of Americans, with Billy Sunday, Homer Rhodeheaver, Ralph Neal, even Dickey Beck et al., to let him see those who provided comfort and solace during vulnerable times, rather than just those who piled up slag heaps while the boy watched his beloved Ohio and Ohio River befouled. Wright "hangs" these subjects in his poems to honor them, just as his hometown library has hung his portrait in a place of honor. In this context, it is important that these subjects do not have to be "social outsiders" to qualify for Wright's love. These poems are portraits of those ordinary people who represent what Wright calls "the river gold," the good that is left after the debris is sifted out and sifted through. Neal is a leader and authority figure with tremendous power, equal to that of Harding or Mark Hanna from the young scouts' perspective, yet one who does not cheat or abuse. Such people exist, Wright says, and despite the ambivalence that that creates in his mind as he contemplates America, the goodness cannot be denied: "The very name of America often makes me sick, and yet Ralph Neal was an American. The country is enough to drive you crazy." I believe the tone of that final line from the poem is positive, almost a sigh of relief as the poet finally admits the obvious.

He not only gathers Americans to him in these poems set in his native land. He also, in a kind of gradual desensitization process, looks at his fears and faces them down, strengthened by the light and love he has absorbed in Europe. The saguaro cactus in "To the Saguaro Catcus in the Desert Rain," thorny and uninviting on the outside, in deserts as hot as the "brutal dry suns" of factories Wright remembers, seems another of the "bitter places / In America, that seemed / Tall and green-rooted in mid-noon." However, it is life-sustaining if one burrows far enough inside and is not fooled by its forbidding exterior, as the elf owl, a resident in the cactus, knows. The owl finds a home in the cactus just as the redwings found a home near the sewer main, just as Wright will find his home in America. After linking the cactus with Ohio through the "brutal dry suns" and "Tall and green-rooted in mid-noon" images, and himself to the elf owl ("the elf owl's face / Is inside me"), Wright allows himself to be "gathered" by the cactus: "Your green arms lower and gather me." The concluding image is clearly one of hope and potential salvation. The cactus becomes like an oasis on his desert journey through life, a place where he can rest and be comforted, a symbol of the possibility of finding isolated green spots (like Ralph Neal and Homer Rhodeheaver) in the "bitter places" where he is forced to live.

"Discoveries in Arizona" immediately follows "To the Saguaro Cactus" and begins with an italicized epigraph:

> All my life so far
> I have been afraid
> Of cactus,
> Spiders,
> Rattlesnakes.

He just overcame his fear of cactus and now confronts a spider, as he continues reconciling himself to things he has hated or feared. (He faces a snake in "In Exile.") The tarantula's burrow is compared to "a blacksnake hole in Ohio, / that I hated," thus linking this poem to Wright's home. He is off the bridge we first saw him on in this book's opening poems. Here he has ventured into enemy territory, the home of the tarantula, and with a guide, not Virgil, but a "tall four-teen-year-old boy." The desert setting is certainly suggestive enough of the wanderer, searching, confronting his doubts and fears, Christ-like without being presumptuous, I think, and also reminds us of the earlier allusion to Dante entering the dark wood in mid-life.

Wright's "discoveries" here bode well for his eventual successful return. He realizes that he has feared the tarantula all his life, "yet I have never even seen / A tarantula turn her face / Away from me." Perhaps there is less to fear than he had once thought. Facing and describing the tarantula, or at least the tarantula's hole, is a way to expand his experience, to include more parts of the world, those parts he has lived in terror of, within his experience. He does not pacify those wild and buried parts but simply faces them down and faces down his own fear in the process. He realizes, in "Discoveries in Arizona" and other of the American poems, that he is stronger than he has imagined, and that what he has feared may be what he needs to face (precisely what he has been declaring others must realize since *The Green Wall* and what he seemed to know as he faced his Furies in *River*).

Thus strengthened by the light he has gathered and the lessons he has learned throughout the early and middle poems of *Pear Tree*, Wright turns to his greatest test, that of rescuing beauty from the literal waste of a sewer pipe, the ditch he began the book with. That test takes place in "Beautiful Ohio," the book's concluding poem and the final poem in the book's closing triptych of hope, love, and life wrested from the grasp of despair and pain, which balances and answers the opening triptych. In the three poems, Wright confronts the ugliness he has long denounced, first by accepting physical and mental deformity in individuals, and then, after seeing that love and beauty can assume the most grotesque forms in individual cases, by finally accepting the ugliness collective man brings forth into the world, something he has resisted doing for five books. In these final poems, he sees through ugliness to beauty and learns that, just as individuals can be flawed yet embody love, can even appear grotesque *because* of their need for love, so too there is beauty to be found in the heart of the society's ugliness.

"Hook" finds the poet a young man "in trouble / With a woman." The poem takes place in the past as Wright begins his process of summing up, taking the long view. We are back in Minneapolis, during that terrible period of Wright's life. He may not redeem the misery of those years, but he can find something positive in them. He is, in effect, writing, or rewriting, his autobiography, drawing his own "face" as he now sees it. The time is winter; the poet is desolate and hopeless: ". . . there was nothing / There but me and dead snow." There is no comfort in this snow, as there was in "The careful fingers of the healing snows" in "The Refusal" (*Saint Judas*). The snow is "dead," and Wright has no illusions about its healing power. He cannot seek shelter in the natural world, as he once might have. In fact, the environment is his adversary now:

> I stood on the street corner
> In Minneapolis, lashed
> This way and that.
> Wind rose from some pit,
> Hunting me.

The last time Wright was in Minneapolis in his poetry, it was not the wind hunting him but other men:

> There are men in this city who labor dawn after
> Dawn to sell by my death.
> ("The Minneapolis Poem")

Now the wind and the snow are his enemies, and it is only another man who can save him. "The young Sioux" who "loomed beside me," his hook hanging at his side, will deliver the stranded poet by giving him "money / To get home on":

> Did you ever feel a man hold
> Sixty-five cents
> In a hook,
> And place it
> Gently
> In your freezing hand?

It is the offer itself, however, and not the sixty-five cents, that gets Wright "home," back from the nothingness he felt in the first stanza:

I took it.
It wasn't the money I needed.
But I took it.

The Sioux reminds us of the old man in "Redwings," and we see the book turning back on itself, completing its poetic vision. The speaker needs the human touch, the warmth of human charity, even if that warm human charity comes in the form of a cold metal hook. The "company" that banishes the "dead snow" and its numbing effects comes from the Sioux's human soul but through his ugly hook. The beauty of the touch transforms the hook from a symbol of human imperfection and frailty to a symbol of love's ability to strengthen and momentarily perfect even weak, imperfect humanity. Though physically deformed, the young Sioux is beautiful in a deeper way, and the "scars" life has given him do not destroy his feelings for his fellow man, where in earlier poems Wright's trials had often made him bitter and unforgiving. The poet is led to realize that only his fellow humans will or can save him.

In the title poem, Wright exchanges roles with the Sioux of "Hook" and becomes the stranger in the snow approached by another needing warmth:

An old man
Appeared to me once
In the unendurable snow.
He had a singe of white
Beard on his face.
He paused on a street in Minneapolis
And stroked my face.
Give it to me, he begged,
I'll pay you anything.

The poet demurs ("I flinched. Both terrified, / We slunk away") but still imaginatively gathers the petitioner to him in sympathy:

. . . the dark
Blood in my body drags me
Down with my brother.

Although he first recoils, Wright sympathizes with the "old man" because he understands the man's extreme need:

> . . . He was so near death
> He was willing to take
> Any love he could get.

Because Wright, too, has been "near death," at least in his poetry, and looking for "any love he could get," he can see himself in the "old man" "dodging / The cruel darts of the cold." And because Wright is human and has felt the need for love, he can understand the man's desperation, while the "pure delicate" pear tree cannot:

> Beautiful natural blossoms,
> How could you possibly
> Worry or bother or care
> About the ashamed, hopeless
> Old man?

The pear tree's beauty is "perfect, beyond my reach" and therefore paradoxically pales in comparison with the old man's ugliness and need. Wright realizes that his task is to express the human, which "unburdened" nature cannot understand:

> For if you could only listen,
> I would tell you something,
> Something human.

The poet commented on this poem in a 1978 interview: ". . . I was trying to say that I am committed to the beauty of nature which I love very much, but that commitment in me anyway always more and more has to be qualified by my returning to my own responsibility as a human being. And the life of a human being is more complicated than the blossoming of a pear tree."[19]

Again we see how far Wright has come since being "nuzzled" by a horse in *Branch* and hoping to blossom. Now he knows that it is neither possible nor desirable for people to step out of their bodies.

Nature is now recognized as an unattainable realm, and as a realm that need not be attained, because the living evidence of our frail humanity borne in our bodies, the evidence of our insignificance, which of all creatures only we can know, is both the source of our pain and disappointment and the source of our ability to sympathize with another's pain, to extend the love that is absent in the nuzzling of a horse or the fragrance of a pear tree's "beautiful natural blossoms." Hank Lazer notes that while Wright "clearly belongs to the American tradition, from Bradstreet to Emerson to Frost to Roethke, that makes nature a symbol of spirit,"[20] in this poem, his attitude is much closer to Frost's than Emerson's. He is too well "versed in country things" to agree with Emerson, in "The American Scholar," that "the ancient precept, 'Know Thyself,' and the modern precept, 'Study Nature,' become at last one maxim."

As I have said, Wright's poetry is a lesson in acceptance and accommodation. But that does not mean it is false or compromised. Wright does what I think every person has to do to live a completed life or to write a fulfilled poetry. Rather than live in anger and write splenetic poems fed by that anger, Wright accepts the fact that his country, culture, and self are imperfect mediums for his artistic and personal growth. In the absence of a perfect medium for his maturation, he makes do with the materials he has been given by nature and the culture. He constructs a poetry of fulfillment, and, judging from the new mood of the poems, a life of fulfillment, by making what he has been given suffice. He learns to see the "secret light" that is part of and essential to the "perilous black" of his country and his soul. Both black and light, death and life, ugliness and beauty, control and release are necessary to constitute a complete life, love, or art. This is the theme we see most clearly in "Beautiful Ohio," the third poem in this volume's concluding triptych. I will quote it in its entirety:

> Those old Winnebago men
> Knew what they were singing.
> All summer long and all alone,
> I had found a way
> To sit on a railroad tie

Above the sewer main.
It spilled a shining waterfall out of a pipe
Somebody had gouged through the slanted earth.
Sixteen thousand and five hundred more or less people
In Martins Ferry, my home, my native country,
Quickened the river
With the speed of light.
And the light caught there
The solid speed of their lives
In the instant of that waterfall.
I know what we call it
Most of the time.
But I have my own song for it,
And sometimes, even today,
I call it beauty.

What a clear indication of the progress Wright has made: Ohio is "beautiful"; Martins Ferry is "my home, my native country"; and even the waste of the culture, for today, is "beauty." The sewer's ugliness is incorporated undiluted into the singer's song, rather than placed next to the beautiful as a separate but equal part of the poet's vision, as was occasionally the case in *Two Citizens*. Here Wright sings the beauty *in* the ugliness, not merely the beauty *and* the ugliness. But what makes that "progress"? Why is this attitude reconciliation rather than a compromised defeat? Because the poet still sees the waste—he does not turn his back to it or choose to write about other, more poetic subjects. His doubts remain, but they are now balanced by and grow out of the same vision as his hopes. He regrets that even for the necessary purpose of carrying away the town's sewage men had to "gouge" a hole in the earth. And while he accepts the "old Winnebago men" as peers, he is teasingly ambivalent about the rest of the residents of Martins Ferry: "more or less" in line 9 squints a bit. It could modify "sixteen thousand and five hundred" and be a neutral modifier of number, or it could modify "people" and be a comment on the unfulfilled lives of the mass of citizens. And finally, he admits that he had to meet beauty halfway. It will not jump across and grab him; he has to *call* it beauty, has to make the choice implied by that verb, has to see, recognize, and identify the beauty around him. He has wanted beauty to overwhelm him. He knows, however, that he has to call its name before it will ever exist for him. That is the poet's and the person's power and duty: to call into human existence the beauty that lies dormant around us. As Marvin Bell said of this volume: "Wright, like the best poets of his generation[,] . . . finds beauty where others might not, looks twice or more where others might not, gives us a chance where others would neither care nor dare to."[21]

The poet is no longer perplexed by the contradiction that beauty needs ugliness, but he embraces it as part of a series of contradictions that are the source of all life (in which death clears the land for new growth), love (in which male and female contribute equally), and art (in which poet and subject illuminate each other). Wright was capable of neither escape nor blissful ignorance, though he was tempted by both, so he had to come to an earned knowledge—one he feels in his bones as well as knows in his brain—of evil, ugliness, and death, a knowledge that is now capable of accepting and redeeming all of life's bitter facts.

7

"To die a good death means to live one's life"

James Wright died of cancer of the tongue on March 25, 1980. *This Journey*, "more or less" completed by Wright before he died, was published by Wright's executrix and wife, Anne, in 1982.[1] I would like to focus on two striking facts about this final volume. The first is that the book is filled with insistent echoes of earlier poems and attitudes, revised now in the "lighter" spirit of *To a Blossoming Pear Tree*. The point is not to deny those earlier, younger words (for "He will not deny, he will not deny his own," *Saint Judas*) but to refine them of their anger and doubt—to acknowledge the facts of life the words point to but to alter the poet's reaction to those facts from rejection and despair to acceptance and hope. Despite his lifelong confrontation with life's horrors, he has managed to do nothing to diminish them. Yet while struggling to overcome what cannot be overcome—humankind's flaws, too numerous and too well known to be listed here, but numbering among them greed, selfishness, willful destruction of beauty, and complacent ignorance—Wright managed, in the process traced by this study, to transform his resistance into acceptance, of others and of himself, his own darkness, his own mortality. As I said in the last chapter, this acceptance, the subtle other side of resistance, strengthened the poet, enlarged his self and his self's power, so that he no longer needed to diminish life's horrors in order to sing life's joys. The result is a continuous consciousness of life's wonders, undiminished by, in fact made more profound by, the equally sharp awareness of life's brutality.

We notice this clearly if we look for a moment at Wright's change in attitude toward death. In his first book, *The Green Wall*, death was the ultimate insult to the young man's aspirations and self-assurance. The initial book was full of the youth's musings on mortality, the brevity of life, the necessity of living one's life now because there may be no later. In other words, *The Green Wall* reads like one long *carpe diem* poem. The death Wright saw in *The Green Wall*, however, was the death of other people and other things, not his own. The result was the arrogance of the smug youth, seemingly confident in his vitality, disdainful of the aged, and condemning others for not living their lives fully. For example, in "The Fisherman," Wright and a friend watch "old men," their "driftwood faces" and "saurian beards." The fishermen are as good as dead to the young poet: "their twine" has "gone slack," and "their blood" has "gone dumb." Behind this arrogance, however, was fear, not confidence: fear that the poet's nerve would fail and that he, too, would become "slack" and "dumb." As Peter Stitt notes, in *The Green Wall*, Wright was "terrified of death."[2]

Those early poems were about all manner of death but were curiously detached from the poet's own experience. Suzanne Juhasz has remarked on a similar trait in Sylvia Plath's early poems. The poems of Plath's first collection, *The Colossus* (1960), were held together, Juhasz claims, by "the perception of the worm in every apple core that breeds . . . a bitter humor, a delight in the knowledge of disintegration and death."[3] This vision is "precocious because it expresses knowledge without experience."[4] The same could be said of the poems in Wright's first book. The poet knew of death but had no real feeling for or "experience" of it. Consequently, he could treat others' mortality as a sign of his superiority. Images of mortality, loss, and separation return in, or rather dominate, this final, posthumous collection. No one, however, would mistake the poems of *This Journey* for those of *The Green Wall*. The attitude and tone of *This Journey* are noticeably different, in part because the death Wright sees now is his own, as Stitt also noted: "the readers of these poems cannot help but feel that the poet is anticipating his *own* death."[5]

This new awareness of his own mortality does not engender the young man's smug delight but the older man's, the dying man's, secure and calm delight. In *This Journey*, again quoting Stitt, "Like Whitman so many years before him, Wright has learned to treat death as a positive force. . . ."[6] The poet's voice here is consistently, rather than occasionally, calm and assured but not at all arrogant, a tribute to the struggles he has made with himself since his first collection of poems. For example, in "The Turtle Overnight," from *This Journey*, the old turtle's "religious face" as it emerges from its shell eradicates all the earlier unpleasant associations of aging: "All the legendary faces of broken old age disappeared from my mind, the thickened muscles under the chins, the nostrils brutal with hatred, the murdering eyes." An "ancient pleasure" replaces the earlier fishermen's "withered" faces, and when the turtle leaves, his absence is not a real loss but simply an opportunity for another part of the world to fill the space vacated by the animal: "So much air left, so much sunlight, and still he is gone."

The poet's attitude has changed also because he now sees that his sources of sustenance are fewer than he had suspected when younger. A young man sees the world as a place of limitless opportunity and wonders why these petrified old men do not take advantage of what life offers. The older poet understands scarcity and desperation and now tells us we would be fools not to take whatever we can get and chew this life to its very roots:

> In Burgundy, beyond Auxerre
> And all the way down the river to Avallon,
> The grass lies thick with sheep
> Shorn only a couple of days ago.
> They shine all over their plump bodies
> In the June mist.
>
> Sheep eat everything
> All the way down to the roots.
>   ("Sheep in the Rain")

Earlier, the sheep's image as cowering, powerless, and frightened ani-
mals would have dominated the poem. Now, the allusion to Chris-
tian sheep, humble and blessed creatures, controls the poem's tone,
and Wright admires the sheep's opportunism:

> Someone has freed them only a little while
> Into the fields, and they have a good life of it
> While it lasts.

In *This Journey*, we see the poet, too, wandering over the fields open
to him and having a "good life of it / While it lasts," chewing every-
thing he sees into a poem. How subtly and almost imperceptibly
the poet has managed to travel in verse from loathing the meta-
phorical sheep he saw in *The Green Wall*, those people who were
content to live dully oblivious to the pain around them, to admiring
the "plump bodies" of these "explorers of the rain," who know how
to feed themselves on whatever they are privileged to find in their
brief lives. And note that this transformation is not capitulation—
Wright has not "given in" to the forces of destruction and hatred he
cursed so vehemently and convincingly earlier. He simply realizes
the sanity of taking what is available and not worrying about what is
unavailable or immutable:

> The trouble with me is
> I worry too much about things that should be
> Left alone.
> The rain-washed stone beside the Adige where
> The lizard used to lie in the sun
> Will warm him again
> In its own time, whether time itself
> Be good or bad.
>   ("Leave Him Alone")

The world is not built on human time. Humankind is not the center.
Sunlight returns, and beauty persists. What should we want to change
about that arrangement? What could we change even if we wanted to?
   Wright takes the evidence of nature's vitality and plenitude to in-

dicate that his life, whatever it may have been or whatever it has come to, and however soon it will end, is justified and good and deserves, rather demands, to be lived out as fully as possible while it is still his. This attitude, this ability to "treat death as a positive force," leading to charity and self-acceptance, is, I suspect, a gift given to only a few as they near the ends of their lives. It is an attitude, however, that is more than a gift in this instance. I would contend, and this study has been an attempt to support this contention, that Wright has earned enlightenment, the wisdom to accept both life and death, by first making peace with the world. His poetry has been, in large part, a quest for the right way to live. And, as these last poems testify, one of the ultimate values of discovering how to live a good life is that it enables one to die a good death.

This discussion of death, and the way Wright's attitude toward it and his tone when discussing it have changed, leads to, and is really inseparable from, the second attribute of *This Journey* that is most striking. As we read the poems, we cannot miss the haunting impression of intense, animal vitality, combined with a keen human awareness of death. Robert Shaw describes that central impression: "Wright's awareness of approaching death can be discerned in these poems—not in any cadaverous quality but rather in a heightened sensitivity to the pulse of vitality everywhere around him."[7] The "vitality" is occasionally human, but often it is the vitality of nature: vines, spiders, hawks, lizards, eels, stingrays, sheep, foxes, butterfly fish, crabs, lightning bugs, tortoises, cicadas, limpets, terns, and sumacs dominate the imagery of *This Journey*. One critic has counted "at least twenty-seven different kinds of animals" in the book.[8] Again like *The Green Wall*, this book is a menagerie, its various animals caught in cages of verse. These animals, however, unlike those in *The Green Wall*, do not bring us lessons of stern refusal or rebellion but lessons of measured acceptance. The poet is checking his conclusions about life against the actual life he meets. The poems are gently didactic; in fact, many poems here mimic the pattern of a sermon: observation of nature (the poet's "text"), reflection, generalization, and then application to the poet's life. Yet the poems are also curiously tentative because we recognize that the poet is testing his philosophy against the standard of verification he has most consistently valued, the natural world. This does not mean that he is turning from humankind's world back to nature's: nature, after *Pear Tree*, can no longer be, as it once was, an impossible standard for imperfect humanity to match. After the lessons of *Pear Tree*, he could never again say, as he did in *The Branch Will Not Break*, "Whatever moon and rain may be, / The hearts of men are merciless" ("Two Poems about President Harding"). Instead, nature is a standard in a new way. The flora and fauna we see are perfect in themselves and are used as mirrors for the poet—"Can I be as content with what I am as these lizards and sumacs are with what they are?" he implicitly asks. The fact that he can use nature as this new kind of standard—as an achievable criterion by which he can measure his human progress, rather than as an alternative to the human world—is in itself evidence of his progress.

Wright is now, as he says, a "jaded pastoralist." The flowers he knows best, he claims, are fireweeds, "the spring leaves of the sumac" (which "Stink only a little less worse / Than the sewer main"), and "the foul trillium" ("Whose varicose bloom swells the soil with its bruise"). He still loves his nature but has no more illusions about its benignity, no need to proclaim its innocence in order to claim its significance. In fact, he claims, "I'm antipastoralist. I've worked on farms and I would never work on another one. I've got up at four o'clock in the morning and shoveled the manure out of the barn and bailed away horse urine. To hell with it."[9] He shows us the continuing "war" that is nature: swallows eat midges, hawks eat swallows, blowflies fatten on the "snaggle" that was once a hawk, and to fly freely is to take "the risk of joy" ("Between Wars"). As Bruce Weigl notes, Wright shows us images of "aggressive, brute nature and the hard lessons of survival learned there."[10] The animals and insects of the world are often indifferent to him because they are secure in their identity, in their bone-knowledge of their existence and place:

> He knows already he is so alive he can leave me alone,
> Peering down, holding his empty mountains.
>   ("Butterfly Fish")

He is not going to visit his palaces
In my sight, he is not going to dance
Attention on the brief amazement of my life.
He is not going to surrender the splendid shadow
Of his throne. Not for my sake. Not even
To kill me.
    ("Entering the Kingdom of the Moray Eel")

Streaked in a green stain,
An insect had flown in,
Quiet on the white leaf, paying
My name no mind.
    ("My Notebook")

She will never know or care how sorry I am that my lungs are not
huge magnificent frozen snows, and that my fingers are not firmly
rooted in earth like the tall cypresses.
    ("Regret for a Spider Web")

Sometimes the animals are openly hostile, which the poet takes humorously:

Once, in some hill trees long ago,
A red-tailed hawk paused
Long enough to look me over
Halfway down the air.
He held still, and plainly
Said, go.
It was no time
For singing about the beauties of nature,
And I went fast.
    ("Contemplating the Front Steps of the Cathedral in Florence
    as the Century Dies")

Wright is not perturbed by hawk's or insect's or eel's reaction because he has become as thick-skinned as the sumac trees of his native southern Ohio, which resist all assaults, including those of hatchet and knife blade, and, almost miraculously, "toward the end of May" open "their brindle buds" and "turn a bewildering scarlet" ("The Sumac in Ohio"). This determination to live is the result, in part, of the sumac's need to resist forces conspiring to kill it: "the sap and coal smoke and soot from Wheeling Steel . . . gather all over the trunk." These are the same forces, of course, that the poet has resisted and gained strength from. Like the tree, he stands his ground ("It is viciously determined to live and die alone, and you can go straight to hell") and is proud of being from this place, "my place / Where I was born and my friends drowned" ("A Flower Passage"). In short, the world of *This Journey* is bountiful, but dangerous. Joy is possible, but risky. Mercy is possible, but "small." Life is good, but brief. Beauty exists, but much of nature is haggard and scarred on the surface. Wright does not simplistically worship nature as a panacea. He does not need to because, even when the sky is dark, as it often is, he has absorbed enough of the sun's rays to warm himself:

> Look, the sea has not fallen and broken
> Our heads. How can I feel so warm
> Here in the dead center of January? I can
> Scarcely believe it, and yet I have to, this is
> The only life I have.
> ("A Winter Daybreak above Vence")

"The only life I have" is a key phrase, and one of the last, in the book. In earlier volumes, Wright had wanted something more than this "only life," but in *This Journey*, stronger now, he takes what he can get, celebrates all vitality, and engages in a dialogue with his former self, whose poems echo through these lines.

"Come, Look Quietly," for example, is a delicate poem that we may compare to "Piccolini" of *Pear Tree*. In "Piccolini," the poet implied, and then just as implicitly rejected, the idea that he had to look at either the fish around his ankles or the Grotte di Catullo. No such need to choose between nature and art is even hinted at in "Come, Look Quietly." Wright looks at a bird, perhaps a nuthatch, on the terrace of his room in Paris:

He has a perfectly round small purple cap on his crown and a
slender long mask from his ears to his eyes all the way across.
Come, look quietly. All the way across Paris. Far behind the bird,
the globes of Sacre Coeur form out of the rain and fade again, all by
themselves. The daylight all across the city is taking its own time.

The poem is unified by the imagery of the bird's "round small purple
cap," repeated in the "globes of Sacre Coeur," and finally reiterated
in the "tiny cones on the outcast Christmas tree" in the last para-
graph. Without changing his perspective, as was necessary in "Pic-
colini," the poet can see both Parisian architecture (humanity's art)
and the bird (explicitly labeled as "wild" to heighten the contrast
between himself and the very domesticated city). By asking us to
look "all the way across" or "all across" three times in the middle
paragraph, Wright asks us to see the metaphyscial connection be-
tween the small bird, the city of Paris, and the people of Paris, all
existing "by themselves" or in their "own time," but all unified by
their quality of being alive, which quality is brought to life for the
reader by the poet's vision, his ability to "look quietly." The poet's
patient attention reveals a world in which no facts are unrelated or
insignificant and in which individual facts do not war with each
other for the poet's allegiance. There is no individual separated from
its context and its life-sustaining role in that field.

In the final paragraph of "Come, Look Quietly," we see that

The plump Parisian wild bird is scoring a light breakfast at the end
of December. He has found the last seeds left in tiny cones on the
outcast Christmas tree that blows on the terrace.

The "outcast" tree (Wright must have read critics' descriptions of his
fondness for outcasts) supports the bird, and the globes of Sacre
Coeur lend the whole poem its sacramental air, making the feeding
of the bird a ritual, investing the work with a religiosity that rounds
out the picture with values as well as facts. Everything contributes
to the poem's atmosphere, which imbues the specific data with
meaning. The atmosphere of the poem is value-laden, making us
forget that facts and values are supposedly separate phenomena.

Even though Wright does not make the theme of the poem explicit, it is clear that the "plump . . . wild bird" (like the spider later in "The Journey") is the focus of the vision because he can gather life (the "light breakfast" of "seeds") from death (the dead and "outcast Christmas tree," appropriately enough, a symbol of the holiday that celebrates the victory over death). Death is again acknowledged as part of life, whereas in "A Christmas Greeting," the poem that set the tone for *Shall We Gather at the River* and the one we recall when reading about this dead Christmas tree, death destroyed the speaker's ability to hope. The cyclical permanence of nature, especially as it engenders hope and affirms the value of human life, which is part of nature, is the theme of this poem and a recurring idea in this volume.

Wright walks a fine line, a line his readers will be familiar with by now, between preciousness and delicacy in "Come, Look Quietly." It is a good poem: he is not sentimental about this cute little bird, yet he clearly draws its frailty; he does not simply appropriate the bird for his own ends but manages to turn the bird's presence to his purpose; he invites the reader to look rather than accuses him of complicity in some crime; he seeks intimacy with the reader without exposing his scars. He is friendly and gentle, without being maudlin. He directs our attention without pushing or raising his voice. He is a good teacher, and, like all the best teachers, he can admit his partial ignorance without allowing that limitation to stifle him. He admits "I don't know" the bird's name in French, but that lack of knowledge does not inhibit him, as it occasionally did in *Two Citizens*. He substitutes his description for the name, replacing a label with a relationship, a static counter with an immediate perception. At one time, Wright would have agreed with Denise Levertov in her poem "The Cold Spring," from *Relearning the Alphabet*:

> What do I know?
> Swing of the
> birch catkins,
> drift of
> watergrass,
> tufts of

> green on the
> trees,
> (flowers, not leaves,
> bearing intricately
> little winged seeds
> to fly in fall)
> and whoever
> I meet now,
> on the path.
> It's not enough.

It *is* enough, now, for Wright: the facts of the world are sufficient. They validate themselves in their "own time," a phrase he repeatedly uses in *This Journey*. It is enough for him to see and point, even if he occasionally takes this attitude to its anti-intellectual limits: "I don't want to know / I want to see," he says in "Small Wild Crabs Delighting on Black Sand."

He is not just teaching us, of course; in an odd way, he is teaching himself, addressing himself as his own reader. He has become so much a part of his poems—his "I" is always present whether that pronoun occurs in a poem or not—that he is like an object in the poem, or a character whose development both writer and reader view with the same interest. Alan Williamson has observed this phenomenon in much "personal poetry" of our era:

> . . . as the poet approaches success in his narcissistic endeavor of
> self-creation, he begins paradoxically to experience his self as if it
> were an external object—circumscribed, defined by laws, imbued
> with its own alien aura or flavor. More and more of himself
> becomes subject to ever broader judgments or prejudicial reactions,
> both others' and, at times, his own. . . . By this strange transaction,
> the poet has become at once subject, for the reader, and object, for
> himself.[11]

I would not call Wright's particular quest for self-creation, "narcissistic," but the rest of Williamson's quotation is applicable. We get the strange sense of the poet-as-external-object most noticeably in those poems of memory. One of the best of those poems, and one of the best in this very good book, is "The Ice House," a one-paragraph work:

> The house was really a cellar deep beneath the tower of the old Belmont Brewery. My father's big shoulders heaved open the door from the outside, and from within the big shoulders of the ice-man leaned and helped. The slow door gave. My brother and I walked in delighted by our fear, and laid our open palms on the wet yellow sawdust. Outside the sun blistered the paint on the corrugated roofs of the shacks by the railroad; but we stood and breathed the rising steam of that amazing winter, and carried away in our wagon the immense fifty-pound diamond, while the old man chipped us each a jagged little chunk and then walked behind us, his hands so calm they were trembling for us, trembling with exquisite care.

The poet becomes a character in an initiation rite. The poem tells of the initiation of the two boys into the hidden mysteries of beauty and magic by two powerful elders. The phrasing is almost biblical ("The slow door gave"), the big-shouldered men are heroic, and the secret is the pure—transient, transparent, but eternal—wonder of life. We can hear the writer trembling with care, for *he* is now the old man in the ice house handing us this fifty-pound diamond for safe-keeping. The transience of ice is misleading, for the memory is as hard as a diamond and will never be worn down, perhaps will even be enhanced, by time. The chunk of ice becomes the Holy Grail retrieved from the Chapel Perilous of a child's memory.

That tone of wonder is characteristic of *This Journey,* and Wright will not allow us to strike it off as a naive or childish response, even if we are sophisticated adult poetry readers who have read too much to be awed easily. He insists that wonder is still a valid, true, and healthy emotional response to the facts of the world. In fact, "The Ice House" serves as an illustration of the idea we were given in the poem immediately prior to it, "Against Surrealism," which begins with an explicit statement of this thesis: "There are some tiny obvious details in human life that survive the divine purpose of boring fools to death." The poet goes on to illustrate with a narrative about an encounter he and his wife had with some chocolate penguins.

They successfully resisted the tempting delectation until "the savage fire of the dog-days" wore them down and they bought three penguins and "snuck them home under cover":

> We set them out on a small table above half the rooftops of Paris. I reached out to brush a tiny obvious particle of dust from the tip of a beak. Suddenly the dust dropped an inch and hovered there. Then it rose to the beak again.

> It was a blue spider.

The world, he repeatedly shows us, is spectacular enough without our improvements, or as Randall Stiffler phrases the idea: "miraculous events take place in real time and real space."[12] The book is comprised of gay, even magical moments, narrated calmly, almost indifferently, as if such moments were only to be expected in this life:

> Laying the foundations of community, she labors all alone. Whether or not God made a creature as deliberately green as this spider, I am not the one to say. If not, then He tossed a star of green dust into one of my lashes. A moment ago, there was no spider there.
> ("Regret for a Spider Web")

In these convincing combinations of unexpected images and ideas with the simplest, most expected sentence structure, we are reminded of the final line of "Lying in a Hammock at William Duffy's Farm in Pine Island, Minnesota" ("I have wasted my life") and of the final three lines of "A Blessing":

> Suddenly I realize
> That if I stepped out of my body I would break
> Into blossom.

That striking combination of the fantastic and the prosaic, both uttered in the most assured of tones, is the standard of these last poems, rather than the exception. The self-consciously oracular tone that used to accompany Wright's pronouncements, as in the final stanza of "The Minneapolis Poem" (*River*), is replaced by a simpler diction and almost Oriental tone of enlightened acceptance here. In *This Journey*, he achieves the religious tone rather plainly and effortlessly, as in "Entering the Kingdom of the Moray Eel":

> Before me, this small bay,
> A beginning of the kingdom,
> Opens its own half-moon.
>
> Solitary,
> Nearly naked, now,
> I move in up to my knees.

He enters the eel's "kingdom" as if he is going to his baptism, but his phrasing is more even and less ceremonial than it would have been in the past. The form (simple sentences in which startling pronouncements or fantastic images are related in a deadpan tone) and the tone become the message—life is a series of amazing moments, and one should never be surprised but always observant and thoughtful.

Even more noticeably than in *Pear Tree*, this book is full of examples of offerings from the world to the observant poet. An anonymous "she" offers him a cluster of grapes in "In Gallipoli"; he is offered "One glittering opihi shell / Bony with light" in "Coming Home to Maui"; "fluttering jewels," a circle of lightning bugs, offer themselves to the poet in "Lightning Bugs Asleep in the Afternoon." The poet, of course, is generous in turn. He offers his hand in "Greetings in New York City" ("Here are mine. They are kind of skinny") and in "To the Silver Sword Shining on the Edge of the Crater" ("Look, I bring you a wild thing, / A token of welcome, a withered thing, / A human hand"). He hands a stone, polished to resemble a tortoise, in "With the Gift of the Alabaster Tortoise." These meetings, greetings, and links proliferate throughout the book, accompanying and reinforcing the unexpected, unsought, and gratuitous leavings of light that he stumbles across. Within everyone and everything, he shows us, there is this secret power of light and life that operates "even if it rains." One simply never knows when beauty is going to be thrust into one's path without warning. In fact, knowing enough to receive gratefully the inexplicable is one's salvation, as the religious imagery in "A Rainbow on Garda" suggests:

> But I am not ready for light
> Where no light was,
> Bardolino risen from the dead, blazing
> A scarlet feather inside a wing.

> Every fool in the world can see this thing,
> And make no more
> Of it than of Christ, frightened and dying
> In the air, one wing broken, all alone.

The poet would not be surprised if, as in Ovid's *Metamorphoses*, trees themselves took new forms:

> Just north of Rome
> An ilex and an olive tangled
> Their roots together and stood one afternoon,
> Caught in a ring of judas
> And double cherry.
> They glared at me, so bitter
> With something they knew,
> I shivered. They knew
> What I knew:
> One of those brilliant skeletons
> Was going to shed her garlands
> One of these days and turn back
> Into a girl
> Again.
>   ("Caprice")

The poet himself just might decide to be transformed:

> I am going home with the lizard,
> Wherever home is,
> And lie beside him unguarded
> In the clear sunlight.

We will lift our faces even if it rains.
We will both turn green.
("Wherever Home Is")

Reality, we understand, is sufficient. Wright "decides," as Weigl notes, "that things are well enough left alone."[13] The longing for escape or a vague transcendence, familiar from earlier volumes, is gone. Death is no longer terrifying. The "tiny obvious" details of life, the blue spiders and jagged pieces of ice, are indeed wonderful in the strictest sense of that world. This idea reminds us of the title of a poem discussed earlier, "Come, Look Quietly": reverently, almost religiously, inspect the world you inhabit. A quotation from Levertov's essay "Some Notes on Organic Form" is appropriate: "It is faithful attention to the experience from the first moment of crystallization that allows those first or those forerunning words to rise to the surface: and with that same fidelity of attention the poet, from that moment of being let in to the possibility of the poem, must follow through, letting the experience lead him through the world of the poem, its unique inscape revealing itself as he goes."[14] "Faithful attention," "the possibility of the poem," "letting the experience lead," "inscape revealing itself"—all ring true for Wright's technique. He is attentive because he trusts that each fact before him is a potential poem, which he can allow to reveal itself if he humbly submits to its presence. The idea goes beyond that, though, as Kevin Stein notes: "Such an attitude possesses a moral and aesthetic urgency, for the duty to keep one's eyes open assumes that there is a preexistent order within the natural world that the attentive person may identify and perhaps learn from."[15] The world, Wright says, contains life-giving, life-sustaining, and meaningful moments so common that one has to be a fool, madman, child, or poet to see them. Or one has to be a fool or madman to overlook them. Yet we have to notice that Wright is not really calling us fools. He has quit accusing us or reminding us of his spiritual superiority. *He* overlooked the chocolate penguins before buying them on a whim; *he* mistook the spider for an irritant to be brushed away. He is too old, wise, and forgiving to take the delight that the young poet took in his superiority to the old fishermen. If we substitute

"Wright" for "Cummings" in this excerpt from one of Randall Jar-
rell's reviews, we have a legitimate complaint about Wright's early
work: "What I least like about Cummings's poems is their pride in
Cummings and their contempt for most other people; the difference
between the *I* and *you* of the poems, and other people, is the poems'
favorite subject. All his work thanks God that he is not as other men
are; none of its says, 'Lord, be merciful to me, a sinner.'"[16] Wright
now asks for mercy and what forgiveness and wisdom he can find.

This notion of reality's plenitude and sufficiency is an idea Wright
has been working with for some time, but I think that if we look
closely we can again see that these last poems are subtly different
from earlier ones that might have enunciated the same philosophy
but with a different attitude. In "With the Shell of a Hermit Crab"
(*Pear Tree*), for instance, the poet looks at a crab, now out of its shell,
and suspects that leaving one's shell may be fatal. In "The Turtle
Overnight," as we recall, the turtle's "emergence" is rejuvenating for
the turtle and poet. The image of gnarled old age, to some extent
surely Wright's self-image, drops from the poet's mind. The shell is
not necessary self-protection but the hopelessly encrusted false im-
ages of aging that need to be shed to reveal the always-young self
beneath. The turtle's "religious face" of paragraph 1, the "impercep-
tible" raising of the turtle's face to the light (there are several such
almost imperceptible raisings of the face to light in the book), and
Wright's reverently phrased "I trust" of paragraph 2 combine to give
the poem its sacramental tone. A faith in what persists informs the
lines. When the turtle leaves, the world converges behind it, as
water converges behind one who walks through it. This could be
taken to indicate the turtle's insignificance or the world's plenitude.
Wright takes it both ways, but without any sorrow that the turtle
(and the poet, too, of course) is unimportant. His ego does not need
to be fulfilled because the world he sees is filled.

His is now an ethics of awareness that does not rely on the unique
moment. In *Pear Tree*, we may get many epiphanies of light. The
light in *This Journey* is more like a continuous glow, not a spotlight
trained on just those special and necessarily rare moments during
which the poet, by some atypical act of intense attention, percep-

tion, or imagination, manages to break through the masks. Wright has always used images of height and depth to describe his quest for values. At times, we feel we should drift off the earth and dig deeper into it simultaneously. This is the intense ambivalence that surrounds the themes of dying and living that run through his work. When images of height and escape dominate, the poems begin to sound deathly, otherworldly, and we sense that the "beyond" is apprehensible only in death or in moments of intense, mystical awareness, scattered in particles like ice floes across a vast, boring ocean of everyday sameness. The beauty and truth of life now seem everywhere, and the poet always looks around him and usually down to the ground, his sight resting almost randomly on the objects that are to become the subjects of his poems. In fact, as Stein says, "The act of attentive seeing is so important to Wright that he can wholly define the value of being human in terms of how good one is at doing it: 'Simply to *be* a man (instead of one more variety of automaton, of which we have some tens of thousands) means to keep one's eyes open.'"[17] Something as simple as the sight of his breath on a cold day is cause for wonder, as if the vapor is his human spirit made visible:

> Somehow I have never lost
> That feeling of astonished flight,
> When the breath of my body suddenly
> Becomes visible.
>   ("Above San Fermo")

We get the impression that even if Wright had not seen the tiny blue spider of "Against Surrealism," he would have seen something else equally remarkable. We sense now that the meanings are here underfoot, rather than above or beyond us, because Wright keeps his attention focused so squarely on the here and now and never contemplates escaping or being lifted away by birds or climbing into the branches of a sycamore. This book truly is, as Weigl notes, "a celebration of the ordinary."[18]

One of the best examples of this "celebration" is the title poem, "The Journey," which finds the poet walking above Anghiari, Italy, when he happens upon a spider web. The web is covered with dust, which Wright loads on with insistent adverbs and participles: the "wind had been blowing . . . for days"; "everything" is "graying gold / With dust"; the spider's web "Reeled heavily and crazily with the dust"; it is "sagging / And scattering shadows among shells and wings." How much can a web bear? There is almost as much dust here as there is snow in Joyce's "The Dead." The mounding on of dust makes the spider's emergence, like the turtle's in an earlier poem, even more unexpected and amazing to the poet: "And then she stepped into the center of air / Slender and fastidious . . . While ruins crumbled on every side of her." She persists, calmly, even fastidiously, literally in the middle of the dust, in the midst of the ruins of human endeavors.

We immediately recognize the spider, of course, as an embodiment of the reality the poet wants to be part of. She could be called a symbol, but that would be to imply that she is not really as remarkable as Wright makes her sound. She would be something the poet temporarily used to make the reader think of another reality. Yet Wright is not using her as a symbol. She is glorious by herself, not as a reminder of something else. She is also very dramatic. She is "the spider." She does not simply walk through a beam of sunlight; she steps "into the center of air," as if she were the only thing moving in the world at the time. And then, as if she did not already have our attention, she pauses for a moment so the poet can reflect on her presence amidst the "ruins." The moment is credible because the poet has slowly narrowed our focus, beginning with all of Anghiari in the opening stanza, narrowing to the hill behind the town, then to the children playing on the hill, then to himself as he stops to rinse his face ("*with* the dust," as Stitt notices, thus making the "omnipresent dust . . . a source of sanctification"[19]), and finally to the small, almost imperceptible spider living quietly and inconspicuously by the side of the road. He narrows our focus because the way to the reality he wants us to see, the way to the spider's reality, is through relaxation, through openness to the possibilities always inherent in the world before our eyes. As he says in another poem in *This Journey*, "You can only hear a spruce tree speak in its own silence" ("A True Voice").

Wright is like the Whitman's poet, described in his 1855 preface to

Leaves of Grass: "He is a seer . . . the others are as good as he, only he sees it and they do not":

> Many men
> Have searched all over Tuscany and never found
> What I found there, the heart of the light
> Itself shelled and leaved, balancing
> On filaments themselves falling.

The others did not find because they sought—"searched" is the key verb here. Wright does not search; he happens upon the truth because he has faith that it will expose itself by itself. Seeking only obscures and blurs the seeker's vision. Notice how Wright discovers the spider in this poem. He walks above Anghiari, through this veritable dust storm, and leans "down to rinse the dust from my face." Then he finds the spider web. He did not seek it; he found it. He did not create the spider's significance; he found it. (Another spider appears to him in a similar fashion in "Regret for a Spider Web." While "thinking about something else," he discovers, "resting beneath my thumbnail," a "star of green dust," a spider.) It is surely difficult to follow this path (and the path image does make us think in religious terms of The Way). It is difficult to need desperately (and Wright has needed as desperately as anyone) and to give oneself up to trust (or faith) in the immanence of value in our everyday world, to avoid the temptation to force significance onto objects (in a symbolist mode) and patiently to seek without seeking. Yet it has to be done. In "To the Cicada," the "Holy Rollers rage all afternoon . . . , Their voices heavy as blast furnace fumes, their brutal / Jesus risen but dumb." When Wright finds, in the same poem, the cicada "asleep on a locust root" one morning, he "carefully breathe[s] on [its] silver body" because the insect is "one of the gods who will rise / Without being screamed at." All Wright's gods rise silently and are found quietly. They never come down to "voices heavy as blast furnace fumes."

How easy it would be with this attitude to be overwhelmed by time, to be daunted by our own insignificance, as simply one mortal creature among many. How difficult to believe in our right and ability to live a dignified life without apology. The spider's message in

"The Journey" is her life, and Wright implies that we each deliver a message by the way we live. Not only his philosophy but also his art are validated by the spider's carefully crafted web, which defies the dust raised by the dissolution of all that is material as well as by the decay of dreams. The tone and message are typical of *This Journey*. Wright does not "rage against the dying of the light" with Thomas or "amaze the ground with anger," as he had done in an earlier poem. He is calmer now because his seeing has taught him something, something much like what Eliot knew in "Burnt Norton":

> To be conscious is not to be in time
> But only in time can the moment in the rose-garden
> The moment in the arbour where the rain beat,
> The moment in the draughty church at smokefall
> Be remembered; involved with past and future.
> Only through time time is conquered.

The difference is, I believe, that Wright does not want to "conquer" time but to live wholly within it. To him, that way of living does not necessitate giving up meaning, for meaning inheres in life's particulars, in its cicadas, spiders, and people, too. Those moments of the "intersection of the timeless / With time," as Eliot called them in "The Dry Salvages," can be had wholly in time. Wright does not seek an escape of time through time, but a deeper appreciation of the values of those numinous moments of time. The final two lines of "Above San Fermo" summarize the poet's attitude toward time: "But spring will do him all right, / For the time being." Everything is transitory, but linked to something permanent, something "all right." Over and over, Wright lovingly examines the small birds and animals he meets in an attempt to "see" them and, in that perception, to apprehend in the temporary and mundane that spiritual food he needs to live, or to confirm, his life. He celebrates what Rilke called the "purely mundane, deeply mundane, blissfully mundane consciousness."[20]

He gives us in the final stanza of "The Journey" a statement that is as close to an overt statement of his philosophy as we will ever get:

> . . . The secret
> Of this journey is to let the wind

> Blow its dust all over your body,
> To let it go on blowing, to step lightly, lightly,
> All the way through your ruins, and not to lose
> Any sleep over the dead, who surely
> Will bury their own, don't worry.

This is his earlier passivity transformed, as was his releasing of the pear-imprisoned bee in "The First Days" (*Pear Tree*). It is an active participation (stepping through) that is respectful rather than willful ("lightly, lightly"). It is a vision that, while recognizing death, is dedicated to life, and that, while aware of life's "dust," is founded on a belief in the fullness of life, not life's emptiness. I am reminded of A. O. Lovejoy's definition of "the principle of plenitude," in particular the provision in the definition that "the world is the better, the more it contains."[21] The "dust" of "The Journey" is the sign of ruin, but also the harbinger of new life, of "more." Wright struggled against the weeds, thickets, and dust in *River*, believing his job was to bring water to dry places. Now he realizes that "the secret" is to take the dust full-face and step through it to the plenitude of which it is part. He steps "through," rather than dreams of flying above. Stepping through is different from transcending—one's feet are on the ground and one's salvation is here, but finding "the secret" still requires intense and precise attention, not passivity. Ahab urges Starbuck to "strike through the mask!" Wright's advice is less violent, less egotistical, and recognizes the role of the mask, or dust or even "them," as part of the plenitude of life for which "the world is the better." The poems become life-affirming, not life-denying; they need not be sentimental to be positive; they can depict sterility without venom and impotent bitterness; they can confront life's "ruins" while only infrequently relying on irony or cynicism to distance and minimize the loss. In short, the poems are simply much more pleasant to read, without any sacrifice in depth of thought or emotion.

The poems of *This Journey* not only go beyond Wright's earlier poems, they build upon each other, and images in the book accumulate richer meanings with each poem. Kathy Callaway identifies a list of "icon-words" in *This Journey* that "are used so repeatedly and conspicuously throughout the book" that they comprise "a single story—or a response, perhaps, to the world."[22] The dust and ruins of "The Journey," for example, work perfectly well within the poem without any outside assistance, but the reader who comes to the poem in the context of *This Journey* is able to appreciate the dust and ruins on another level as well. The book begins in Diana's temple in Nîmes, as the poet thinks of "stone-eyed legions of the rain" and walks between pillars covered with vine leaves. He asks to "find the beginning of one vine leaf there" ("Entering the Temple in Nîmes"). "Stems" and "a heavy ritual stone" appear again in the second poem. A sycamore leaf falls on three-hundred-pound Old Bud Romick in the fourth poem ("Old Bud"). Wright celebrates the "tough leaf branches" of sumacs in the sixth poem, "The Sumac in Ohio." The tree's skin will "turn aside hatchets," we are told. A stone grave monument is the focus of the seventh poem. In the ninth poem, "Wherever Home Is," a "basalt stone" statue of Leonardo da Vinci is covered with wisteria vines, "turning gray and dying / All over his body." The vines and sea wind combine to "crumble Leonardo down." In "The Vestal in the Forum," the twelfth poem, a "cold wind" and roses slip their "fingers into the flaws" of "a stone girl / Pitted by winter." Earlier, in the tenth poem, "A Dark Moor Bird," Wright refers to himself as "standing here, / Turning to stone." By the time we get to "The Journey," the twenty-sixth poem, we have begun to associate stone statues and monuments with crumbling ruins and the poet's own mortality, as contrasted with nature's vines and leaves that persist, that live off the detritus of humankind. So the spider emerging from the world's dust and ruins in "The Journey," a spider with which the poet identifies, is an image of Wright's own resurrection. The echoes in our ears from the other poems not only contribute to our understanding and appreciation of the spider in this poem, they also constitute a "response . . . to the world": humanity's monuments to themselves, constructed specifically to preserve their image, crumble (here we are forced to remember "Ozymandias"); the flaw in our nature, our own mortality (and we have to think also of Adam's flaw), lets the vines and wind wear us down, despite our best efforts to preserve ourselves. In addition, humanity's ego, the motivation for the statues, has to be worn down before enlightenment will present itself. The spider, we realize now, does not accidentally emerge from the ruins; it can *only* emerge from the ruins. The goal is to notice the spider or to grasp the vine leaf, not have a statue built in one's honor.

The passive tone of the poems, then, is not related to physcial passivity at all—"I have to move," he says, "or die" ("Regret for a Spider Web")—but is more an answer to man's delusions of grandeur, his statue-building impulses. The passive stance is an attempt to achieve the "harmony with nature" that Matthew Arnold claims is impossible. Wright addresses the critic directly in "A Reply to Matthew Arnold on My Fifth Day in Fano," which begins with an epigraph from Arnold: "In harmony with Nature? Restless fool. . . . Nature and man can never be fast friends. . . ." The poem itself consists of two paragraphs. Here are the end of the first and beginning of the second paragraphs:

> Briefly in harmony with nature before I die, I welcome the old
> curse:
>
> a restless fool and a fast friend to Fano, I have brought this wild
> chive flower down from a hill pasture.

In the past, when Wright began to long for "harmony with nature" as an escape from the "human town," he increasingly relied on images of sleep, stasis, and death. The implication was that to be like nature is to be dead, for nature is nonhuman, and the only way to achieve harmony with it is to die as a human, to become nothing more than organic matter. Here we see that Wright approaches the task of reconciling himself with nature by imagining a living eternity, something he feels in his bones while alive. He is as old as, older than, the sea:

> To carefully split yet another infinitive, I seem to have been here
> forever or longer, longer than the sea's lifetime and the lifetimes of
> all the creatures of the sea, than all the new churches among the
> hill pastures and all the old shells wandering about bodiless just off
> the clear shore.

He is not dead, but he, or his imagination, is in touch with some-
thing more durable than a human life. "Harmony with nature" in
this context is not a defeat of the poet's humanness, but a sense of
communion with the "infinitive," if you will. Because he no longer
rejects his humanness, he no longer celebrates nature as an escape
from that humanness. He can, therefore, accept nature and incorpo-
rate it in all its forms into his poems without implying by that ac-
ceptance a rejection of, or a need to escape from, the human and
temporal world. He is part of both worlds—nature's and mankind's,
time's and eternity's—which are really one, and no longer makes
himself or the reader choose between the two. This larger vision
allows him to see that his temporal limits are not limits at all, just
as his spatial boundaries do not contain him: he offers a part of him-
self to the sea in the form of a flowering seed:

> I am not about to claim that the sea does not care. It has its own
> way of receiving seeds, and today the sea may as well have a
> flowering one, with a poppy to float above it, and the Venetian navy
> underneath.

This state of cosmic harmony is difficult to understand and cer-
tainly difficult to maintain—he is only "briefly in harmony with
nature"—but it is emphatically not, now, a longing for the death of
his humanness. We hear in the last line a regret that the poet cannot
stay alive with the sea: "Goodbye to the living place, and all I ask it
to do is stay alive." We could read this as a plea by the poet to stay
alive himself, or as a plea by the poet for the sea to stay alive. The
confusion is appropriate in a poem announcing the speaker's union
with nature. The poet will die, but he knows others will continue:

> All I am doing is standing here,
> Turning to stone,
> Believing he will build a strong nest
> Along the Adige, hoping
> He will never die.
>   ("A Dark Moor Bird")

And the poet's death will not really be his end. He will go "to seed among the pear trees," he tells us ("In View of the Protestant Cemetery in Rome") in a line that reminds us of Whitman's "If you want me again look for me under your boot-soles" near the end of "Song of Myself." "The sky holds," he says in another poem ("In Gallipoli"), and that is proof enough for him that there is a "centre" somewhere, or everywhere, and that, despite Yeats, it can "hold."

When we hear the authenticity that we hear in Wright's work in this volume, we know that the poems are not simplistic but are the fruits of a deep understanding of life, the sort of understanding personified by his characters as early as *The Green Wall* and now revealed in the very heart of the poems. The verses are no longer about others who have achieved this "peace that passeth understanding" but are the products of just such an understanding that can see the mysterious in the common and can hammer that insight into art:

> A young man, his face dark
> With the sea's fire,
> Quickens his needle bone through webbing,
> And passes away.
> He moves out of my sight
> And back again, as the moon
> Braces its shoulders and disappears
> And appears again. The young face
> Begins to turn gray
> In the evening light that cannot
> Make up for loss.
> It is morning and evening again, all over the water.
> I know it is only moonlight that changes him, I know
> It does not matter. The sea's fire
> Is only the cold shadow of the moon's,
> And the moon's
> Fire itself only the cold
> Shadow of the young
> Fisherman's face:
> The only home where now, alone in the evening,
> The god stays alive.
> ("Apollo")

The world is a seamless web: the moon has human characteristics ("shoulders"); the fisherman's face takes on the look of moonlight; the "sea's fire" is only the reflection of the moon's light; and the moon's light is only a reflection of the fisherman's face. After reading "the moon's / Fire itself only the cold / Shadow of the . . . ," we expect to see "sun." Instead, we see "the young / Fisherman's face." The man is the source of light but also the beneficiary of the moonlight, which makes him look godlike. Animate and inanimate, fire and water, present (this god of the night water) and past (the gods of mythology), all illuminate one another, gain meaning from one another, become more beautiful because of the other's presence. Apollo, god and man, part of both worlds, is perfectly at home here, for this world is divine. The "light" is diffused equally on all objects: the reflected light of the sea is an active agent, making the man's face look dark and young; the reflected light of the moon is also an active agent, making the man's face look gray and older; the sea itself only reflects the light of the moon, which only reflects the light of the sun, which is associated with the moon. There is no end or beginning to this circle of interdependence.

Circularity, I suppose, is the key: death circles back to life, rejection to acceptance, evil to goodness, and *This Journey* to *The Green Wall*. The book as a whole also forms a circle, the closing poems commenting upon the opening ones. As I said earlier, in this volume's first poem, set in the Temple of Diana in Nîmes, the speaker announces that he does not need much to live, only a small portion of beauty, a square foot of space, before he dies:

> Allow me to walk between the tall pillars
> And find the beginning of one vine leaf there,
> Though I arrive too late for the last spring
> And the rain still mounts its guard.
>   ("Entering the Temple of Nîmes")

He wants to start life over, to find "the beginning" of life, but he realizes that he has missed "the last spring" and that all his beginnings are in the past. The poem starts the book on a mildly plaintive note, as the poet realizes he can never return to what he has left behind. In the book's penultimate poem, entitled "Leaving the Temple of Nîmes" and clearly meant as an answer to the first poem, the poet tells us that he has found what he needs: not a new leaf bud, but instead four mature leaves. The spring that he hoped for in "Entering the Temple of Nîmes" has not really arrived, but the vine, hidden in "the wet darkness of the winter moss," makes it seem like spring. This is not exactly the life he has been searching for, but it is what he has, what his hands can reach, and will therefore have to do, will, in fact, do quite nicely:

> I couldn't see the top of the branches,
> I stood down there in the pathway so deep.
> But a vine held its living leaves all the way down
> To my hands. So I carry away with me
> Four ivy leaves.

This is one more, one final, offering. The last poem in the volume, one that fittingly completes Wright's work, is "A Winter Daybreak above Vence." He ends his career with a poem about daybreak, and with the final word "sunlight." It is a poem about life by a man who knew his own death was near. Clearly, as Thoreau tells us in *Walden*, Wright recognizes that "darkness bear[s] its own fruit," that his darkness has "blossomed," and that what he sees while sitting "on top of the sunlight" is not eternal night but an image of life's fullness and potential. Thoreau's final words in his masterpiece seem an appropriate conclusion for a study of James Wright's poetry: "There is more day to dawn. The sun is but a morning star."

Notes

INTRODUCTION

1. Peter Stitt, *The World's Hieroglyphic Beauty: Five American Poets* (Athens: University of Georgia Press, 1985), 161.
2. Hank Lazer, "'The Heart of Light,'" *Virginia Quarterly Review* 59 (1983): 711.
3. Stitt, *Hieroglyphic Beauty*, 162.
4. Robert Langbaum, *The Poetry of Experience: The Dramatic Monologue in Modern Literary Tradition* (1957; rpt. New York: W. W. Norton, 1971), 16–17.
5. Langbaum, 20.
6. Langbaum, 20.
7. Stitt, *Hieroglyphic Beauty*, 162.
8. T. S. Eliot, "What Is Minor Poetry?", in *On Poetry and Poets* (New York: Farrar, Straus and Cudahy, 1957), 47. Hank Lazer makes this same point in his essay, noted above, p. 723.

CHAPTER 1

1. I have taken my quotations of the poetry in this chapter from Wright's *Collected Poems* (Middletown, Conn.: Wesleyan University Press, 1971).

The Green Wall was originally published by Yale University Press (New Haven, 1957).

2. Northrop Frye, *The Great Code: The Bible and Literature* (New York: Harcourt, Brace, Jovanovich, 1982), 15. Frye uses these terms in a discussion of three types of language (the language of immanence, the language of transcendence, and descriptive language) associated with Vico's three ages of history. I do not mean to appropriate all of the connotations Frye associates with these terms but could not resist employing them since they fit the conflict we hear in *The Green Wall* so well.

3. Lazer, 719.

4. Jerome Mazzaro, "Dark Water: James Wright's Early Poetry," *Centennial Review* 27, no. 2 (Spring 1983): 138.

5. Mazzaro, 144.

6. W. H. Auden, "Introduction" to *The Green Wall*, xiii.

7. This discussion is informed by my reading of Charles Altieri's excellent book, *Enlarging the Temple: New Directions in American Poetry during the 1960's* (Lewisburg, Pa.: Bucknell University Press, 1979). The reader familiar with Altieri's book will notice that it has influenced my reading of contemporary American poetry.

8. James Wright, "The Pure Clear Word: An Interview with Dave Smith," in Wright's *Collected Prose*, ed. Anne Wright (Ann Arbor: University of Michigan Press, 1983), 233.

9. James Seay, "A World Immeasurably Alive and Good: A Look at James Wright's *Collected Poems*," in *The Pure Clear Word: Essays on the Poetry of James Wright*, ed. Dave Smith (Urbana: University of Illinois Press, 1982), 12. (First published in *Georgia Review* 27 (Spring 1973): 71–81.)

10. R. D. Laing, *The Politics of Experience* (New York: Ballantine Books, 1972), 120.

11. C. G. Jung, *The Collected Works of Carl Gustav Jung*, trans. R. F. C. Hull, ed. Sir Herbert Read, Michael Fordham, and Gerhard Adler, vol. 8 (New York: Pantheon Books, 1960), 34–35.

12. R. W. Emerson, "The Poet," in *Selected Writings of Ralph Waldo Emerson*, ed. William H. Gilman (New York: New American Library, 1965), 319.

13. I am indebted to Hank Lazer's article, mentioned above, for an excellent discussion of light in Wright's later books.

14. Chuang Tzu, "Cook Ting," in *The Complete Works of Chuang Tzu*, trans. Burton Watson (New York: Columbia University Press, 1968), 50.

15. Chuang Tzu, 50.

16. Wright explains his relation with Doty in his interview with Dave Smith, reprinted in Wright's *Collected Prose:*

> Some people believe that I was sympathizing with the criminal rather than with the victim. Well, I sympathize with the victim all right. As I have replied at least ten times to people from Martins Ferry who have written to me to protest that poem, I sympathize with the victim. I'm just saying that I sympathize with George Doty, too. I think what annoyed them is somehow that the person who committed this crime ought to be cut off from human fellowship; that is, they believed this and I did not believe it. (212)

17. Robert Frost, "The Figure a Poem Makes," in *Complete Poems of Robert Frost* (New York: Holt, Rinehart and Winston, 1949), vi.

18. Gerald Graff, "The Politics of Anti-Realism," *Salmagundi,* no. 42 (Summer–Fall 1978): 5.

19. Graff, 5.

20. Stephen Stepanchev, *American Poetry since 1945: A Critical Study* (New York: Harper and Row, 1965), 209.

21. Stepanchev, 209.

22. Peter Stitt, "The Art of Poetry XIX: James Wright," *Paris Review* 16 (Summer 1975): 53.

23. Stitt, "The Art of Poetry," 50.

24. Charles Molesworth, *The Fierce Embrace: A Study of Contemporary American Poetry* (Columbia: University of Missouri Press, 1979), 203.

25. Wright admired Lowell's courage in abandoning a style that had proved so successful: "After all *Lord Weary's Castle* is certainly one of the formal masterpieces, not only of American literature but of all poetry in the English language. And yet Lowell became dissatisfied with that and moved on to try something new; this is one of the things that makes him a great writer" ("Something to Be Said for the Light: A Conversation with James Wright," in Wright, *Collected Prose,* 157.)

26. James E. B. Breslin, *From Modern to Contemporary: American Poetry, 1945–1965* (Chicago: University of Chicago Press, 1984), 39. The ten books Breslin mentions (38) are William Meredith, *Love Letter from an Impossible Land* (1944); Reed Whittemore, *Heroes and Heroines* (1946); Howard Moss, *The Wound and the Weather* (1946); Howard Nemerov, *The Image and the Law* (1947); Louis Simpson, *The Arrivistes* (1949); Peter Viereck, *Terror and Decorum* (1950); James Merrill, *First Poems* (1951); Adrienne Rich, *A Change of World* (1951); W. S. Merwin, *A Mask for Janus*

(1952); and John Ashbery, *Some Trees* (1956). Wright's first book, of course, was published in 1957.

27. A. N. Kaul, *The American Vision* (New Haven: Yale University Press, 1963), 16.

28. Roy Harvey Pearce, *The Continuity of American Poetry* (Princeton: Princeton University Press, 1961), 5.

29. Kaul, 14.

CHAPTER 2

1. James Wright, *Saint Judas* (Middletown, Conn.: Wesleyan University Press, 1959).

2. Robert Bly, "The Work of James Wright," in Smith, ed., *The Pure Clear Word*, 83. The essay originally appeared with the same title in *The Sixties*, no. 8 (1966): 52–78, under the pseudonym Crunk. I chose to refer to the reprinted version, assuming it is more accessible to the reader who might want to read the essay in its entirety.

3. William Meredith, "A Steady Stream of Consciousness: Theodore Roethke's Long Journey Out of the Self," in *Theodore Roethke: Essays on the Poetry*, ed. Arnold Stein (Seattle: University of Washington Press, 1965), 47.

4. Bly, "Work," 81.

5. Karl Malkoff, *Escape from the Self* (New York: Columbia University Press, 1977), 84.

6. Malkoff, 84.

7. Malkoff, 84.

8. Matthew Arnold, "The Study of Poetry," in *The Complete Prose Works of Matthew Arnold*, ed. R. H. Super, vol. 9 (Ann Arbor: The University of Michigan Press, 1973), 161.

9. Bly, "Work," 83–84.

10. Bly, "Work," 81.

11. Mazzaro, 142.

12. Mazzaro, 142.

13. Molesworth, 10.

14. Roland Barthes, *Writing Degree Zero*, trans. Annette Lavers and Colin Smith (New York: Hill and Wang, 1977), 75.

15. Barthes, 75.

16. Christopher Clausen, *The Place of Poetry: Two Centuries of an Art in Crisis* (Lexington: The University Press of Kentucky, 1981), 26, 119.

17. Clausen, 1.

18. Clausen, 119.

19. Wright, *Collected Prose*, 213. Peter Stitt, in *The World's Hieroglyphic Beauty*, shows that Wright knew he was leaving behind his past style when he wrote the poem. He dedicated it to James Dickey ("J.L.D."), with whom Wright had "a vigorous correspondence that ultimately led Wright to question his commitment to the traditional forms of English poetry." The dedication is thus "a tribute to the way [Dickey] had inspired Wright towards a greater directness in his work" (168).

A quick glance at the original version of "At the Executed Murderer's Grave," first published in *Poetry* 92 (August 1958): 277–79, shows how much Wright's work matured in the few years after *The Green Wall*. The early version of "Grave" is far different from the form we find in *Saint Judas*. Wright never mentions his name in the 1958 version, and the poem is just a much simpler variation on the *mea culpa* theme:

> . . . Father and citizen,
> Myself, I killed this man:
> For the blind Judges in my heart cried *Stone,*
> Stone the murderer down!

The version in *Saint Judas* is the work of a different poet—it is more direct, less allusive, more a true testament than an attempt to testify while keeping one's hands clean by employing a diction that confesses yet shows that one is still among the anointed:

> Have we not hallowed life by naming life,
> Not shaped the vacant air with the stars' names,
> Lucifer, Venus, out of our savage grief,
> Out of our stupid shames?

The poet of the earlier version is more interested in showing us that he can mention Venus and Lucifer, with the promise that he can also name the stars, than he is in confessing his shame: the situation is reversed in the later version of the poem, and it is that later version that marks the beginning of his poetic "liberation." (I relied on Belle M. McMaster's bibliography, "James Arlington Wright: A Checklist," *Bulletin of Bibliography and Magazine Notes* 31, no. 2 (April–June 1974): 71–82, 88, to help me find the earlier version.)

20. Altieri, Enlarging, 22.

21. Warner Berthoff, *A Literature without Qualities: American Writing since 1945* (Berkeley: University of California Press, 1979), 47.

22. Richard Howard, *Alone with America: Essays on the Art of Poetry in the United States since 1950* (New York: Antheneum, 1969), 578.

23. Mazzaro, 143.

24. Mazzaro, 143.

25. Stitt, *Hieroglyphic Beauty*, 169.

26. Bly, "Work," 82.

27. Lazer, 720.

28. Lazer, 720.

29. Langbaum, 16.

CHAPTER 3

1. James Wright, *The Branch Will Not Break* (Middletown, Conn.: Wesleyan University Press, 1963).

2. Bly, "Work," 92. For similar reactions to *Branch*, see Robert Hass, "James Wright," in Smith, ed., *The Pure Clear Word*, 196–220 (first published in *Ironwood* 10 (1977): 74–96); George S. Lensing and Robert Moran, *Four Poets of the Emotive Imagination: Robert Bly, James Wright, Louis Simpson, and William Stafford* (Baton Rouge: Louisiana State University Press, 1976), 110; Ralph J. Mills, Jr., "Introductory Notes on the Poetry of James Wright," *Chicago Review* 17, nos. 2–3 (1964): 137–39; Shirley Clay Scott, "Surrendering the Shadow: James Wright's Poetry," *Ironwood* 10 (1977): 53; and Stepanchev, 183.

3. Wright, *Collected Prose*, 145.

4. Nicholas Gattuccio, "Now My Amenities of Stone Are Done: Some Notes on the Style of James Wright," *Scape: Seattle, New York*, no. 1 (1981): 31–44 (rpt. in *Concerning Poetry* 15, no. 1 (1983): 61–76).

5. Wright, *Collected Prose*, 82.

6. T. S. Eliot, *Selected Prose of T. S. Eliot*, ed. Frank Kermode (New York: Farrar, Straus and Giroux, 1975), 42.

7. Charles Altieri, *Self and Sensibility in Contemporary American Poetry* (Cambridge, England: Cambridge University Press, 1984), 39, 40.

8. Altieri, *Self*, 36.

9. Altieri, *Self*, 43.

10. Altieri, *Self*, 46–47.

11. Altieri, *Self,* 46.

12. Mazzaro, 150.

13. Alan Williamson, *Introspection and Contemporary Poetry* (Cambridge: Harvard University Press, 1984), 79.

14. Wright, *Collected Prose,* 174.

15. Altieri, *Enlarging,* 25.

16. Altieri, *Enlarging,* 31.

17. Altieri, *Enlarging,* 31.

18. Altieri, *Enlarging,* 36.

19. Williamson, *Introspection,* 68.

20. See, for example, Thom Gunn, "Modes of Control," *Yale Review* 53, no. 3 (Spring 1964): 455; Geoffrey Hartman, "Beyond the Middle Style," *Kenyon Review* 25, no. 4 (Autumn 1963): 752; Howard, *Alone in America,* 578–85; Judson Jerome, "For Summer, a Wave of New Verse," *Saturday Review* 46, no. 27 (6 July 1963): 30; Paul Lacey, *The Inner War: Forms and Themes in Recent American Poetry* (Philadelphia: Fortress Press, 1972) 64; Louis D. Rubin, Jr., "Revelations of What Is Present," *The Nation* 197, no. 2 (13 July 1963): 39. Also see the articles of Mills, Scott, and Stepanchev, mentioned above in n. 2 for this chapter.

21. The letter is in the Theodore Roethke collection of the University of Washington library. I take my quotation from James E. B. Breslin, "James Wright's *The Branch Will Not Break,*" *American Poetry Review,* 11, no. 2 (March–April 1982): 139.

22. Wright, *Collected Prose,* 83.

23. Wright, *Collected Prose,* 83–84.

24. Wright, *Collected Prose,* 276.

25. Wright, *Collected Prose,* 114.

26. Seay, 114.

27. Smith, ed., "Introduction" to *The Pure Clear Word,* xviii.

28. I am concentrating exclusively on those poems Wright translated and as he translated them, rather than on all of Trakl, Vallejo, and Neruda, because, first, I am not an authority on these poets and would not presume to consider the accuracy of Wright's translations or other poems that he did not translate; and second, I am concerned with the poets' influence on Wright, and for that all we need to know is how he understood them, even if his understanding is incomplete or flawed, although I have read no one who claims it is either.

29. Jean Franco, *Cesar Vallejo: The Dialectics of Poetry and Silence* (Cambridge, England: Cambridge University Press, 1976), 252–53.

30. Seay, 114.

31. Williamson, *Introspection*, 82.

32. Wright, *Collected Prose*, 293.

33. Wright, *Collected Prose*, 293.

34. Wright did not play high school football but did play "a lot of football on a sort of semi-pro team," a fact disclosed in an interview with Dave Smith, reprinted in Wright's *Collected Prose*, 191.

35. Breslin, *From Modern to Contemporary*, 42.

36. Hass, 211.

37. Hass, 211.

38. Hass, 210.

39. Berthoff, 37.

40. A. Poulin, Jr., "Contemporary American Poetry: The Radical Tradition," in *Contemporary American Poetry* (Boston: Houghton Mifflin, 1975), 464.

41. Williamson, *Introspection*, 70.

42. Breslin, *From Modern to Contemporary*, 42.

43. Stitt, *Hieroglyphic Beauty*, 174.

44. Frost, vi.

45. Stitt, *Hieroglyphic Beauty*, 175.

46. Breslin, *From Modern to Contemporary*, 43.

47. Stitt, *Hieroglyphic Beauty*, 174.

48. Breslin, *From Modern to Contemporary*, 45.

49. Breslin, *From Modern to Contemporary*, 45.

50. Breslin, *From Modern to Contemporary*, 45.

51. Stitt, *Hieroglyphic Beauty*, 178–79.

52. John Martone, "'I Would Break / Into Blossom': Neediness and Transformation in the Poetry of James Wright," *Publications of the Arkansas Philological Association* 9, no. 1 (Spring 1983): 71.

53. Martone, 66.

54. Williamson, *Introspection*, 66.

55. See the introduction ("Imagined Lives") to David Kalstone, *Five Temperaments* (New York: Oxford University Press, 1977), 3–11.

56. Robert Bly, "The Dead World and the Live World," *The Sixties*, no. 8 (1966): 6.

57. An interesting comparison could be made of "Two Hangovers" and Hardy's "The Darkling Thrush."

58. Bly, "The Dead World," 2.

59. Bly, "The Dead World," 3.

60. Breslin, *From Modern to Contemporary*, 44.
61. James Dickey, *The Suspect in Poetry* (Madison, Minn.: The Sixties Press, 1964), 55–56.
62. In several interviews, Wright refers to himself as "a craftsman, as a Horatian" (see, for example, Stitt, "The Art of Poetry," 38). And he usually revised poems that had appeared in periodicals before allowing them into his books. See McMaster's bibliography for a detailed history of Wright's publications until 1974.
63. Stitt, *Hieroglyphic Beauty*, 171.

CHAPTER 4

1. James Wright, *Shall We Gather at the River* (Middletown, Conn.: Wesleyan University Press, 1968).
2. Stitt, *Hieroglyphic Beauty*, 181.
3. Mazzaro, 152.
4. Renato Poggioli, *The Theory of the Avant-Garde*, trans. Gerald Fitzgerald (New York: Harper and Row, 1971), 110.
5. Stitt, *Hieroglyphic Beauty*, 181.
6. Poggioli, 110.
7. Stitt, *Hieroglyphic Beauty*, 179.
8. Mazzaro, 154.
9. Mazzaro, 154.
10. Stitt, *Hieroglyphic Beauty*, 179.
11. Mazzaro, 154.
12. Stitt, "The Art of Poetry," 52.
13. Edward Lense, "'This Is What I Wanted': James Wright and the Other World," *Modern Poetry Studies* 11, nos. 1–2 (1982): 26.
14. Lense, 26.
15. Maud Bodkin, *Archetypal Patterns in Poetry: Psychological Studies of Imagination* (London: Oxford University Press, 1963), 274.
16. Bodkin, 274.
17. M. L. Rosenthal, *The New Poets: American and British Poetry since World War II* (New York: Oxford University Press, 1967), 17.
18. Emerson, 309.
19. Emerson, 316.
20. Emerson, 320–21.
21. Emerson, 315.

22. Larzer Ziff, *Literary Democracy: The Declaration of Cultural Independence in America* (New York: The Viking Press, 1981), 241.

23. Ziff, 241.

24. Mazzaro, 155.

25. Mazzaro, 154.

26. Albert Camus, *The Myth of Sisyphus and Other Essays*, trans. Justin O'Brien (New York: Random House, 1955), 3.

27. William V. Spanos, "Abraham, Sisyphus, and the Furies: Some Introductory Notes on Existentialism," in *A Casebook on Existentialism* (New York: Thomas Y. Crowell, 1966), 10.

28. William Barrett, *Irrational Man: A Study in Existential Philosophy* (Garden City, N.Y.: Doubleday, 1962), 276.

29. Spanos, 10.

30. See, for example, C. G. Jung, "The Relation between the Ego and the Unconscious," in *Two Essays on Analytical Psychology*, trans. R. F. C. Hull (New York: Meridian Books, 1960), 182–253; "A Study in the Process of Individuation," *The Collected Works of C. G. Jung*, vol. 9, pt. 1; and "Definition 29," *Psychological Types*, in *The Collected Works of C. G. Jung*, vol. 6.

31. Rosenthal, 238.

32. John Bayley, "On John Berryman," *Contemporary Poetry in America: Essays and Interviews*, ed. Robert Boyers (New York: Shocken Books, 1974), 67.

33. Bayley, 67.

34. Bayley, 68.

35. Williamson, *Introspection*, 12.

36. Williamson, *Introspection*, 25.

37. Stitt, *Hieroglyphic Beauty*, 184.

38. Thomas Hardy, *The Return of the Native* (1878; rpt. New York: Penguin Books, 1978), 123.

CHAPTER 5

1. James Wright, *Two Citizens* (New York: Farrar, Straus and Giroux, 1973).

The reader may want to know that although I am calling these poems the beginning of Wright's mature work, the poet seems to have disagreed. Wright himself was not happy with the book and said so in his *Paris Review* interview (16 (Summer 1975): 34–61) with Peter Stitt: "I've never written any book I've detested so much. No matter what anybody thinks about it, I know this book is final. God damn me if I ever write another" (56). In a 1979 interview (published in 1980 in *American Poetry Review* and reprinted in Wright's *Collected Prose*, from which I quote) he says: "I forget what I was thinking of at the time. I feel this way about almost everything in my book *Two Citizens*. The book is just a bust. I will never reprint it (222)."

I should also mention here that I do not plan to discuss the "New Poems" as a unit because I do not think they are a unit. They seem to me to be a loose collection of poems that Wright apparently liked, but which he thought did not fit together well enough to be a book themselves and did not fit the pattern of *Two Citizens* or any other book well enough to be included there. Some of the "New Poems," however, are relevant to the points I make in this chapter and will be discussed as the need arises.

2. Williamson, *Introspection*, 66.

3. Smith, ed., *The Pure Clear Word*, 177. Smith defends Wright's language in *Two Citizens*, but others have been more critical. See especially Edward Butscher, "The Rise and Fall of James Wright," *Georgia Review* 28 (Spring 1974): 257–68, and Calvin Bedient, "Two Citizens," *New York Times Book Review*, 11 August 1974, 6.

4. Wright, *Collected Prose*, 291.

5. Laurence Lieberman, "The Shocks of Normality," *Yale Review* 63, no. 3 (Spring 1974): 468.

6. Williamson, *Introspection*, 69.

7. Seay, 116.

8. James Wright, "From a Letter," in *Naked Poetry: Recent American Poetry in Open Forms*, ed. Stephen Berg and Robert Mezey (New York: Bobbs-Merrill, 1969), 287.

9. Seay, 122.

10. Seay, 121. Seay is speaking specifically of "A Secret Gratitude" and "Blue Teal's Mother" in "New Poems," but the remarks are relevant to "Ars Poetica" also.

11. Harry Stack Sullivan, *Conceptions of Modern Psychiatry* (1940; rpt. New York: W. W. Norton, 1953), 44.

12. Kevin Stein, *James Wright, the Poetry of a Grown Man: Constancy and Transition in the Work of James Wright* (Athens: Ohio University Press, 1989), 117

13. Stein, 117.

14. Stein, 117.

15. Smith, ed., *The Pure Clear Word*, 187.

16. Wright, *Collected Prose,* 252.

17. Williamson, *Introspection,* 85.

18. Smith, ed., *The Pure Clear Word,* 186.

19. Wright, *Collected Prose,* 293.

20. I am relying here on a reproduction of the painting in James H. Beck, *Raphael* (New York: Abrams, 1976), 148–49.

21. Lieberman, 472.

22. Smith, ed., *The Pure Clear Word,* 176.

23. Lieberman, 471.

CHAPTER 6

1. James Wright, *To a Blossoming Pear Tree* (New York: Farrar, Straus and Giroux, 1977).

The reader will notice that many of the poems discussed here are what we commonly call "prose poems." I would like not to get into a debate over terminology. Wright rejected the term *prose poem* in an interview conducted by David Smith, first published in 1980 in the *American Poetry Review* and reprinted in Wright's *Collected Prose,* from which the following is taken: "The French can talk about the prose-poem and do so effectively just because they can use a phrase like that and everybody knows that people may disagree with one another about these terms. But everybody in the controversy also knows that the prose-poem is a term of convenience (209)." The matter of finding a term, then, for these poems, or these prose pieces, is not a primary problem. First, we must read them carefully, as we must any product of a poet's mind. Second, we must notice that they seem a natural last step in the evolution of Wright's poetic form, from metered and rhymed verse to free verse and finally to prose poetry. And third, we should remember that Wright's formal changes are parts of a continually evolving artistic and personal relationship to the world. For example, the prose form he now uses freely gives the poem the look of a logical, orderly movement, something Wright has tried to avoid in his poems since *Saint Judas.* Prose is often thought of as the practical medium, the medium of ratiocination and logic, as opposed to poetry, the medium of the imagination. Wright's use of prose to create a poem indicates that he feels strong enough now to use "their" form, confident in his status as person and poet, and not worried that he will be implicated, for instance, in their destruction of the redwings we see in the first poem in *Pear Tree.*

2. Wright, *Collected Prose*, 232–33.

3. Peter Serchuk, "James Wright: The Art of Survival," *Hudson Review,* 31, no. 3 (Autumn 1978): 549.

In addition to those reviews quoted in the text, see also Robert Pinsky, "Light, Motion, Life," *Saturday Review,* 21 January 1978, 47–49; and Peter Stitt, "Poetry Chronicle," *Georgia Review* 32, no. 3 (Fall 1978): 691–99.

4. Randall Stiffler, "The Renconciled Vision of James Wright," *Literary Review* 28, no. 1 (1984): 77.

5. Linda Pastan, review of *To a Blossoming Pear Tree, Library Journal,* 15 December 1977, 2503.

6. Hayden Carruth, "The Passionate Few," *Harper's* 256 (June 1978): 87.

7. Stitt, "The Art of Poetry," 52.

8. Serchuk, 548.

9. Joseph Campbell, *The Hero with a Thousand Faces* (Princeton: Princeton University Press, 1968), 29.

10. Campbell, 37.

11. Campbell, 37.

12. Campbell, 41.

13. Here I must disagree somewhat with a point Kevin Stein makes in his very helpful book on Wright. Stein contends that in *Pear Tree* and *This Journey,* when Wright "addresses his reader as 'you,' he now embraces rather than shuns that reader, effectively ending his isolation from both audience and poem" (144). I agree that Wright here does not "shun" the reader, but he does not "embrace" the reader, either. Instead, he accuses the reader, which, since Wright calls himself guilty also, does effectively end "his isolation from [his] audience," but not, I think, in the form of an "embrace."

14. Serchuk, 548.

15. Stiffler, 91.

16. Richard Howard, "James Wright's Transformations," *New York Arts Journal,* no. 8 (February–March, 1978): 23.

17. Stein, 144.

18. Campbell, 29.

19. Wright, *Collected Prose,* 186.

20. Lazer, 721.

21. Marvin Bell, "That We Keep Them Alive," *Poetry* 136 (June 1980), 165.

CHAPTER 7

1. James Wright, *This Journey* (New York: Random House, 1982). The phrase "more or less" is taken from "A Note on the Text of *This Journey*," written by Anne Wright.

The "Note" is a handy bit of information to have, but its second paragraph leaves out some useful information. Anne Wright reports that when Donald Hall, Jane Kenyon, Galway Kinnell, Ines Kinnell, and she met to discuss the poems and the comments others had made on the poems in manuscript (the others including Robert Bly, Hayden Carruth, John Logan, and Robert Mezey), "it was decided to remove two unfinished poems and three others, and a few changes in the order of the poems were made." One wonders what changes in the order were made and why, on what basis the two poems were deemed "unfinished," and why those "three others" were omitted without explanation. Since James Wright described the book as only "more or less done," one assumes that the poet was contemplating some changes, but were the changes that the group made those changes that the poet was considering? Did the poet express reservations about those poems deleted? About the order of the poems? Of course, the poet's wife and executrix had the right to do what she wanted with the poems, even not publish them, and considering the talent of those reading the manuscript, one has to grant that the book may be better with the changes. But as these are Wright's last poems and this is his final book, the juggling of the order and omitting of five poems could be explained in more detail. (I should mention that Bruce Weigl, in "How Lovely a Music We Make: James Wright's *This Journey*, *Poet Lore* 78, no. 2 (Summer 1983): 103–14, also expresses reservations about the "ambiguous note" (104) on the text.)

2. Stitt, *Hieroglyphic Beauty*, 191.

3. Suzanne Juhasz, *Naked and Fiery Forms: Modern American Poetry by Women, a New Tradition* (New York: Harper and Row, 1976), 91.

4. Juhasz, 91.

5. Stitt, *Hieroglyphic Beauty*, 189.

6. Stitt, *Hieroglyphic Beauty*, 191.

7. Robert B. Shaw, "Exploring the Ruins," *The Nation* 235, no. 4 (7–14 August 1982): 118.

8. Kathy Callaway, "The Very Rich Hours of the Duke of Fano," *Parnassus* 11, no. 1 (Fall–Winter 1983): 64.

9. Wright, quoted in Stitt, *Hieroglyphic Beauty*, 187.

10. Weigl, 110.

11. Williamson, *Introspection*, 12.

12. Stiffler, 78.

13. Weigl, 108.

14. Denise Levertov, "Some Thoughts on Organic Form," in *The Poet in the World* (New York: New Directions, 1973), 9.

15. Stein, 164.

16. Randall Jarrell, "A Poet's Own Way," in *Kipling, Auden & Co.: Essays and Reviews, 1935–1964* (New York: Farrar, Straus and Giroux, 1980), 202.

17. Stein, 164.

18. Weigl, 111.

19. Stitt, *Hieroglyphic Beauty*, 190.

20. Rainer Maria Rilke, *Duino Elegies*, trans. J. B. Leishman and Stephen Spender (New York: W. W. Norton, 1963), 128.

21. Arthur O. Lovejoy, *The Great Chain of Being: A Study of the History of an Idea* (Cambridge: Harvard University Press, 1942), 52.

22. Callaway, 63–64.

Bibliography

I. WORKS BY JAMES WRIGHT

A. Poetry, Arranged Chronologically

The Green Wall. New Haven: Yale University Press, 1957.

Saint Judas. Middletown, Conn.: Wesleyan University Press, 1959.

The Lion's Tale and Eyes: Poems Written Out of Laziness and Silence. Madison, Minn.: The Sixties Press, 1962. (Includes poems written by William Duffy, Robert Bly, and Wright.)

The Branch Will Not Break. Middletown, Conn.: Wesleyan University Press, 1963.

Shall We Gather at the River. Middletown, Conn.: Wesleyan University Press, 1968.

Collected Poems. Middletown, Conn.: Wesleyan University Press, 1971.

Two Citizens. New York: Farrar, Straus and Giroux, 1973.

Moments of the Italian Summer. Washington, D.C.: Dryad Press, 1976.

To a Blossoming Pear Tree. New York: Farrar, Straus and Giroux, 1977.

A Reply to Matthew Arnold. Durango, Colo.: Logbridge-Rhodes, 1981.

Leave It to the Sunlight. Durango, Colo.: Logbridge-Rhodes, 1981.

The Summers of James and Anne Wright. New York: Sheep Meadow Press, 1981.

This Journey. New York: Random House, 1982.

A Secret Field. Ed. Anne Wright. Durango, Colo.: Logbridge-Rhodes, 1985.

B. Prose

Collected Prose. Ed. Anne Wright. Ann Arbor: University of Michigan Press, 1983. (Several of Wright's reviews are not included in this volume, including the following: "Delicasies, Horse-Laughs, and Sorrows," *Yale Review* 47, no. 4 (Summer 1958): 608–13; "Some Recent Poetry," *Sewanee Review* 66, no. 4 (Autumn 1958): 657–58; "Son of *New Poets*," *Minnesota Review* 3, no. 1 (Fall 1962): 133–36.)

The Delicacy and Strength of Lace: Letters between Leslie Marmon Silko and James Wright. Ed. Anne Wright. St. Paul: Graywolf Press, 1986.

C. Translations

Char, Rene. *Hypnos Waking.* Trans. James Matthews, with Barbara Howes, W. S. Merwin, William Jay Smith, Richard Wilbur, William Carlos Williams, and Wright. New York: Random House, 1956.

Guillen, Jorge. *Cantico: A Selection.* Ed. Norman Thomas di Giovanni. Boston: Little, Brown, 1965.

Hesse, Herman. *Poems.* New York: Farrar, Straus and Giroux, 1970.

Hesse, Herman. *Wanderings: Notes and Sketches.* New York: Farrar, Straus and Giroux, 1973.

Neruda, Pablo. *Twenty Poems.* Trans. Wright and Robert Bly. Madison, Minn.: The Sixties Press, 1968.

Neruda, Pablo, and Cesar Vallejo. *Selected Poems,* New York: Signet, 1964.

Storm, Theodor. *The Rider on the White Horse.* New York: Signet, 1964.

Trakl, George. *Twenty Poems of George Trakl.* Trans. Wright, Robert Bly, and John Knoepfle. Madison, Minn.: The Sixties Press, 1961.

Vallejo, Cesar. *Twenty Poems of Cesar Vallejo.* Trans. Wright, Robert Bly, and John Knoepfle. Madison, Minn.: The Sixties Press, 1962.

II. SECONDARY SOURCES

Alteri, Charles. *Enlarging the Temple: New Directions in American Poetry during the 1960's.* Lewisburg, Pa.: Bucknell University Press, 1979.

———. *Self and Sensibility in Contemporary American Poetry.* Cambridge, England: Cambridge University Press, 1984.

Auden, W. H. "Introduction" to *The Green Wall,* by James Wright. New Haven: Yale University Press, 1957.

Berg, Stephen, and Robert Mezey, eds. *Naked Poetry: Recent American Poetry in Open Forms.* New York: Bobbs-Merrill, 1969.

Berthoff, Warner. *A Literature without Qualities: American Writing since 1945.* Berkeley: University of California Press, 1979.

Blakeley, Roger. "Form and Meaning in the Poetry of James Wright." *South Dakota Review* 25, no. 2 (Summer 1987): 20–30.

Bly, Robert. "The Dead World and the Live World." *The Sixties,* no. 8 (1966): 2–7.

———. *Leaping Poetry: An Idea with Poems and Translations.* 1972; rpt. Boston: Beacon Press, 1975.

———. "A Note on James Wright." *Ironwood* 10 (1977): 64–65.

———. "The Work of James Wright." In *The Pure Clear Word: Essays on the Poetry of James Wright,* ed. Dave Smith, 78–98. Urbana: University of Illinois Press, 1982. (First published by Crunk [pseudo.] in *The Sixties,* no. 8 (1966): 52–78.)

Breslin, James E. B. *From Modern to Contemporary: American Poetry, 1945–1965.* Chicago: University of Chicago Press, 1984.

———. "James Wright's *The Branch Will Not Break.*" *American Poetry Review* 11, no. 2 (March–April 1982): 139–46.

Breslin, Paul. "How to Read the New Contemporary Poetry." *American Scholar* 47 (Summer 1978): 357–70.

Brooks, Cleanth. *Modern Poetry and the Tradition.* 1939; rpt. Chapel Hill: University of North Carolina Press, 1967.

Bugeja, Michael. "James Wright: The Mastery of Personification in *This Journey.*" *Mid-American Review* 4, no. 2 (Fall 1984): 106–15.

Butscher, Edward. "The Rise and Fall of James Wright." *Georgia Review* 28 (Spring 1974): 257–68.

Cambon, Glauco. *The Inclusive Flame: Studies in American Poetry.* Bloomington: Indiana University Press, 1965.

Carroll, Paul. *The Poem in Its Skin.* Chicago: Follett, 1968.

Clausen, Christopher. *The Place of Poetry: Two Centuries of an Art in Crisis.* Lexington: The University Press of Kentucky, 1981.

Coles, Robert. "James Wright: One of Those Messengers." *American Poetry Review* 2, no. 4 (1973): 36–37.

Collier, S. J. "Max Jacob and the 'Poeme en Prose.'" *Modern Language Review* 51, no. 4 (October 1956): 522–35.

Costello, Bonnie. "James Wright: Returning to the Heartland." *New Boston Review* 5 (August–September 1980): 12–14.

Davis, William V. "'A Grave in Blossom': A Note on James Wright." *Contemporary Poetry: A Journal of Criticism* 4, no. 3 (1982): 1–3.

DeFrees, Madeline. "James Wright's Early Poems: A Study in 'Convulsive' Form." *Modern Poetry Studies* 2 (1979): 241–51.

Dickey, James. *Babel to Byzantium: Poets and Poetry Now.* New York: Farrar, Straus and Giroux, 1967.

———. "In the Presence of Anthologies." *Sewanee Review* 66 (Spring 1958): 294–314.

———. *The Suspect in Poetry.* Madison, Minn.: The Sixties Press, 1964.

Dougherty, David C. "James Wright: The Murderer's Grave in the New Northwest." *The Old Northwest: A Journal of Regional Life and Letters* 2, no. 1 (1976): 45–54.

———. "The Skeptical Poetry of James Wright." *Contemporary Poetry: A Journal of Criticism* 2, no. 2 (1977): 4–10.

Engel, Bernard F. "The Universality of James Wright." *Society for the Study of Midwestern Literature Newsletter* 10, no. 3 (1980): 26–28.

Friedman, Norman. "The Wesleyan Poets III: The Experimental Poets." *Chicago Review* 19, no. 2 (1967): 52–73.

Gattuccio, Nicholas. "Now My Amenities of Stone Are Done: Some Notes on the Style of James Wright." *Scape: Seattle, New York,* no. 1 (1981): 31–44. Rpt. in *Concerning Poetry* 15, no. 1 (1983): 61–76.

Gerke, Robert S. "Ritual, Myth, and Poetic Language in the Poetry of James Wright." *Bulletin of the West Virginia Association of College English Teachers* 7 (Spring 1982): 17–23.

Graves, Michael. "Crisis in the Career of James Wright." *Hollins Critic* 22, no. 5 (December 1985): 1–9.

———. "A Look at the Ceremonial Range of James Wright." *Concerning Poetry* 16, no. 2 (1983): 43–54.

Hall, Donald, ed. *Contemporary American Poetry.* Harmondsworth, England: Penguin Books, 1962.

Harris, Victoria. "James Wright's Odyssey: A Journey from Dualism to Incorporation." *Contemporary Poetry: A Journal of Criticism* 3, no. 3 (1978): 56–74.

Hass, Robert. "James Wright." In *The Pure Clear Word: Essays on the Poetry of James Wright,* ed. Dave Smith, 196–220. Urbana: University of Illinois Press, 1982. (First published in *Ironwood* 10 (1977): 74–96.)

Heffernan, Michael. "'To Catch a Lizard by the Shoulder': James Wright as Crypto-Sonneteer." *Poet and Critic* 18, no. 1 (Fall 1986): 50–53.

Howard, Richard. *Alone with America: Essays on the Art of Poetry in the United States since 1950.* New York: Atheneum, 1969.

———. "James Wright's Transformations." *New York Arts Journal,* no. 8 (February–March 1978): 22–23.

———. "My Home, My Native Country: James Wright." *Ironwood* 10 (1977): 101–10.

Ignatow, David. "What I Feel at the Moment Is Always True." *Ironwood* 10 (1977): 45–46.

Jackson, Richard. "The Time of the Other: James Wright's Poetry of Attachments." *Chowder Review* 10–11 (1978): 126–144.

Janssens, G. A. M. "The Present State of American Poetry: Robert Bly and James Wright." *English Studies* 51, no. 2 (April 1970): 112–37.

Jarrell, Randall. *Poetry and the Age.* New York: Knopf, 1953.

Jauss, David. "Wright's 'Lying in a Hammock at William Duffy's Farm in Pine Island, Minnesota.'" *Explicator* 41, no. 1 (Fall 1982): 54–55.

Kalaidjian, Walter. "'Many of Our Waters': The Poetry of James Wright." *Boundary 2: A Journal of Postmodern Literature* 9, no. 2 (1981): 101–21.

Kelly, Robert. "Notes on the Poetry of the Deep Image." *Trobar* 2 (1961): 14–16.

Lacey, Paul. *The Inner War: Forms and Themes in Recent American Poetry.* Philadelphia: Fortress Press, 1972.

Langbaum, Robert. *The Poetry of Experience: The Dramatic Monologue in Modern Literary Tradition.* 1957; rpt. New York: W. W. Norton, 1971.

Lense, Edward. "'This Is What I Wanted': James Wright and the Other World." *Modern Poetry Studies* 11, nos. 1–2 (1982): 19–32.

Lensing, George S., and Ronald Moran. *Four Poets of the Emotive Imagination: Robert Bly, James Wright, Louis Simpson, and William Stafford.* Baton Rouge: Louisiana State University Press, 1976.

Lieberman, Laurence. *Unassigned Frequencies: American Poetry in Review, 1964–1977.* Urbana: University of Illinois Press, 1977.

Logan, John. "The Prose of James Wright." *Ironwood* 10 (1977): 154–55.

McDonald, Walter. "Blossoms of Fire: James Wright's Epiphany of Joy." *Conference of the College Teachers of English Proceedings* 46 (September 1981): 22–28.

McPherson, Sandra. "You Can Say That Again (Or Can You?)." *Iowa Review* 3, no. 3 (Summer 1972): 70–75.

Malkoff, Karl. *Escape from the Self: A Study of Contemporary American Poetry and Poetics.* New York: Columbia University Press, 1977.

Martone, John. "'I Would Break / Into Blossom': Neediness and Transformation in the Poetry of James Wright." *Publications of the Arkansas Philological Association* 9, no. 1 (Spring 1983): 64–75.

Matthews, William. "The Continuity of James Wright's Poems." *Ohio Review* 18, no. 2 (Spring–Summer 1977): 44–57.

Mazzaro, Jerome. "Dark Water: James Wright's Early Poetry." *Centennial Review* 27, no. 2 (Spring 1983): 135–55.

Mills, Ralph J., Jr. *Contemporary American Poetry.* New York: Random House, 1965.

———. *Creation's Very Self.* Fort Worth: Texas Christian University Press, 1969.

———. *Cry of the Human: Essays on Contemporary American Poetry.* Urbana: University of Illinois Press, 1975.

———. "Introductory Notes on the Poetry of James Wright." *Chicago Review* 17, nos. 2–3 (1964): 128–43.

Molesworth, Charles. *The Fierce Embrace: A Study of Contemporary American Poetry.* Columbia: University of Missouri Press, 1979.

———. "James Wright and the Dissolving Self." In *Contemporary Poetry in America: Essays and Interviews,* ed. Robert Boyers, 267–78. New York: Schocken Books, 1974.

Morgan, Bruce. "In Ohio: A Town and the Bard Who Left It." *Time,* 19 October 1987, 9–10.

Nathan, Leonard. "The Traditional James Wright." *Ironwood* 10 (1977): 131–37.

———. "The Tradition of Sadness and the American Metaphysic: An Interpretation of the Poetry of James Wright." In *The Pure Clear Word: Essays on the Poetry of James Wright,* ed. Dave Smith, 159–74. Urbana: University of Illinois Press, 1982.

Nelson, Cary. *Our Last First Poets: Vision and History in Contemporary American Poetry.* Urbana: University of Illinois Press, 1981.

Orlen, Steven. "The Green Wall." *Ironwood* 10 (1977): 109–28.

Pearce, Roy Harvey. "The Burden of Romanticism: Toward the New Poetry." *Iowa Review* 2 (Spring 1971): 109–28.

———. *The Continuity of American Poetry.* Princeton: Princeton University Press, 1961.

Pinsky, Robert. *The Situation of Poetry: Contemporary Poetry and Its Traditions.* Princeton: Princeton University Press, 1976.

Poggioli, Renato. *The Theory of the Avant-Garde.* Trans. Gerald Fitzgerald. New York: Harper and Row, 1971.

Poulin, A., Jr. *Contemporary American Poetry.* Boston: Houghton Mifflin, 1975.

Rosenthal, M. L. *The New Poets: American and British Poetry since World War II.* New York: Oxford University Press, 1967.

Saunders, William S. "Indignation Born of Love: James Wright's Ohio Poems." *The Old Northwest: A Journal of Regional Life and Letters* 4 (1978): 353–69.

———. *James Wright: An Introduction.* Columbus: State Library of Ohio, 1979.

Scott, Shirley Clay. "Surrendering the Shadow: James Wright's Poetry." *Ironwood* 10 (1977): 46–63.

Serchuk, Peter. "On the Poet, James Wright." *Modern Poetry Studies* 10, nos. 2–3 (1981): 85–90.

Smith, Dave. "That Halting, Stammering Movement." *Ironwood* 10 (1977): 111–30.

———, ed. *The Pure Clear Word: Essays on the Poetry of James Wright.* Urbana: University of Illinois Press, 1982.

Spendal, R. J. "Wright's 'Lying in a Hammock at William Duffy's Farm in Pine Island, Minnesota.'" *Explicator* 34, no. 9 (May 1976): item 64.

Stein, Kevin. *James Wright, the Poetry of a Grown Man: Constancy and Transition in the Work of James Wright.* Athens: Ohio University Press, 1989.

Stepanchev, Stephen. *American Poetry since 1945: A Critical Study.* New York: Harper and Row, 1965.

Stiffler, Randall. "The Reconciled Vision of James Wright." *Literary Review* 28, no. 1 (1984): 77–92.

Stitt, Peter. "The Garden and the Grime." *Kenyon Review* 6, no. 2 (1984): 76–91.

———. "The Poetry of James Wright." *Minnesota Review* 2 (Spring 1972): 13–29.

———. "The Quest Motif in *The Branch Will Not Break.*" In *The Pure Clear Word: Essays on the Poetry of James Wright,* ed. Dave Smith, 65–77. Urbana: University of Illinois Press, 1982.

———. *The World's Hieroglyphic Beauty: Five American Poets.* Athens: University of Georgia Press, 1985.

Taylor, Henry. "In the Mode of Robinson and Frost." In *The Pure Clear*

Word: Essays on the Poetry of James Wright, ed. Dave Smith, 49–64. Urbana: University of Illinois Press, 1982.

Thompson, Phyllis Hoge. "James Wright: His Kindliness." *Ironwood* 10 (1977): 97–100.

Van den Heuvel, Cor. "The Poetry of James Wright." *Mosaic* 7 (Spring 1974): 163–70.

Williams, Miller. "James Wright, His Poems: A Kind of Overview, in Appreciation." In *The Pure Clear Word: Essays on the Poetry of James Wright*, ed. Dave Smith, 234–46. Urbana: University of Illinois Press, 1982.

Williamson, Alan. "History Has to Live with What Was Here." *Shenandoah* 25 (Winter 1974): 85–91.

———. *Introspection and Contemporary Poetry.* Cambridge: Harvard University Press, 1984.

———. "Language against Itself: The Middle Generation of Contemporary Poets." In *American Poetry since 1945: Some Critical Perspectives*, ed. Robert Shaw, 55–67. Cheadle, England: Carcanet Press, 1973.

Wright, Anne. "A Horse Grazes in My Long Shadow: A Short Biography of James Wright." *E.N.V.O.Y.*, Spring–Summer 1981, 1–5.

Wright, Franz. "Some Thoughts on My Father." *Poets and Writers Magazine* 15, no. 1 (1987): 20–21.

Yenser, Stephen. "Open Secret." *Parnassus* 6 (1978): 125–42.

III. REVIEWS

A. The Green Wall

Booth, Phillip. "World Redeemed." *Saturday Review,* 20 July 1957, 18.

Fitts, Dudley. "Five Young Poets." *Poetry* 94, no. 5 (August 1959): 333–39.

Mazzaro, Jerome. Review of *The Green Wall. Poetry Broadside* 1, no. 3 (Winter 1957): 6, 10.

Nathan, Leonard. Review of *The Green Wall. Voices* 165 (1958): 51–53.

Nemerov, Howard. "Younger Poets: The Lyric Difficulty." *Kenyon Review* 20 (Winter 1958): 25–37.

Palmer, J. E. "The Poetry of James Wright: A First Collection." *Sewanee Review* 65 (Autumn 1957): 687–93.

Simon, John. Review of *The Green Wall. Audience* 5, no. 2 (1958): 98–102.

Simpson, Louis, "Poets in Isolation." *Hudson Review* 10 (1957): 458–64.

Whittemore, Reed. Review of *The Green Wall*. *New Orleans Poetry Journal* 4, no. 2 (1958): 38–43.

B. Saint Judas

Booth, Phillip. "Four Modern Poets." *New York Times Book Review*, 27 September 1959, 22.

Deutsch, Babette. Review of *Saint Judas*. *New York Herald Tribune Book Review*, 15 November 1959, 8.

Galler, David. "Three Poets." *Poetry* 96, no. 3 (June 1960): 185–90.

Gunn, Thom. "Excellence and Variety." *Yale Review* 49, no. 2 (Winter 1960): 295–305.

Hall, Donald. Review of *Saint Judas*. *Encounter* 15, nos. 1–3 (1960): 83.

Hecht, Anthony. "The Anguish of the Spirit and the Letter." *Hudson Review* 12, no. 4 (Winter 1959–60): 593–603.

Hoffman, Daniel. "Between New Voice and Old Master." *Sewanee Review* 68 (Autumn 1960): 674–80.

Robie, B. A. Review of *Saint Judas*. *Library Journal*, 15 September 1959, 2645.

Scott, Winfield T. "Four New Voices in Verse." *Saturday Review*, 21 May 1960, 39–40.

C. The Branch Will Not Break

Baro, Gene. "Curiosity and Illumination." *New York Times Book Review*, 1 September 1963, 5.

Gunn, Thom. "Modes of Control." *Yale Review* 53, no. 3 (Spring 1964): 447–58.

Hartman, Geoffrey. "Beyond the Middle Style." *Kenyon Review* 25, no. 4 (Autumn 1963): 751–57.

Jerome, Judson. "For Summer, a Wave of New Verse." *Saturday Review* 46, no. 27 (6 July 1963): 30–32.

Logan, John. "Poetry Shelf." *The Critic* 22 (August–September 1963): 85–86.

Nemerov, Howard. Review of *The Branch Will Not Break*. *The New Leader*, 13 May 1963, 20.

Rubin, Louis D., Jr. "Revelations of What Is Present." *The Nation* 197, no. 2 (13 July 1963): 38–39.

Smith, Ray. Review of *The Branch Will Not Break*. *Library Journal*, 1 June 1963, 2259.

Strickhausen, Harry. "In the Open." *Poetry* 102, no. 6 (September 1963): 391–92.

Weeks, Robert. "The Nature of the 'Academic.'" *Chicago Review* 16, no. 3 (1963): 138–44.

D. Shall We Gather at the River

Benedict, Estelle. Review of *Shall We Gather at the River*. *Library Journal*, 15 September 1968, 3145.

Brownjohn, Alan. "Dark Forces." *The New Statesman*, 12 September 1969, 346–47.

Dickey, William. "A Place in the Country." *Hudson Review* 22, no. 2 (1969): 347–68.

French, Robert. "Shall We Gather at the River." *Minnesota Review* 8 (Fall 1968): 382–83.

Ignatow, David. "Shall We Gather at the River." *New York Times Book Review*, 9 March 1969, 31.

Kessler, Jascha. "The Caged Sybil." *Saturday Review*, 14 December 1968, 34–36.

Lieberman, Laurence. "A Confluence of Poets." *Poetry* 114, no. 1 (April 1969): 40–58.

Matthews, William. "Entering the World." *Shenandoah* 20 (Summer 1969): 80–93.

Meyers, Bert. "Our Inner Life." *Kayak* 18 (1969): 71–74.

Moss, Stanley. "Joy Out of Terror." *The New Republic* 160, no. 13 (29 March 1969): 30–32.

Stepanchev, Stephen. Review of *Shall We Gather at the River*. *The New Leader*, 2 December 1968, 18.

Zweig, Paul. "Pieces of a Broken Mirror." *The Nation* 209, no. 1 (7 July 1969): 20–22.

E. Collected Poems

Carruth, Hayden. "Here Today: A Poetry Chronicle." *Hudson Review* 24, no. 2 (Summer 1971): 320–36.

Cushman, Jerome. Review of *Collected Poems*. *Library Journal*, 15 February 1971, 642.

Davidson, Peter. "Three Visionary Poets." *Atlantic Monthly* 229 (February 1972): 106–7.

Deutsch, Babette. "A Fashionable Poet?" *The New Republic* 165 (17 July 1971): 27.

Ditsky, John. "James Wright Collected: Alterations on the Monument." *Modern Poetry Studies* 2 (1973): 252–59.

Goldstein, Laurence. Review of *Collected Poems*. *Michigan Quarterly Review* 40 (Summer 1972): 214–17.

Hecht, Roger. "Poems from a Dark Country." *The Nation*, 2 August 1971, 88–89.

Hughes, J. W. "Humanism and the Orphic Voice." *Saturday Review*, 22 May 1971, 31–33.

Landess, Thomas H. "New Urns for Old: A Look at Six Recent Volumes of Verse." *Sewanee Review* 81, no. 1 (Winter 1973): 137–57.

Seay, James. "A World Immeasurably Alive and Good: A Look at James Wright's *Collected Poems*." In *The Pure Clear Word: Essays on the Poetry of James Wright*, ed. Dave Smith, 113–23. Urbana: University of Illinois Press, 1982. (First published in *Georgia Review* 27 (Spring 1973): 71–81.)

Spender, Stephen. "The Last Ditch." *New York Review of Books*, 22 July 1971, 3–4.

Stitt, Peter. "James Wright Knows Something about the Pure Clear Word." *New York Times Book Review*, 16 May 1971, 7.

Williamson, Alan. "Pity for the Clear Word." *Poetry* 119, no. 5 (Feburary 1972): 296–300.

Zweig, Paul. "Making and Unmaking." *Partisan Review* 15, no. 2 (1973): 269–79.

F. Two Citizens

Bedient, Calvin. "Two Citizens." *New York Times Book Review*, 11 August 1974, 6.

Cooney, Seamus. Review of *Two Citizens*. *Library Journal*, 15 April 1973, 1291.

Deutsch, Babette. "Chiefly Ironists." *The New Republic*, 28 April 1973, 25.

Engelberg, Edward. "Discovering America and Asia: The Poetry of Wright and Merwin." *Southern Review* 11 (1975): 440–43.

Henry, Gerrit. "Starting from Scratch." *Poetry* 124, no. 5 (August 1974): 292–99.

Lieberman, Laurence. "The Shocks of Normality." *Yale Review* 63, no. 3 (Spring 1974): 453–73.

Perloff, Marjorie. "The Corn-Pone Lyric: Poetry 1972–73," *Contemporary Literature* 16, no. 1 (Winter 1975): 84–125.

Pritchard, William. Review of *Two Citizens. Hudson Review* 26, no. 3 (Autumn 1973): 581.

Ramsey, Paul. "American Poetry in 1973." *Sewanee Review* 82 (Spring 1974): 393–406.

G. To a Blossoming Pear Tree

Bell, Marvin. "That We Keep Them Alive." *Poetry* 136 (June 1980): 164–70.

Carruth, Hayden. "The Passionate Few." *Harper's* 256 (June 1978): 85–89.

Kazin, Alfred. "James Wright: The Gift of Feeling." *New York Times Book Review,* 20 July 1980, 13.

Kenner, Hugh. Review of *To a Blossoming Pear Tree. New York Times Book Review,* 12 February 1978, 12.

Kinzie, Mary. "Through the Looking Glass." *Ploughshares* 5, no. 1 (1979): 202–40.

Pastan, Linda. Review of *To a Blossoming Pear Tree. Library Journal,* 15 December 1977, 2503.

Pinsky, Robert. "Light, Motion, Life." *Saturday Review,* 21 January 1978, 47–49.

Ramsey, Paul. "One Style—And Some Others: American Poetry in 1977." *Sewanee Review* 86, no. 3 (Summer 1978): 454–60.

Serchuk, Peter. "James Wright: The Art of Survival." *Hudson Review* 31, no. 3 (Autumn 1978): 548–50.

Stitt, Peter. "Poetry Chronicle." *Georgia Review* 32, no. 3 (Fall 1978): 691–99.

H. This Journey

Callaway, Kathy. "The Very Rich Hours of the Duke of Fano." *Parnassus* 11, no. 1 (Fall–Winter 1983): 58–72.

Garrison, James. Review of *This Journey. Library Journal* 107 (15 March 1982): 640.

Harmon, William. "James Wright, the Good Poet." *Sewanee Review* 90, no. 4 (Fall 1982): 612–23.

Hirsch, Edward. "Stepping through the Ruins." *New York Times Book Review,* 18 April 1982, 15, 37.

Lazer, Hank. "'The Heart of Light.'" *Virginia Quarterly Review* 59 (1983): 711–24.

Shaw, Robert B. "Exploring the Ruins." *The Nation* 235, no. 4 (7–14 August 1982): 118–19.

Weigl, Bruce. "How Lovely a Music We Make: James Wright's *This Journey.*" *Poet Lore* 78, no. 2 (Summer 1983): 103–14.

Williamson, Alan. "An American Lyricist." *The New Republic* 188, no. 4 (31 January 1983): 36–37.

IV. INTERVIEWS

Andre, Michael. "An Interview with James Wright." *Unmuzzled Ox* 1, no. 2 (February 1972): 3–18.

Henricksen, Bruce. "Poetry Must Think." *New Orleans Review* 6, no. 3 (1978): 201–7.

Heyen, William, and Jerome Mazzaro. "Something to Be Said for the Light: A Conversation with James Wright." *Southern Humanities Review* 6 (1972): 134–53.

Smith, Dave. "James Wright: The Pure Clear Word, an Interview with Dave Smith." In *Collected Prose,* ed. Anne Wright, 191–235. Ann Arbor: University of Michigan Press, 1983. (First published in *American Poetry Review* 9, no. 3 (1980): 19–30.)

Stitt, Peter. "The Art of Poetry XIX: James Wright." *Paris Review* 16 (Summer 1975): 34–61.

V. BIBLIOGRAPHIES

Ironwood 10 (1977): 156–65.

McMaster, Belle M. "James Arlington Wright: A Checklist." *Bulletin of Bibliography and Magazine Notes* 31, no. 2 (April–June 1974): 71–82, 88.

Smith, Dave, ed. *The Pure Clear Word: Essays on the Poetry of James Wright.* Urbana: University of Illinois Press, 1982.

Stein, Kevin. *James Wright, the Poetry of a Grown Man: Constancy and Transition in the Work of James Wright.* Athens: Ohio University Press, 1989.

Index